ISBN 978-1-331-64297-8
PIBN 10216952

FB &c Ltd, Dalton House, 60 Windsor Avenue, London, SW19 2RR.
Company number 08720141. Registered in England and Wales.

For support please visit www.forgottenbooks.com

EVERYMAN'S LIBRARY
EDITED BY ERNEST RHYS

POETRY AND THE DRAMA

THE NEW GOLDEN TREASURY OF SONGS AND LYRICS

LONDON: J. M. DENT & SONS, LTD.
NEW YORK: E. P. DUTTON & CO.

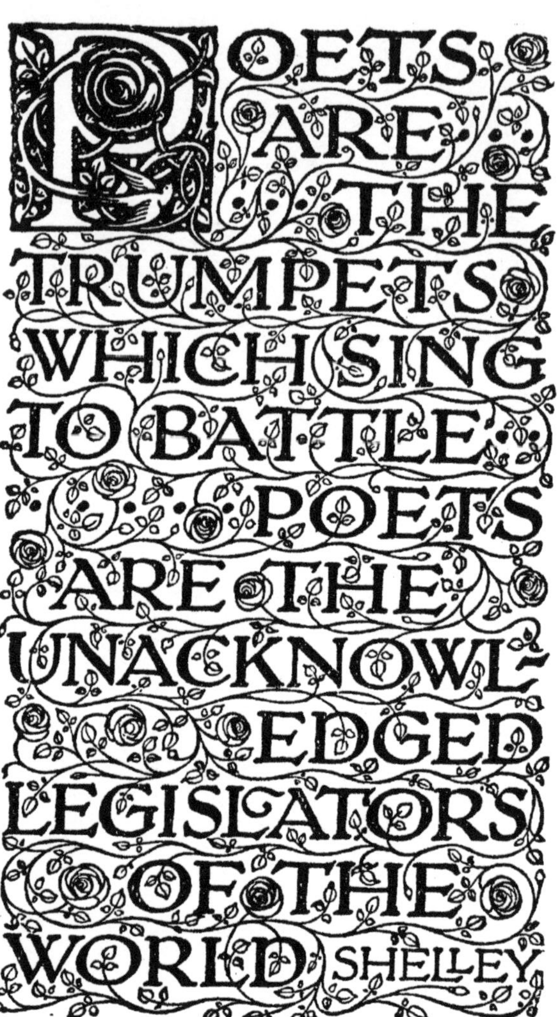
POETS ARE THE TRUMPETS WHICH SING TO BATTLE: POETS ARE THE UNACKNOWL-EDGED LEGISLATORS OF THE WORLD
SHELLEY

THE NEW GOLDEN TREASURY OF SONGS & LYRICS *by* ERNEST RHYS

LONDON: PUBLISHED
by J·M·DENT·&·SONS·LTD
AND IN NEW YORK
BY E·P·DUTTON&CO

INTRODUCTION

THE present anthology is a companion book to the old *Golden Treasury*, ranging farther back in time and farther forward, and adding many poets who have enriched the lyric tongue, omitted in those pages. Here the delicious early songs, in particular, written before or during Chaucer's time, that give the true April note to our poetry, have been brought into the first group; while into the last come many of the poets who were still writing when Palgrave and Tennyson talked over the final limits of their selection. Two periods are thus added to the record, and the volume falls naturally into a division of six books—the *First* leading up to and away from Chaucer, ranges on to Tudor times; the *Second* leads from Wyatt and Surrey to Shakespeare; the *Third*, from Ben Jonson to the last of the Lutanists, including Campion and Herrick; the *Fourth* gives the eighteenth-century men, but pauses at the advent of William Blake; the *Fifth* adds the poets from Blake to Shelley and Keats, who broke with the town poetry and brought the revolution; and the *Sixth* brings down the lyric line to those writers of yesterday who, if fate had been kinder, might have still been writing—John Davidson, Lionel Johnson and Francis Thompson among them.

In this long succession we find the art passing through many hard seasons, and coming out of each with new vigour. The foreign invasions might seem at a first glance to threaten the English idiom; yet the cuckoo song was an old French strain, and Chaucer took music from Italy before Wyatt went there for his new instrument, and Shakespeare's ear was affected by echoes of the Provençal love-poets. The straitening of the eighteenth century verse was followed by the lyric and romantic deliverance to be seen in Burns and Chatterton, Coleridge and Wordsworth. If the poets, of all writers, are those who make light of chronology, we can, as we do with the thrushes, mark when their note passes its spring innocence and grows ripe with summer, without losing our zest for their music. As the songs by the unknown first poets seem to run on inevitably to Chaucer, who after them gives us an idea of what larger developments of poetry might come about, so the beauty and force, the mixed naturalness and art, of the

Elizabethan lyric do not lose anything by the discovery that there was a spring before their summer. In these pages Palgrave's own principle of selection has been followed; but for the sake of convenience and in order to individualise the poets, the work of each writer has been given in sequence, and where no name follows a poem, it means that the writer is anonymous. In general the order of the book is chronological, but it is varied here and there, in order to allow for the fact that the poets have not always consented to fit themselves into periods, and that half a century may sometimes divide a lyric writer from his nearest relation and fondest disciple.

Another consideration bound to weigh with the anthologist lies in the discovery that every anthology has a law of its own. It needs for its total effect and the finer correspondence of its parts, a variety in its excellence, and no single note, however taking to the ear, must be repeated too often. There are poems which, while not perfect as works of art, yet become of value in such a collection because they add an indispensable something, a word, a phrase, a memorable epithet, to the lyric dialect. The boundaries are more open here than in the old *Golden Treasury*, while the maintenance of the singing note in the verse has perhaps been kept more clear. As we turn the pages of the old music and song books, or the poets like Campion and Herrick who wrote with the cadence of the lute in their ears, we become aware that a lyric, like a flower or like a crystal, has a symmetry and a unity of its own. But it never hardens absolutely into a type. It keeps adding something new and strange of its own, with every relay, to the given melody, breaking from the type with every heaven-sent impulse of the poet; and all these accessions need to be shown in the lyric anthology.

One thing there is by which this book has inevitably to suffer, by the omission of many connective, characteristic poems, which have already been printed in Palgrave. But the reader, by taking the two books together, and taking up the thread in the one where it is dropped in the other, will easily complete the account for himself. Yet another limitation is that of space; for every song or lyric that has gone into these pages, a couple of others with like claims, has had to be left out. In fact, only those who have worked over the ground for the same purpose can estimate what the lyric wealth of our poetry actually is, or how many exquisite songs and poems, which to-day we are in danger of forgetting, still await their resurrection.

Special mention should be made of those who have given formal consent for the reprinting of copyright poems. The thanks of compiler and reader, public and publisher, are due to Mrs. John Davidson and Mr. Grant Richards for a poem of John Davidson's; Mr. John Lane, for poems by W. B. Rands and Ernest Dowson; Mr. Elkin Mathews, for two poems by Lionel Johnson; Messrs. Chatto & Windus, for two poems by R. L. Stevenson, and a sonnet by Mathilde Blind; Messrs. Longmans & Co., for two sonnets by Andrew Lang; and Mr. Wm. Meredith and Messrs. Constable for two poems of George Meredith. Further acknowledgement is due to those who have generously put poems at the editor's free disposal; Mr. Watts-Dunton for three poems of Swinburne; Mr. Wilfrid Meynell for three poems of Francis Thompson; Dr. Greville MacDonald for two poems of George MacDonald; Mr. Bertram Dobell for a poem by James Thomson; Mr. Walter Scott for a lyric by Joseph Skipsey; and Mrs. William Sharp and Mr. William Heinemann for two poems by "Fiona Macleod" and Wm. Sharp.

E. R.

BIBLIOGRAPHY IN BRIEF
OF ENGLISH LYRIC ANTHOLOGIES

Ane Compendious Buik of Godlie Psalmes and Spirituall Sangis (1545?)
Arber, Ed. The English Garner, 1877.
Beeching, H. C. Paradise of English Poetry, 1893.
Bright, J. W., and Kittredge, G. L. The Albion Series of Anglo-Saxon and Middle English Poetry, 1900.
Bryant, W. C. New Library of Poetry and Song, 1876.
Bullen, A. H. England's Helicon (1600), ed. by, 1887.
" " Lyrics from Elizabethan Dramatists, 1889.
" " Lyrics from Elizabethan Song-Books, 1887.
" " More Lyrics from Elizabethan Song-Books, 1888.
" " Poems from Elizabethan Romances, 1890.
Campbell, T. Specimens of the British Poets, 1841.
Chambers, E. K. English Pastorals, 1895.
Chambers, E. K., and Sidgwick, F. Early English Lyrics, 1907.
Collier, J. Payne. Lyrical Poems, 1844.
Cox, F. A. English Madrigals, 1899.
Davison, Francis. A Poetical Rapsody, 1602.
Dircks, W. H. Cavalier and Courtier Lyrists, 1891.
Douglas, Sir George. Book of Scottish Poetry, 1911.
Hazlitt, W. C. Remains of the Early Popular Poetry of England. 4 vols. 1864–66.
Henley, W. E. English Lyrics, Chaucer to Poe, 1340–1809, 1897.
Jones, Robt. England's Parnassus.
Locker-Lampson, F. Lyra Elegantiarum, 1867; enlarged 1891.

MacDonald, G. England's Antiphon, 1868.
Meynell, Alice. A Seventeenth Century Anthology, 1903.
Miles, A. H. The Poets and Poetry of the Century, 1891–99.
Morley, Henry. Companion Poets, 1891–92.
Morris, R. Specimens of Early English (Poetry), 1866. (Part I revised by W. W. Skeat, 1882; 2nd edition revised 1885.)
Munday, A. Banquet of Dainty Conceits, 1581.
Palgrave, F. T. Golden Treasury, 1861. Revised and enlarged 1896. Second Series, 1897. Treasury of Sacred Song, 1889.
Park, T. *Heliconia*, 1815.
Percy, T. Reliques of Ancient English Poetry, 1765.
Quiller-Couch, Sir A. T. Oxford Book of English Verse, 1250–1900, 1900. The Golden Pomp: a procession of lyrics from Surrey to Shirley, 1895. Oxford Book of Victorian Verse, 1912. Oxford Book of Ballads, 1910.
Ramsay, Allan. Tea Table Miscellany, 1724–7.
Ritson, John. Ancient Songs and Ballads, 1792. Ancient Popular Poetry, 1791. Collection of English Songs, 1813.
Saintsbury, G. E. B. Seventeenth Century Lyrics, 1900.
Sharp, C. J. English Folk Carols, 1911.
Sharp, Eliz. A. Lyra Celtica, 1896.
Sharp, Wm. A Century of Sonnets, 1887.
Songs of Scotland (ed. by R. Chambers), 1862.
Southey, E. British Poets, 1831.
Stedman, E. C. A Victorian Anthology, 1837–95, 1896.
Sylvester, Joshua. Christmas Carols and Ballads. n. d.
The Paradise of Dainty Devices, 1576.
The Phoenix Nest, 1593.
Tottel's Miscellany, 1557.
Ward, T. H. The English Poets, selections, 4 vol., 1883.
White, Gleeson. Ballades and Rondeaux, 1893.
Works of the English Poets, ed. by A. Chalmers, 21 vol. 1810.
Works of the Poets of Great Britain and Ireland, ed, by Dr. Samuel Johnson, 8 vol., 1800.
Wright, Thos. Songs and Carols, 1836.
,, ,, Specimens of Lyric Poetry, ed. from Harleian MS. in British Museum, 1842.
,, ,, Songs and Ballads, 1860.

E NEW GOLDEN TREASURY

BOOK FIRST

SUMMER IS I-COMEN IN

Summer is i-comen in,
Loud sing cuckoo;
Groweth seed and bloweth mead,
And springeth the wood new.
  Sing cuckoo!
Ewe bleateth after lamb,
Loweth after calfe cow,
Bullock sterteth,
Bucke verteth,
Merrie sing cuckoo!
  Cuckoo, cuckoo;
Well thou singest, cuckoo!
Nor cease thou never now.

WYNTER WAKENETH AL MY CARE

Wynter wakeneth al my care,
Nou this leves waxeth bare;
Ofte y sike ant mourne sare
  When hit cometh in my thoht
  Of this worldes joie, how hit goth al to noht.

Now hit is, ant now hit nys,
Also hit ner nere y wys,
That moni mon seith soth hit ys,
  Al goth bote Godes wille
  Alle we shule deye, thah us like ylle.

MERRY IT IS

Merry it is while summer i-last
    With fowle's song;
Och, me nigheth winde's blast,
    And weather strong.
Ei, ei, what this night is long!
And I, with well mickle wrong
Sorrow and mourn and fast.

IV BLOW, NORTHERN WIND

Blow, northern wind,
Send thou me my sweeting:
Blow, northern wind:
  Blow, blow, blow.

I wot a burde in bower bright
That sully seemly is on sight,
Menskful maiden of might
  Fair and free to fond.
In all this worthliche won,
A burde of blood and of bone
Never yet I knew none
  Lovesomer in lond.
A better burde never was.

She is dear worth by day
Gracious, stout and gay,
Gentle, jolly as the jay;
  Worthliche when she waketh:
Maiden, merriest of mouth
By east, by west, by north, by south,
That is not fickle nor trouth
  That such mirths maketh.

V ALYSOUN

Bytuene Mershe ant Averil
  When spray biginneth to springe,
The lutel foul hath hire wyl
  On hyre lud to synge;
Ich libbe in love-longinge
For semlokest of alle thynge,
He may me blisse bringe,
  Icham in hire baundoun.
An hendy hap ichabbe y-hent,
Ichot from heuene it is me sent,
From alle wymmen mi loue is lent
  Ant lyht on Alysoun.

On heu hire her is fayr y-noh,
Hire browe broune, hire eye blake,
With lossum chere he on me loh;
With middel smal ant wel y-make;

Bote he me wolle to hire take,
Forte buen hire owen make,
Longe to lyuen ichulle forsake,
Ant feye fallen a-doun.

Nihtes when y wende ant wake,
For-thi myn wonges waxeth won;
Levedi al for thine sake
Longinge is y-lent me on.
In world nis non so wyter mon
That al hire bounté telle con;
Hire swyre is whittore then the swon,
Ant feyrest may in toune.

Icham for wowyng al for-wake,
Wery so water in wore;
Lest eny reve me my make,
Ychabbe y-yyrned yore.
Betere is tholien whyle sore,
Then mournen euermore.
Geynest under gore,
Herkne to my roune.
An hendy hap ichabbe y-hent,
Ichot from heuene it is me sent,
From alle wymmen mi loue is lent
   Ant lyht on Alysoun.

VI LENTEN IS COME WITH LOVE TO TOWN

Lenten is come with love to town,
With blossom and with briddes roune,
   That all this blisse bryngeth;
Dayes-eyes in the dales,
Notes sweet of nightingales,
   Each fowl song singeth.
The threstelcock him threatneth oo,
Away is their wynter woe,
   When woodruff springeth;
The fowls singeth ferly fele,
And wlyteth on their winter wele,
   That all the wood ringeth.

The rose rayleth her rood,
The leaves on the light wood
   Waxen all with wille;

The moon yieldeth her blee,
The lily is lovesome to see,
  The fennel and the fille;
Woo now the wilde drakes
Maids murgeth their makes,
  As stream that striketh stille;
Moody moaneth, so doth mo,
I wot am one of tho',
  For love that likes ille.

The moon yieldeth her light,
So doth the seemly sonne bright,
  When briddes singeth breme;
Dewes donketh the downes,
Dears with their derne runes,
  Doomes forte deme;
Wormes woweth under clod,
Women waxeth wonder proud,
  So well it will them seeme,
If I shall want will of one:
This joy will I well foregone,
  And wight in wood be fleme.

VII MY DEATH I LOVE, MY LIFE I HATE

My deth I love, my lyf I hate,
  For a levedy shene;
Heo is briht so daiés light,
  That is on me wel sene.
Al I falewe so doth the lef,
  In somer when hit is grene;
Yef mi thoht helpeth me noht,
  To whom shall I me mene?

Sorrow and syke and drery mod
  Byndeth me so faste;
That I wene to walke wod,
  Yef hit me lengore laste.
My sorewe, my care, al with a word
  He myhte away caste.
Whet helpeth thee, my suete lemmon,
  My lyf thus forte gaste?

VIII LULLY, LULLEY; LULLY, LULLEY!

  Lully, lulley; lully, lulley!
  The falcon hath borne my mate away!
He bare him up, he bare him down,
He bare him into an orchard brown.
In that orchard there was a hall
That was hangèd with purple and pall.
And in that hall there was a bed,
It was hangèd with gold so red.
And in that bed there lieth a knight,
His wounds bleeding day and night.
By that bedside kneeleth a may,
And she weepeth both night and day.
And by that bedside there standeth a stone
Corpus Christi written thereon.
  Lully, lulley; lully, lulley!

IX SOME TIME AN ENGLISH SHIP WE HAD

Some time an English ship we had;
  Noble it was and high of tow'r
Thro' all Christendom it was drad
  And stiff would stand in every stour,
  And best durst bide a sharp show'r
And other storms, small and great.
  Now is that ship that bare the flow'r
Seldom seen and soon forget.

Unto that ship there longed a Rudder
  That steered the ship and governed it:
In all this world n'is such another
  As me thinketh in my wit;
  While Ship and Rudder together was knit
They dread neither tempest, dry nor wet.
  Now be they both asunder flit:
That seldom seen is soon forget.

Sharp waves that Ship has sailed
  And assayed all seas at adventure;
For wind nor weather never it failed
  While the Rudder might endure;

Though the sea were rough or well demure,
Good havens that Ship would get:
Now is that Ship, I am well sure
Seldom seen and soon forget.

X

IN PRAISE OF WOMEN

I am as light as any roe
To praise women where that I go.

To onpraise women it were a shame,
For a woman was thy dame.
Our blessèd Lady beareth the name
Of all women where that they go.

A woman is a worthy thing;
They do thee wash and do thee wring;
"Lullay, lullay!" she doth thee sing;
And yet she hath but care and woe.

A woman is a worthy wight;
She serveth a man both day and night;
Thereto she putteth all her might;
And yet she hath but care and woe.

XI

MY SWEET SWEETING

Ah my sweet sweeting,
My little pretty sweeting,
My sweeting will I love wherever I go:

She is so proper and so pure,
Full steadfast, stable and demure,
There is none such, ye may be sure,
As my sweet sweeting.

In all this world, as thinketh me
Is none so pleasant to my eye,
That I am glad so oft to see,
As my sweet sweeting.

When I behold my sweeting sweet,
Her face, her hands, her minion feet,
They seem to me there is none so sweet
As my sweet sweeting.

Above all other praise must I
And love my pretty piggésnie
For none I find so womanly
As my sweet sweeting.

XII THE LITTLE PRETTY NIGHTINGALE

The little pretty nightingale
Among the leavés green,
I would I were with her all night.
But yet ye wot not whom I mean.

The nightingale sat on a brere
Among the thornes sharp and keen,
And comfort me with merry cheer.
But yet ye wot not whom I mean.

She did appear of all her kind
A lady right well to be seen;
With words of love told me her mind.
But yet ye wot not whom I mean.

It did me good upon her to look;
Her corse was closèd all in green;
Away from me her heart she took.
But yet ye wot not whom I mean.

"Lady," I cried with rueful moan,
"Have mind of me that true hath been;
For I love none but you alone."
But yet ye wot not whom I mean.

XIII THE BAILEY BEARETH THE BELL AWAY

The maidens came
When I was in my mother's bower;
I had all that I would.
The bailey beareth the bell away;
The lily, the rose, the rose I lay.
The silver is white red is the gold;
The robes they lay in fold.
The bailey beareth the bell away;
The lily, the rose, the rose I lay.
And through the glass window shines the sun.
How should I love, and I so young?
The bailey beareth the bell away;
The lily, the lily, the rose I lay.

XIV THE HOLLY AND THE IVY (I)

Holly and Ivy made a great party,
Who should have the mastery
  In lands where they go.

Then spake Holly, "I am fierce and jolly,
I will have the mastery
  In lands where we go."

Then spake Ivy, "I am loud and proud,
And I will have the mastery
  In lands where we go."

Then spake Holly, and bent him on his knee,
"I pray thee, gentle Ivy,
Assay me no villainy
  In lands where we go."

XV THE HOLLY AND THE IVY (II)

The Holly and the ivy,
  Now are both well grown.
Of all the trees that are in the wood
  The Holly bears the crown.
    O, the rising of the sun,
      The running of the deer,
    The playing of the merry organ,
      The singing in the choir.

The holly bears a blossom
  As white as the lily flower,
And Mary bore sweet Jesus Christ
  To be our sweet Saviour.

The holly bears a berry
  As red as any blood,
And Mary bore sweet Jesus Christ
  To do poor sinners good.

The holly bears a prickle
  As sharp as any thorn,
And Mary bore sweet Jesus Christ
  On Christmas day in the morn.

The holly bears a bark
  As bitter as any gall,
And Mary bore sweet Jesus Christ
  For to redeem us all.

The Holly and the Ivy
  Now are both well grown,
Of all the trees that are in the wood
  The Holly bears the crown.

XVI I SAW THREE SHIPS COME SAILING IN

I saw three ships come sailing in,
On Christmas Day, on Christmas Day:
I saw three ships come sailing in
On Christmas Day in the morning.

And who was in those ships all three,
On Christmas Day, on Christmas Day?
And who was in those ships all three,
On Christmas Day in the morning?

Our Saviour Christ and his ladye,
On Christmas Day, on Christmas Day;
Our Saviour Christ and his ladye
On Christmas Day in the morning.

Pray whither sailed those ships all three,
On Christmas Day, on Christmas Day?
Pray whither sailed those ships all three
On Christmas Day in the morning?

O they sailed into Bethlehem,
On Christmas Day, on Christmas Day;
O they sailed into Bethlehem,
On Christmas Day in the morning.

And all the bells on Earth shall ring,
On Christmas Day, on Christmas Day;
And all the bells on Earth shall ring,
On Christmas Day in the morning.

And all the angels in Heaven shall sing,
On Christmas Day, on Christmas Day;
And all the angels in Heaven shall sing,
On Christmas Day in the morning.

And all the souls on Earth shall sing,
On Christmas Day, on Christmas Day;
And all the souls on Earth shall sing,
On Christmas Day in the morning.

XVII NOEL

Noel, Noel, Noel, Noel,
Tidings good I think to tell.

The boar's head, that we bring here,
Betokeneth a prince without peer
Is born to-day to buy us dear;
Noel.

The boar he is a sovereign beast,
And acceptable at every feast;
So might this lord be to greatest and least;
Noel.

This boar's head we bring with song,
In worship of him that thus sprung
From a virgin to redress all wrong;
Noel.

XVIII THE BOAR'S HEAD

The boar's head in hand bring I,
With garlands gay and rosemary;
I pray you all sing merrily,
Qui estis in convivio.

The boar's head, I understand,
Is the chief service in this land;
Look wherever it be found,
Servite cum cantico.

XIX WELCOME YULE

Welcome be thou heavenly King,
Welcome, born on this morning,
Welcome, for whom we shall sing
Welcome Yule.

Welcome be ye Stephen and John,
Welcome Innocents every one,
Welcome Thomas Martyr one,
Welcome Yule.

Welcome be ye good New Year,
Welcome Twelfth day both in fere,
Welcome Saints loved and dear,
Welcome Yule.

Welcome be ye Candlemass,
Welcome be ye Queen of Bliss,
Welcome both to more and less,
Welcome Yule.

Welcome be ye that are here,
Welcome all, and make good cheer,
Welcome all, another year,
Welcome Yule.

XX MAKE WE MERRY, BOTH MORE AND LESS

Make we merry, both more and less,
For now is the time of Christmas!
Let no man come into this hall,
Groom, page, nor yet marshal,
But that some sport he bring withal.

If that he say he cannot sing,
Some other sport then let him bring,
That it may please at this feasting.

If he say he can nought do,
Then, for my love, ask him no more,
But to the stocks then let him go.

XXI SHEPHERDS' SONG

I

As I out rode this enderes' night,
Of three jolly shepherds I saw a sight,
And all about their fold a star shone bright;
They sang, Terli, terlow;
So merrily the shepherds their pipes can blow.

II

Down from heaven, from heaven so high,
Of angels there came a great company,
With mirth, and joy, and great solemnity
They sang, Terli, terlow;
So merrily the shepherds their pipes can blow.

XXII LULLY, LULLAY

Lully, lulla, thou little tiny child;
By, by, lullay, lullay, thou little tiny child;
By, by, lully, lullay.

O sisters too! how may we do,
For to preserve this day
This poor youngling, for whom we do sing
By, by, lully, lullay.

Herod, the king, in his raging,
Chargëd he hath this day
His men of might, in his own sight,
All young children to slay.

That woe is me, poor child for thee!
And ever morn and day,
For thy parting neither say nor sing,
By, by, lully, lullay.

XXIII NEITHER IN HALLS, NOR YET IN BOWERS

I

Neither in halls, nor yet in bowers,
Born would he not be,
Neither in castles, nor yet in towers,
That seemly were to see,
But at his Father's will,
The prophecy to fulfil,
Betwixt an ox and an ass
Jesu this king born he was;
Heaven he bring us till!

II

Forth they went, and glad they were;
Going they did sing,
With mirth and solace, they made good cheer,
For joy of that new tiding.

And after as I heard them tell,
He rewarded them full well
He granted them heaven therein to dwell.
In are they gone with joy and mirth,
And their song it is Noël.

WHEN I SEE BLOSSOMS SPRING

When I see blossoms spring
  And hear fowle's song
A sweete love-longing
  My herte throughout stung,
Al for a love newe,
That is so swete and trewe
  That gladieth all my song;
I wot al myd i-wisse
My joie and eke my blisse
  On him is al y-long.

When I myself stonde
  And with mine eyen see
Thurled foot and honde
  With great nails three.
Bloody was his head
On him nes none believed
  That was of peynes free;
Wel, wel onte myn herte
For his love to smerte,
  And sick and sorry be.

MY LADY CLEAR

Who shall have my fair lady?
Who but I? Who but I—who?
Who shall have my fair lady?
Who hath more right thereto?

This lady clear
That I show here,
Man's soul it is, trust ye;
To Christ most dear
It hath no peer;
Therefore this song sing we.

For love sweetness
And joy endless
I made my lady free;
Unto my likeness
I gave her quickness
In Paradise to be.

O my sweet store,
My true love therefore
Thy place it is above;
What man may do more
Than only die therefore,
Lady, for thy love?

XXVI MY TRUEST TREASURE

My trewest tresowre sa trayturly taken,
So bytterly bondyn wyth bytand bandes:
How sone of thi servandes was thou forsaken,
And lathly for my lufe hurld with thair handes.

My hope of my hele sa hye to be hanged,
Sa charged with thi crosce, and corond with thorne,
Ful sare to thi hert thi steppes tha stanged
Me thynk thi bak burd breke, it bendes for-borne.

RICHARD ROLLE

XXVII LOVE IS A LIGHT BURTHEN

Love is a light burthen; Love gladdens young and old,
Love is withouten pine; as lovers have me told;
Love is a ghostly wine, that makes men big and bold
Of love shall he nothing tyne, that it in heart will hold.

Love is the sweetest thing, that man in earth has ta'en,
Love is God's darling, Love bindes blood and bane.
In Love be our liking; I wot no better wane
For me and my Loving, Love makes both be ane.

RICHARD ROLLE

XXVIII THE JOLLY SHEPHERD

Can I not sing but "Hoy,"
Whan the joly shepard made so much joy.

The shepard upon a hill he satt;
He had on him his tabard and his hat,
His tarbox, his pipe, and his flagat;
His name was called Joly Joly Wat,
For he was a gud herde's boy.
Ut hoy!
For in his pipe he made so much joy.

The shepard upon a hill was laid:
His dog to his girdell was taid;
He had not slept but a litill braid,
But "*Gloria in excelsis*" was to him said.
Ut hoy!
For in his pipe he made so much joy.

The shepard on a hill he stode;
Round about him his shepe they yode;
He put his hand under his hode,
He saw a star as rede as blode.
Ut hoy!
For in his pipe he made so much joy.

The shepard said anon right,
"I will go see yon farly sight,
Where as the angel singeth on hight
And the star that shineth so bright."
Ut hoy!
For in his pipe he made so much joy.

"Now must I go wher Crist was born;
Farewell! I cum again to morn.
Dog, kepe well my shepe fro ye corn,
And warn well 'Warroke' when I blow my horn!"
Ut hoy!
For in his pipe he made so much joy.

XXIX THE JOLLY FORESTER

I am a jolly foster, I am a jolly foster,
And have been many a day
And foster will I be still,
For shoot right well I may.

Wherefore should I hang up my bow
  Upon the green wood bough?
I can bend and draw a bow
  And shoot well enow.

Wherefore should I hang up my arrow
  Upon the green wood lind?
I have strength to make it flee,
  And kill both hart and hind.

Wherefore should I hang up my horn
  Upon the green wood tree?
I can blow the death of a deer as well
  As any that ever I see.

Wherefore should I tie up my hound
  Upon the green wood spray?
I can lodge and make a suit
  As well as any in May.

XXX EARTH UPON EARTH

Earth upon Earth would be a king
How Earth shall to Earth, he thinkest nothing;
When Earth biddeth Earth his rent home bring
Then shall Earth fro' the Earth have a hard parting,
                                        With Care;
For Earth upon Earth wots never wherefore to fare.

Earth upon Earth wins castles and towers,
Then saith Earth to Earth, all this is ours;
When Earth upon Earth has built all his bowers,
Then shall Earth fro' the Earth suffer May's showers,
                                        And smart.
Man, amend thee betime; thy life is but a start.

XXXI SONG OF THE PENNY

Go bet, penny; go bet, go!
For thou may maken both friend and foe.

Penny is an hardy knight;
Penny is mickle of might;
Penny of wrong he maketh right
  In every country where he go.

Though I have a man i-slaw
And forfeited the king's law;
I shall guiden a man of law,
  Will taken my penny and let me go.

And if I have to do, far or near
And penny be mine messenger
Then am I nothing in fear;
  My cause shall be well i-do.

And if I have pence both good and fine,
Men will bidden me to the wine;
"That I have, shall be thine!"
  Truly they will feign so.

And when I have none in my purse,
Penny better, nor penny the worse;
Of me, they holden but little force.
  He was a man, let him go!

XXXII FREEDOM

A! fredome is a nobill thing!
Fredome mayse man to haiff liking!
Fredome all solace to man giffis:
He levys at ese that frely levys;
A noble hart may haiff nane ease,
Na ellys nocht that may him plese,
Gyff fredome failythe: for fre liking
Is yearnyt ow'r all othir thing
Na he, that ay hase levyt fre,
May nocht knaw weill the propyrte,
The angyr, na the wrechyt dome,
That is cowplyt to foule thyrldome.
Bot gyff he had assayit it,
Than all perquer he suld it wyt;
And suld think fredome mar to pryse
Than all the gold in warld that is.

BARBOUR

XXXIII THE CARELESS MAID

She that is careless is never steadfast;
  She that is careless, though her friends should die,

She that is careless, her care is soon past;
  She that is careless shall never love truly.

She that is careless tenders no man's smart;
  She that is careless is now out and now in;
She that is careless is ever overthwart;
  She that is careless, who loseth her doth win.

XXXIV SONG OF THE ROSE

Then all the birdis sang with voice on height,
  Whose mirthful sound was marvellous to hear;
The mavis sang, "Hail, Rose, most rich and right,
  That does up flourish under Phœbus' sphere;
  Hail, plant of youth; hail, Princess, daughter dear;
Hail, blossom breaking out of the blood royal,
  Whose precious virtue is imperial."

The merle she sang, "Hail, Rose of most delight,
  Hail, of all flowers queen and sovereign:"
The lark she sang, "Hail, Rose, both red and white,
  Most pleasant flower, of mighty colours twane:"
  The nightingale sang, "Hail, Nature's suffragane,
In beauty, nurture, and every nobleness,
In rich array, renown, and gentleness."

Dunbar

XXXV THE PRAISE OF AGE

At matin hour, in middis of the night,
Wakenèd of sleep, I saw beside me soon,
Ane aged man, seemèd sixty years of sight,
This sentence set, and sung it in good tune—
Omnipotent, and eterne God in trone!
To be content and love thee I have cause
That my light youth-head is opprest and done,
  Honour with age to every virtue draws.

Green youth, to age thou mon obey and bow,
They folly lustis lastis scant ane May;
That then was wit, is natural folly now,
As worldly honour, riches, or fresh array,

Defy the devil, dread God and doomisday.
For all shall be accusèd as thou knawis;
Blessed be God, my youth-head is away;
  Honour with age to every virtue drawis.

O bitter youth! that seemis so delicious;
O holy age! that sometimes seemèd sour,
O restless youth! hie, hait, and vicious;
O honest age! fulfillèd with honour;
O froward youth! fruitless and feedand flowr,
Contrar to conscience, both to God and lawis
Of all vain glore the lamp and the mirrour:
  Honour with age till every virtue drawis.

This world is set for to deceive us even,
Pride is the net, and covetous the train;
For no reward, except the joy of heaven,
Would I be young into this world again.
The ship of faith, tempestuous wind and rain
Drives in the sea of Lolledry, that blawis;
My youth is gane, and I am glad and fain:
  Honour with age to every virtue drawis.

Law, love, and lawtie, graven low they lie;
Dissimulance has borrowed conscience clais;
Aithis, writ, wax nor seals are nought set by;
Flattery is fostered both with friends and faes.
The son, to bruik it that his father has,
Would see him dead: Sathanus sic seed sawis
Youth-head, adieu! ane of my mortal faes:
  Honour with age to every virtue drawis.

WALTER KENNEDY

XXXVI TO THEE FOR ME

Sweet nightingale! in holene green that haunt,
To sport thyself, and special in the Spring;
Thy chivring chirls whilk changingly thou chants,
Make all the roches round about thee ring;
Whilk slaiks my sorrow, so to hear thee sing,
And lights my loving languor at the least;
Yet thou sees not, silly saikless thing!
The piercing pike-prods at thy bony breast:

Even so am I, by pleasure likewise prest,
In greatest danger where I most delight:
But since thy song, for shoring, has not ceased,
Should feeble I, for fear, my conquest quit?
Na, na—I love thee freshest Phœnix fair,
In beauty, birth, in bounty but compare.

Alex. Montgomery

XXXVII THE COMPLAINT TO HIS EMPTY PURSE

To you, my purse, and to none other wight
Complain I, for ye be my lady dear!
I am so sorrow, now that ye be light;
For certës, but ye make me heavy cheer,
Me were as lief be laid upon my bier;
For which unto your mercy thus I cry:
Be heavy again, or elles might I die!

Now voucheth safe this day, or it be night,
That I of you the blissful sound may hear,
Or see your colour like the sun bright
That of yellowness had never a peer.
Ye be my life, ye be my hertës stere,
Queen of comfort and of good company:
Be heavy again, or elles might I die!

Now purse, that be to me my life's light,
And saviour, as down in this world here,
Out of this toune help me through your might,
Since that ye wole not be my treasurer;
For I am shaved as nigh as any frere.
But yet I pray unto your courtesy
Be heavy again, or elles might I die!

O Conqueror of Brutë's Albion
Which that by line and free electiön
Be very king, this song to you I send;
And ye, that mighten all our harm amend,
Have mind upon my supplicatiön!

Chaucer

XXXVIII ROUNDELS

I

Your eyën two will slay me suddenly:
I may the beauty of hem not sustene,
So woundeth it through-out my hertë kene.

And but your word will helen hastily
My hertë woundë, while that is green,
  Your eyën two will slay me sodenly:
  I may the beauty of hem not sustene.

Upon my troth I say you faithfully,
That ye be of my life and death the queen,
For with my death the truthë shall be seen:
  Your eyën two will slay me sodenly:
  I may the beauty of hem not sustene,
  So woundeth it through-out my hertë kene.

II

So hath your beauty from your hertë chased
Pity, that me ne availeth not to plain:
For Daunger halt your mercy in his chain.

Guiltless my death thus have ye me purchased;
I say you sooth, me needeth not to feign:
  So hath your beauty from your hertë chased
  Pity, that me ne availeth not to plain.

Alas! that nature hath in you compassed
So great beautỳ, that no man may attain
To mercy, though he stervë for the pain!
  So hath your beauty from your hertë chased
  Pity, that me ne availeth not to plain;
  For Daunger halt your mercy in his chain.

CHAUCER

XXXIX WELCOME SUMMER

Now welcome somer, with thy sonnë softe
That hast this wintrès weders over-shake
And driven away the longë nightës blake.
Seynt Valentyn, that art full hy in lofte,
Thus singen smalë foulës for thy sake
"*Now welcome somer, with thy sonnë softe*
That hast this wintrès weders over-shake."

Wel hav they causë for to gladen ofte
Sith ech of hem recoverëd hath his make:
Ful blisful may they singen whan they wake

"Now welcome somer, with thy sonnë softe
That hast this wintrës weders over-shake
And driven away the longë nightës blake."

CHAUCER

XL SAWEST NOT YOU MY OXEN

I have twelfe oxen, that be faire and brown,
And they go a grasing down by the town.
With hey! with how! with hey!
Saweste not you my oxen, you litill prety boy?

I have twelfe oxen, and they be faire and white,
And they go a grasing down by the dyke.
With hey! with how! with hey!
Saweste not you mine oxen, you litill prety boy?

I have twelfe oxen, and they be faire and blak,
And they go a grasing down by the lak.
With hey! with how! with hey!
Saweste not you mine oxen, you litill prety boy?

I have twelfe oxen, and they be faire and rede,
And they go a grasing down by the mede.
With hey! with how! with hey!
Saweste not you mine oxen, you litill prety boy?

XLI LO, WHAT IT IS TO LOVE

Lo, what it is to love,
Learn ye that list to prove,
By me, I say, that no ways may
The ground of grief remove,
But still decay both night and day:
Lo, what it is to love!

Love is ane fervent fire,
Kindled without desire,
Short pleasure, lang displeasure,
Repentance is the hire;
Ane puir tressour, without measour;
Love is ane fervent fire.

To love and to be wise,
To rage with good advice;
Now thus, now than, so goes the game,
Uncertain is the dice;
There is no man, I say, that can
Both love and to be wise.

Flee always from the snare,
Learn at me to beware;
It is ane pain, and double trane
Of endless woe and care:
For to refrain that danger plain,
Flee always from the snare.

ALEXANDER SCOTT

XLII ILL THRIFT

He that hath lafte the hosier's crafte,
  And fallth to makyng shoon;
The smyth that shall to painting fall,
  His thrift is well nigh done.
A black draper with whyte paper,
  To goe to writing schole,
An old butler become a cutler
  I wene shall prove a fole.
And an old trot, than can God wot,
  Nothing but kyss the cup,
With her physicke will kepe one sicke,
  Till she hath soused hym up.
A man of law that never sawe
  The wayes to buy and sell,
Wenyng to ryse by merchandyse,
  I pray God spede him well!
A merchaunt eke, that will go seke
  By all the meanes he may,
To fall in sute till he dispute
  His money cleane away;
Pletyng the lawe for every stray
  Shall prove a thrifty man,
With bate and strife, but by my life
  I cannot tell you whan.

SIR T. MORE

XLIII PASTIME WITH GOOD COMPANY

Pastime with good company
I love and shall until I die.
Grudge who lust, but none deny
So God be pleased thus live will I,
For my pastime, Hunt, sing and dance;
  My heart is set;
All goodly sport For my comfort.
Who shall me let?

Youth must have some dalliance,
Of good or ill some pastance,
Company me-thinks the best
All thoughts and fancies to digest,
For idleness Is chief mistress
  Of vices all!
Then who can say But mirth and play
Is best of all?

Company with honesty
Is virtue vices to flee;
Company is good and ill,
But every man has his free will.
The best ensue, the worst eschew!
  My mind shall be
Virtue to use, Vice to refuse;
Thus shall I use me.

Henry VIII

XLIV MERRY MARGARET

Merry Margaret,
As midsummer flower,
Gentle as falcon,
Or hawk of the tower;
With solace and gladness,
Much mirth and no madness,
All good and no badness;
So joyously,
So maidenly,
So womanly,
Her demeaning,
In everything,

Far, far passing
That I can indite,
Or suffice to write,
Of merry Margaret,
As midsummer flower,
Gentle as falcon,
Or hawk of the tower;
As patient and as still,
And as full of goodwill,
As fair Isiphil,
Coliander,
Sweet Pomander,
Good Cassander;
Stedfast of thought,
Well made, well wrought,
Far may be sought,
Ere you can find
So courteous, so kind,
As merry Margaret,
This midsummer flower,
Gentle as falcon,
Or hawk of the tower.

Skelton

XLV ISABEL

Star of the morrow gray,
The blossom on the spray,
The freshest flower of May;

Ennewèd, your colour
Is like the daisy flower
After the April shower!

Maidenly demure,
Of womanhood the lure,
Wherefore I make you sure:

It were an heavenly health,
It were an endless wealth,
A life for God himself,

To hear this nightingale,
Among the birds smale,
Warbling in the vale:—

Dug, dug ;
Jug, jug !
Good year and good luck,
With chuk, chuk, chuk, chuk !

SKELTON

XLVI THE GARMENT OF GOOD LADIES

Would my good lady love me best,
  And work after my will,
I should a garment goodliest
  Gar make her body till.

Of high honoúr should be her hood,
  Upon her head to wear,
Garnished with governance, so good
  Na deeming should her deir.

Her sark should be her body next,
  Of chastity so white :
With shame and dread together mixt,
  The same should be perfyte.

Her kirtle should be of clean constance,
  Lacit with lesum love ;
The mailies of continuance,
  For never to remove.

Her gown should be of goodliness,
  Well ribboned with renown ;
Purfilled with pleasure in ilk place,
  Furrit with fine fashioún.

Her belt should be of benignity,
  About her middle meet ;
Her mantle of humility,
  To thole both wind and weït.

Her hat should of fair havíng,
  And her tippet of truth ;
Her patelet of good pansíng,
  Her hals-ribbon of ruth.

Her sleeves should be of esperance,
  To keep her fra despair :
Her glovis of good governance,
  To hide her fingers fair.

Her shoon should be of sickerness,
  In sign that she nought slide;
Her hose of honesty, I guess,
  I should for her provide.

Would she put on this garment gay,
  I durst swear by my seill,
That she wore never green nor gray
  That set her half so weel.

HENRYSON

ENVOI TO BOOK FIRST

O reverend Chaucer! rose of rhetoris all,
As in our tongue ane flower imperial,
That raise in Britain ever, who reads right,
Thou bears of makaris the triumph riall,
Thy fresh enamelled terms celicall:
This matter could illumined have full bright.
Was thou not of our English all the light,
Surmounting every tongue terrestrial,
As far as Mayis morrow does midnight.

DUNBAR

BOOK SECOND

XLVII JOLLY ROBIN

"Ah! Robin!
Jolly Robin!
Tell me how thy leman doth,
And thou shalt know of mine."

"My lady is unkind, perdie!"—
"Alack, why is she so?"—
"She loveth another better than me,
And yet she will say, no."—
"I find no such doubleness;
I find women true.
My lady loveth me doubtless,
And will change for no new."—
"Happy art thou while that doth last;
But I say as I find:
That woman's love is but a blast,
And turneth like the wind."

"But if thou wilt avoid thy harm,
This lesson learn of me:
At others' fires thyself to warm,
And let them warm with thee."
"Such folks shall take no harm by love,
That can abide their turn;
But I, alas! can no way prove
In love, but lack and mourn."

WYATT

XLVIII MY LUTE, AWAKE

My lute, awake, perform the last
Labour that thou and I shall waste,
And end that I have now begun,
And, when this song is sung and past,
My lute, be still, for I have done!

As to be heard where ear is none,
As lead to grave in marble stone,
My song may pierce her heart as soon:
Should we, then, sigh or sing or moan?
No, no, my lute, for I have done!

The rocks do not so cruelly
Repulse the waves continually,
As she my suit and affectiòn:
So that I am past remedy:
Whereby my lute and I have done!

Proud of the spoil that thou hast got
Of simple hearts thorough Love's shot,
By whom unkind thou hast them won,
Think not he hath his bow forgot,
Although my lute and I have done!

Vengeance shall fall on thy disdain,
That mak'st but game of earnest pain,
Trow not alone under the sun
Unquit to cause thy lover's plain,
Although my lute and I have done.

Now cease, my lute, this is the last
Labour that thou and I shall waste,
And ended is that we begun:
Now is this song both sung and past—
My lute, be still, for I have done.

Wyatt

LIX GIVE PLACE, YE LOVERS

Give place, ye lovers, here before
That spent your boasts and brags in vain;
My lady's beauty passeth more
The best of yours, I dare well sayen,
Than doth the sun the candle light
Of brightest day the darkest night.

And thereto hath a troth as just
As had Penelope the fair;
For what she saith, ye may it trust,
As it by writing sealed were:
And virtues hath she many moe
Than I with pen have skill to show.

I could rehearse, if that I would,
The whole effect of Nature's plaint,
When she had lost the perfect mould,
The like to whom she could not paint:
With wringing hands, how she did cry,
And what she said, I know it, I.

I know she swore with raging mind,
Her kingdom only set apart,
There was no loss by law of kind
That could have gone so near her heart;
And this was chiefly all her pain;
"She could not make the like again."

Sith Nature thus gave her the praise,
To be the chiefest work she wrought;
In faith, methinks! some better ways
On your behalf might well be sought,
Than to compare, as ye have done,
To match the candle with the sun.

SURREY

L SUMMER IS COME

The soote season, that bud and bloom forth brings,
With green hath clad the hill, and eke the vale.
The nightingale with feathers new she sings;
The turtle to her mate hath told her tale.
Summer is come, for every spray now springs,
The hart hath hung his old head on the pale;
The buck in brake his winter coat he slings;
The fishes flit with new repaired scale;
The adder all her slough away she slings;
The swift swallow pursueth the flies smale;
The busy bee her honey now she mings;
Winter is worn that was the flowers' bale.
  And thus I see among these pleasant things
  Each care decays, and yet my sorrow springs!

SURREY

LI EPITAPH ON CLERE

Norfolk sprung thee, Lambeth holds thee dead;
Clere, of the Count of Cleremont, thou hight;
Within the womb of Ormond's race thou bred,
And saw'st thy cousin crowned in thy sight.

Shelton for love, Surrey for lord thou chase;
(Aye me! whilst life did last that league was tender)
Tracing whose steps thou sawest Kelsal blaze,
Landrecy burnt, and battered Boulogne render.
At Montreuil gates, hopeless of all recure,
Thine Earl, half dead, gave in thy hand his will;
Which cause did thee this pining death procure,
Ere summers four times seven thou couldst fulfill.
  Ah! Clere! if love had booted, care, or cost,
  Heaven had not won, nor earth so timely lost.

SURREY

LII THE OLD SHEPHERD'S MAY SONG

Is not thilke the mery moneth of May,
When love-lads masken in fresh aray?
How falles it, then, we no merrier bene,
Ylike as others, girt in gawdy greene?
Our bloncket liveryes bene all to sadde
For thilke same season, when all is ycladd
With pleasaunce: the grownd with grasse, the Woods
With greene leaves, the bushes with bloosming buds.
Yougthes folke now flocken in every where,
To gather May bus-kets and smelling brere:
And home they hasten the postes to dight,
And all the Kirke pillours eare day light,
With Hawthorne buds, and swete Eglantine,
And girlonds of roses, and Sopps in wine.
Such merimake holy Saints doth queme,
But we here sitten as drownd in a dreme.

. . . . .

Sicker this morrowe, no lenger agoe,
I sawe a shole of shepeheardes outgoe
With singing, and shouting, and jolly chere:
Before them yode a lusty Tabrere,
That to the many a Horne-pype playd,
Whereto they dauncen, eche one with his mayd.
To see those folkes make such jovysaunce,
Made my heart after the pype to daunce:
Tho to the greene Wood they speeden hem all,
To fetchen home May with their musicall:
And home they bringen in a royall throne,
Crowned as king: and his Queene attone

Was Lady Flora, on whom did attend
A fayre flocke of Faeries, and a fresh bend
Of lovely Nymphs. (O that I were there,
To helpen the Ladyes their Maybush beare !)

SPENSER

LIII HER NAME

One day I wrote her name upon the strand;
But came the waves, and washed it away:
Agayne, I wrote it with a second hand;
But came the tyde, and made my paynes his pray.
Vayne man, sayd she, that doest in vaine assay
A mortall thing so to immortalize;
For I my selve shall lyke to this decay,
And eek my name bee wyped out lykewize.
Not so, quod I; let baser things devize
To dy in dust, but you shall live by fame:
My verse your vertues rare shall éternize,
And in the hevens wryte your glorious name,
Where, whenas death shall all the world subdew
Our love shall live, and later life renew.

SPENSER

LIV THE MERRY CUCKOW

The merry Cuckow, messenger of Spring,
His trompet shrill hath thrise already sounded,
That warnes al lovers wayt upon their king,
Who now is comming forth with girland crowned.
With noyse whereof the quyre of Byrds resounded,
Their anthemes sweet, devized of loves prayse,
That all the woods theyr ecchoes back rebounded,
As if they knew the meaning of their layes.
But mongst them all, which did Loves honor rayse,
No word was heard of her that most it ought;
But she his precept proudly disobayes,
And doth his ydle message set at nought.
Therefore, O Love, unlesse she turne to thee
Ere Cuckow end, let her a rebell be.

SPENSER

LV THIS HOLY SEASON

This holy season, fit to fast and pray,
Men to devotion ought to be inclynd:
Therefore, I lykewise, on so holy day,
For my sweet Saynt some service fit will find.
Her temple fayre is built within my mind,
In which her glorious ymage placed is;
On which my thoughts doo day and night attend,
Lyke sacred priests that never thinke amisse!
There I to her, as th' author of my blisse,
Will builde an altar to appease her yre;
And on the same my hart will sacrifise,
Burning in flames of pure and chast desire:
  The which vouchsafe, O goddesse, to accept,
  Amongst thy deerest relicks to be kept.

SPENSER

LVI EASTER DAY

Most glorious Lord of Life, that on this day
  Didst make thy triumph over Death and Sin;
And having harrow'd hell, didst bring away
  Captivity thence captive, us to win:

This joyous day, dear Lord, with joy begin,
  And grant that we for whom thou diddest die,
Being with thy dear blood clean wash'd from sin,
  May live for ever in felicity;

And that thy love we weighing worthily,
  May likewise love thee for the same again:
And for thy sake, that all like dear didst buy,
  With love may one another entertain.

So let us love, dear Love, like as we ought,
Love is the lesson which the Lord us taught.

SPENSER

LVII THE LULLABY

Sing lullabies, as women do,
  With which they charm their babes to rest;
And lullaby can I sing too,
  As womanly as can the best.

With lullaby theystill the child,
And, if I be not much beguiled,
Full many wanton babes have I
Which must be still'd with lullaby.

First lullaby my youthful years;
  It is now time to go to bed;
For crooked age and hoary hairs
  Have wore the haven within mine head.
With lullaby, then, Youth, be still,
With lullaby content thy will;
Since courage quails and comes behind,
Go sleep, and so beguile thy mind.

Next lullaby my gazing Eyes
  Which wonted were to glance apace;
For every glass may now suffice
  To shew the furrows in my face.
With lullaby, then, wink awhile;
With lullaby your looks beguile;
Let no fair face or beauty bright
Entice you eft with vain delight.

And lullaby my wanton Will,
  Let Reason's rule now rein thy thought,
Since all too late I find by skill
  How dear I have thy fancies bought.
With lullaby now take thine ease,
With lullaby thy doubt appease;
For, trust in this, if thou be still,
My body shall obey thy will.

Thus lullaby my Youth, mine Eyes,
  My Will, my ware and all that was;
I can no more delays devise,
  But welcome pain, let pleasure pass.
With lullaby now take your leave,
With lullaby your dreams deceive:
And when you rise with waking eye,
Remember then this lullaby.

G. GASCOIGNE

LVIII A DIRGE

Ring out your bells, let mourning shews be spread;
For Love is dead:

All Love is dead, infected
With plague of deep disdain:
Worth, as nought worth, rejected,
And Faith fair scorn doth gain.
From so ungrateful fancy,
From such a female frenzy,
From them that use men thus,
Good Lord, deliver us!

Weep, neighbours, weep; do you not hear it said
That Love is dead?
His death-bed, peacock's folly;
His winding-sheet is shame;
His will, false-seeming wholly;
His sole executor, blame.
From so ungrateful fancy,
From such a female frenzy,
From them that use men thus,
Good Lord, deliver us!

Let dirge be sung, and trentals rightly read,
For Love is dead;
Sir Wrong his tomb ordaineth
My mistress' marble heart;
Which epitaph containeth,
"Her eyes were once his dart."
From so ungrateful fancy,
From such a female frenzy,
From them that use men thus,
Good Lord, deliver us!

Alas, I lie: rage hath this error bred;
Love is not dead;
Love is not dead, but sleepeth
In her unmatchèd mind,
Where she his counsel keepeth,
Till due deserts she find.
Therefore from so vile fancy,
To call such wit a frenzy,
Who Love can temper thus,
Good Lord, deliver us!

SIR PHILIP SIDNEY

LIX DESIRE

Thou blind man's mark, thou fool's self-chosen snare,
Fond fancy's scum, and dregs of scattered thought:
Band of all evils; cradle of causeless care;
Thou web of will, whose end is never wrought:
Desire! Desire! I have too dearly bought,
With price of mangled mind, thy worthless ware;
Too long, too long, asleep thou hast me brought,
Who should my mind to higher things prepare.
But yet in vain thou hast my ruin sought;
In vain thou mad'st me to vain things aspire;
In vain thou kindlest all thy smoky fire;
For Virtue hath this better lesson taught,—
Within myself to seek my only hire,
Desiring nought but how to kill Desire.

Sidney

LX ETERNAL LOVE

Leave me, O Love, which reachest but to dust;
And thou, my mind, aspire to higher things;
Grow rich in that which never taketh rust;
Whatever fades, but fading pleasure brings.
Draw in thy beams, and humble all thy might
To that sweet yoke where lasting freedoms be;
Which breaks the clouds, and opens forth the light
That doth both shine, and give us sight to see.
O take fast hold; let that light be thy guide
In this small course which birth draws out to death,
And think how ill becometh him to slide,
Who seeketh heaven, and comes of heavenly breath.
Then farewell, world; thy uttermost I see:
Eternal Love, maintain thy life in me!

Sidney

LXI THE IMPATIENT LOVER

Be your words made, good Sir, of Indian ware,
That you allow me them by so small rate?
Or do you curted Spartans imitate?
Or do you mean my tender ears to spare,

That to my questions you so total are?
When I demand of Phoenix-Stella's state,
You say, forsooth, you left her well of late:
O God, think you that satisfies my care?
I would know whether she did sit or walk;
How clothed; how waited on; sighed she, or smiled;
Whereof,—with whom,—how often did she talk;
With what pastimes Time's journey she beguiled;
If her lips deigned to sweeten my poor name:
Say all; and all well said, still say the same.

SIDNEY

LXII GREENSLEEVES

Alas, my love, ye do me wrong,
  To cast me off discourteously,
And I have lovèd you so long,
  Delighting in your company.
    Greensleeves was all my joy,
      Greensleeves was my delight:
    Greensleeves was my heart of gold,
      And who but Lady Greensleeves.

I have been ready at your hand,
  To grant whatever you would crave,
I have both wagèd life and land,
  Your love and goodwill for to have.

I bought thee kerchers to thy head,
  That were wrought fine and gallantly:
I kept thee both at board and bed,
  Which cost my purse well favouredly.

I bought thee petticoats of the best,
  The cloth so fine as fine might be:
I gave thee jewels for thy chest,
  And all this cost I spent on thee.

Thy smock of silk, both fair and white,
  With gold embroidered gorgeously:
Thy petticoat of sendal right:
  And thus I bought thee gladly.

Thy girdle of the gold so red,
  With pearls bedeckèd sumptuously:
The like no other ladies had,
  And yet thou wouldst not love me.

Thy purse and eke thy gay gilt knives,
  Thy pincase gallant to the eye:
No better wore the burgess' wives,
  And yet thou wouldst not love me.

Thy crimson stockings all of silk,
  With gold all wrought above the knee,
Thy pumps as white as was the milk,
  And yet thou wouldst not love me.

Thy gown was of the grassy green,
  Thy sleeves of satin hanging by:
Which made thee be our harvest queen,
  And yet thou wouldst not love me.

Thy garters fringèd with the gold,
  And silver aglets hanging by,
Which made thee blithe for to behold,
  And yet thou wouldst not love me.

LXIII HARK! HARK! THE NIGHTINGALE

Hark, hark, hark! the nightingale
  In her mourning lay,
She tells her story's woful tale,
  To warn ye if she may:
"Fair maids, take ye heed of love,
  It is a perilous thing;
As Philomel herself did prove,
    Abusèd by a king;
    If kings play false, believe no men,
      That make a scanty outward show;
    But caught once, beware then,
      For then begins your woe.
    They will look babies in your eyes,
      And speak so fair as fair may be;
    But trust them in no wise,
      Example take by me."

"Fie, fie!" said the threstle-cock,
  "You are much to blame,
For one man's fault all men to blot,
  Impairing their good name.

Admit you were used amiss
  By that ungentle king,
It does not follow that you for this
  Should all men's honours wring.
    There be good, and there be bad,
      And some are false, and some are true;
    As good choice is still had
      Amongst us men as you.
    Women have faults as well as we,
    Some say for our one they have three.
    Then smite not, nor bite not,
      When you as faulty be."

"Peace, peace," quoth Madge-Howlet then,
  Sitting out of sight;
"For women are as good as men,
  And both are good alike."
"Not so," said the little wren,
  "Difference there may be,
The cock always commands the hen;
  Then men shall go for me."
    Then Robin Redbreast stepping in
      Would needs take up this tedious strife,
    Protesting true loving
      In either lengthen'd life.
    "If I love you, and you love me
    Can the e be better harmony?
    Then ending contending
    Love must the umpire be."

SHEPHERD TONY

LXIV THE SOUL'S ERRAND

Go, Soul, the body's guest,
  Upon a thankless arrant:
Fear not to touch the best;
  The truth shall be thy warrant:
Go, since I needs must die,
And give the world the lie.

Say to the Court, it glows
  And shines like rotten wood;
Say to the Church, it shows
  What's good, and doth no good:

If Church and Court reply,
Then give them both the lie.

Tell Potentates, they live
  Acting by others' action ;
Not loved unless they give,
  Not strong, but by a faction :
If Potentates reply,
Give Potentates the lie.

Tell men of high condition,
  That manage the estate,
Their purpose is ambition,
  Their practice only hate :
And if they once reply,
Then give them all the lie.

Tell them that brave it most,
  They beg for more by spending,
Who, in their greatest cost,
  Seek nothing but commending :
And if they make reply,
Then give them all the lie.

Tell Zeal it wants devotion ;
  Tell Love it is but lust ;
Tell Time it is but motion ;
  Tell Flesh it is but dust ;
And wish them not reply,
For thou must give the lie.

Tell Age it daily wasteth ;
  Tell Honour how it alters ;
Tell Beauty how she blasteth ;
  Tell Favour how it falters :
And as they shall reply,
Give every one the lie.

Tell Wit how much it wrangles
  In tickle points of niceness ;
Tell Wisdom she entangles
  Herself in over-wiseness :
And when they do reply,
Straight give them both the lie.

Tell Physic of her boldness;
 Tell Skill it is pretension;
Tell Charity of coldness;
 Tell Law it is contention:
And as they do reply,
So give them still the lie.

Tell Fortune of her blindness;
 Tell Nature of decay;
Tell Friendship of unkindness;
 Tell Justice of delay:
And if they will reply,
Then give them all the lie.

Tell Arts they have no soundness,
 But vary by esteeming;
Tell Schools they want profoundness,
 And stand too much on seeming:
If Arts and Schools reply,
Give arts and schools the lie.

Tell Faith it's fled the city;
 Tell how the country erreth;
Tell, manhood shakes off pity:
 Tell, virtue least preferreth:
And if they do reply,
Spare not to give the lie.

So when thou hast, as I
 Commanded thee, done blabbing,—
Although to give the lie
 Deserves no less than stabbing:—
Stab at thee he that will,
No stab the Soul can kill.

Sir W. Raleigh

XV A VISION UPON SPENSER'S "FAERY QUEEN"

Methought I saw the grave where Laura lay,
Within that temple where the vestal flame
Was wont to burn; and passing by that way,
To see that buried dust of living fame,
Whose tomb fair Love and fairer Virtue kept;
All suddenly I saw the Faery Queen;

At whose approach the soul of Petrarch wept;
And from henceforth those graces were not seen,
For they this Queen attended: in whose stead
Oblivion laid him down on Laura's hearse:
Hereat the hardest stones were seen to bleed,
And groans of buried ghosts the heavens did pierce,
  Where Homer's sprite did tremble all for grief,
  And cursed th' access of that celestial thief.

RALEIGH

LXVI THE BEGGAR AT THE DOOR

Pity refusing my poor Love to feed,
  A Beggar starv'd for want of help he lies,
  And at your mouth, the Door of Beauty, cries,
That thence some alms of sweet grants may proceed.
But as he waiteth for some almès-deed
  A cherry-tree before the door he spies:
  "Oh dear," quoth he, "two cherries may suffice,
Two only life may save in this my need."
"But beggars can they nought but cherries eat?"
  "Pardon my Love, he is a goddess' son,
And never feedeth but on dainty meat,
  Else need he not to pine as he hath done:
For only the sweet fruit of this sweet tree
Can give food to my Love, and life to me."

CONSTABLE

LXVII THE BROKEN CHARM

Thrice toss these oaken ashes in the air,
  And thrice three times tie-up this true love-knot;
Thrice sit thee down in this enchanted chair,
  And murmur soft, She will, or she will not.

Go burn these poisoned weeds in that blue fire,
  This cypress gathered at a dead man's grave;
These screech-owl's feathers, and this pricking briar,
  That all thy thorny cares an end may have.

Then come, you fairies, dance with me a round:
  Dance in this circle, let my love be centre;
Melodiously breathe out a charming sound;
  Melt her hard heart, that some remorse may enter.

In vain are all the charms I can devise!
She hath an art to break them with her eyes.

J. SYLVESTER

LXVIII MAY

When May is in his prime, then may each heart rejoice;
When May bedecks each branch with green, each bird strains forth his voice,
The lively sap creeps up into the blooming thorn,
The flowers, which cold in prison kept, now laugh the frost to scorn.
All Nature's imps triúmph, while joyful May doth last;
When May is gone, of all the year the pleasant time is past.

May makes the cheerful hue, May breeds and brings new blood,
May marcheth throughout every limb, May makes the merry mood.
May pricketh tender hearts, their warbling notes to tune,
Full strange it is, yet some, we see, do make their May in June.
Thus things are strangely wrought, whiles joyful May doth last;
Take May in time, when May is gone, the pleasant time is past.

All ye that live on earth, and have your May at will,
Rejoice in May, as I do now, and use your May with skill.
Use May, while that you May, for May hath but his time;
When all the fruit is gone, it is too late the tree to climb,
Your liking, and your lust is fresh whiles May doth last,
When May is gone of all the year the pleasant time is past.

R. EDWARDES

LXIX AMANTIUM IRÆ

In going to my naked bed, as one that would have slept,
I heard a wife sing to her child, that long before had wept.
She sighed sore, and sang full sweet, to bring the babe to rest,
That would not cease, but cried still, in sucking at her breast.
She was full weary of her watch, and grieved with her child;
She rocked it, and rated it, until on her it smiled;
Then did she say: "Now have I found the proverb true to prove,
The falling out of faithful friends renewing is of love."

Then took I paper, pen, and ink, this proverb for to write,
In register for to remain of such a worthy wight.
As she proceeded thus in song unto her little brat,
Much matter uttered she of weight in place whereas she sat;
And proved plain, there was no beast, nor creature bearing life,
Could well be known to live in love without discord and strife:
Then kissed she her little babe, and sware by God above,
"*The falling out of faithful friends renewing is of love.*"

"I marvel much, pardie," quoth she, "for to behold the rout,
To see man, woman, boy, and beast, to toss the world about;
Some kneel, some crouch, some beck, some check, and some can smoothly smile,
And some embrace others in arms, and there think many a wile.
Some stand aloof at cap and knee, some humble, and some stout,
Yet are they never friends indeed until they once fall out."
Thus ended she her song, and said, before she did remove:
"*The falling out of faithful friends renewing is of love.*"

R. EDWARDES

LXX FANCY AND DESIRE

Come hither, shepherd's swain.—"Sir, what do you require?"
I pray thee, show to me thy name.—"My name is Fond Desire."
When wert thou born, Desire?—"In pomp and pride of May."
By whom, sweet boy, wert thou begot?—"By Fond Conceit, men say."
Tell me, who was thy nurse?—"Fresh youth in sugared joy."
What was thy meat and daily food?—"Sad sighs with great annoy."
What hadst thou then to drink?—"The savoury lover's tears."
What cradle wert thou rocked in?—"Hope devoid of fears."
What lull'd thee then asleep?—"Sweet speech, which likes me best."
Tell me, where is thy dwelling-place?—"In gentle hearts I rest."

What thing doth please thee most?—"To gaze on beauty still."
Whom dost thou think to be thy foe?—"Disdain of my good will."
Doth company displease?—"Yes, surely, many one."
Where doth Desire delight to live?—"He loves to live alone."
Doth either time or age bring him unto decay?—
"No, no, Desire both lives and dies a thousand times a day."
Then, Fond Desire, farewell, thou art no mate for me;
I should be loth, methinks, to dwell with such a one as thee.

Ed. Vere (Earl of Oxford)

LXXI LOVE

Turn I my looks unto the skies,
Love with his arrows wounds mine eyes
If so I gaze upon the ground,
Love then in every flower is found;
Search I the shade to fly my pain,
Love meets me in the shade again;
Want I to walk in secret grove,
E'en there I meet with sacred love;
If so I bathe me in the spring,
E'en on the brink I hear him sing;
If so I meditate alone,
He will be partner of my moan;
If so I mourn, he weeps with me,
And where I am there will he be!

Thomas Lodge.

LXXII SONG OF GRIEF

I see there is no sort
Of things that live in grief,
Which at some time may not resort,
Whereas they find relief.

The chacéd deer hath soil,
To cool him in his heat;
The ass, after his weary toil,
In stable is up set.

The coney hath its cave,
The little bird its nest,
From heat and cold themselves to save,
At all times as they list.

The owl, with feeble sight,
Lies lurking in the leaves;
The sparrow, in the frosty night,
May shroud her in the eaves.

But, woe to me, alas!
In sun, nor yet in shade,
I cannot find a resting-place
My burthen to unlade.

LXXIII SAMELA

Like to Diana in her summer-weed,
Girt with a crimson robe of brightest dye,
Goes fair Samela;

Whiter than be the flocks that straggling feed,
When washed by Arethusa Fount they lie,
Is fair Samela;

As fair Aurora in her morning-grey,
Decked with the ruddy glister of her love,
Is fair Samela;

Like lovely Thetis on a calmed day,
Whenas her brightness Neptune's fancy move,
Shines fair Samela;

Her tresses gold, her eyes like glassy streams,
Her teeth are pearl, the breasts are ivory
Of fair Samela;

Her cheeks, like rose and lily, yield forth gleams,
Her brows bright arches framed of ebony:
Thus fair Samela

Passeth fair Venus in her bravest hue,
And Juno in the show of majesty,
For she's Samela;

Pallas in wit, all three, if you well view,
For beauty, wit, and matchless dignity,
Yield to Samela.

GREENE

LXXIV CONTENT

Sweet are the thoughts that savour of content;
The quiet mind is richer than a crown;
Sweet are the nights in careless slumber spent;
The poor estate scorns fortune's angry frown:

Such sweet content, such minds, such sleep, such bliss,
Beggars enjoy, when princes oft do miss.

The homely house that harbours quiet rest;
The cottage that affords no pride nor care;
The mean that 'grees with country music best;
The sweet consort of mirth and music's fare;
Obscured life sets down a type of bliss:
A mind content both crown and kingdom is.

GREENE

LXXV DILDIDO, DILDIDO

Dildido, dildido,
O love, O love,
I feel thy rage rumble below and above!
In summer-time I saw a face,
Trop belle pour moi, hélas, hélas!
Like to a stoned-horse was her pace:
Was ever young man so dismayed?
Her eyes, like wax-torches, did make me afraid:
Trop belle pour moi, voilà mon trépas.

Thy beauty, my love, exceedeth supposes;
Thy hair is a nettle for the nicest roses,
Mon dieu, aide moi!
That I with the primrose of my fresh wit
May tumble her tyranny under my feet:
Hé donc, je serai un jeune roi!
Trop belle pour moi, hélas, hélas,
Trop belle pour moi, voilà mon trépas.

GREENE

LXXVI CHOPCHERRY

Whenas the rye reach to the chin,
And chopcherry, chopcherry ripe within,
Strawberries swimming in the cream,
And schoolboys playing in the stream;
Then, O, then, O, then, O, my true love said,
Till that time come again
She could not live a maid.

PEELE

LXXVII SOWING AND REAPING

"All ye that lovely lovers be,
Pray you for me.
Lo, here we come a-sowing,
a-sowing,
And sow sweet fruits of love,
In your sweet hearts well may it prove.

Lo, here we come a-reaping,
a-reaping,
To reap our harvest-fruit;
And thus we pass the year so long,
And never be we mute."

PEELE

LXXVIII SPREAD, TABLE, SPREAD

Spread, table, spread,
Meat, drink, and bread,
Ever may I have
What I ever crave,
When I am spread,
Meat for my black cock,
And meat for my red.

PEELE

LXXIX YOUTH'S WANING

His golden locks time hath to silver turned;
O time too swift, O swiftness never ceasing!
His youth 'gainst time and age hath ever spurned,
But spurned in vain; youth waneth by increasing:
Beauty, strength, youth, are flowers but fading seen;
Duty, faith, love, are roots, and ever green.

His helmet now shall make a hive for bees,
And, lovers' sonnets turned to holy psalms,
A man-at-arms must now serve on his knees,
And feed on prayers, which are age his alms:
But though from court to cottage he depart,
His saint is sure of his unspotted heart.

And when he saddest sits in homely cell,
He'll teach his swains this carol for a song,—
"Blessed be the hearts that wish my sovereign well,
Cursed be the souls that think her any wrong."
Goddess, allow this aged man his right,
To be your beadsman now that was your knight.

PEELE

LXXX FAIR AND FAIR, AND TWICE SO FAIR

(*For Two Singers.*)

I. Fair and fair, and twice so fair,
As fair as any may be;
The fairest shepherd on our green,
A love for any lady.

II. Fair and fair, and twice so fair,
As fair as any may be;
Thy love is fair for thee alone,
And for no other lady.

I. My love is fair, my love is gay,
As fresh as bin the flowers in May,
And of my love my roundelay,
My merry, merry, merry roundelay,
Concludes with Cupid's curse,—
They that do change old love for new,
Pray gods they change for worse!

I. and II. They that do change old love for new,
Pray gods they change for worse.

I. My love can pipe, my love can sing,
My love can many a pretty thing,
And of his lovely praises ring
My merry, merry roundelays,
Amen to Cupid's curse.

PEELE

XXXI SUMMER'S DROOPING

Fair summer droops, droop men and beasts therefore;
So fair a summer look for never more:
All good things vanish less than in a day,
Peace, plenty, pleasure, suddenly decay
Go not yet away, bright soul of the sad year,
The earth is hell when thou leav'st to appear.

What, shall those flowers that decked thy garland erst,
Upon thy grave be wastefully dispersed?
O trees, consume your sap in sorrow's source,
Streams, turn to tears your tributary course.
  Go not yet hence, bright soul of the sad year,
  The earth is hell when thou leav'st to appear.

THOMAS NASHE

LXXXII SPRING'S WELCOME

What bird so sings, yet so does wail?
O 'tis the ravished nightingale.
"Jug, jug, jug, jug, tereu," she cries,
And still her woes at midnight rise,
Brave prick-song! who is't now we hear?
None but the lark so shrill and clear;
Now at heaven's gates she claps her wings,
The morn not waking till she sings.
Hark, hark, with what a pretty throat,
Poor robin redbreast tunes his note;
Hark how the jolly cuckoos sing,
Cuckoo to welcome in the spring!
Cuckoo to welcome in the spring!

LYLY

LXXXIII SYRINX

Pan's Syrinx was a girl indeed,
Though now she's turned into a reed;
From that dear reed Pan's pipe does come,
A pipe that strikes Apollo dumb;
Nor flute, nor lute, nor gittern can
So chant it as the pipe of Pan:
Cross-gartered swains and dairy girls,
With faces smug and round as pearls,
When Pan's shrill pipe begins to play,
With dancing wear out night and day;
The bagpipe's drone his hum lays by,
When Pan sounds up his minstrelsy;
His minstrelsy! O base! this quill,
Which at my mouth with wind I fill,
Puts me in mind, though her I miss,
That still my Syrinx' lips I kiss.

LYLY

LXXXIV THE FAIRY FROLIC

By the moon we sport and play,
With the night begins our day:
As we frisk the dew doth fall:
Trip it, little urchins all!
Lightly as the little bee,
Two by two, and three by three:
And about go we, and about go we!

First Fairy.

I do come about the copse
Leaping upon flowers' tops;
Then I get upon a fly,
She carries me about the sky,
And trip and go.

Second Fairy.

When a dewdrop falleth down,
And doth light upon my crown,
Then I shake my head and skip,
And about I trip.

Fairies sing.

Round about, round about, in a fine ring a,
Thus we dance, thus we dance and thus we sing a;
Trip and go, to and fro, over this green a,
All about, in and out, for our brave queen a.

LYLY

LXXXV THE COUNTRY LAD

Who can live in heart so glad
As the merry country lad,
Who upon a fair green baulk
May at pleasure sit and walk,
And amid the azure skies
See the morning sun arise?
While he hears in every spring
How the birds do chirp and sing;
Or before the hounds in cry
See the hare go stealing by;
Or, along the shallow brook,
Angling with a baited hook,

See the fishes leap and play
In a blessed sunny day;
Or to hear the partridge call
Till she have her covey all;
Or to see the subtle fox,
How the villain plies the box;
After feeding on his prey
How he closely sneaks away,
Through the hedge and down the furrow
Till he gets into his burrow;
Then the bėe to gather honey;
And the little black-haired coney
On a bank for sunny place
With her forefeet wash her face:
Are not these with thousands moe
Than the courts of kings do know,
The true pleasing spirit's sights,
That may breed true love's delights?
But with all this happiness
To behold that shepherdess
To whose eyes all shepherds yield
All the fairest of the field;
Fair Aglaia; in whose face
Lives the shepherd's highest grace;
For whose sake I say and swear,
By the passions that I bear,
Had I got a kingly grace,
I would leave my kingly place
And in heart be truly glad
To become a country lad!

N. Breton

LXXXVI

A PASTORAL OF PHYLLIS AND CORYDON

On a hill there grows a flower,
  Fair befall the dainty sweet!
By that flower there is a bower,
  Where the heavenly Muses meet.

In that bower there is a chair,
  Fringèd all about with gold;
Where doth sit the fairest fair,
  That ever eye did yet behold.

It is Phyllis fair and bright,
  She that is the shepherds' joy;
She that Venus did despite,
  And did blind her little boy.

This is she, the wise, the rich,
  That the world desires to see;
This is *ipsa quæ* the which
  There is none but only she.

Who would not this face admire?
  Who would not this saint adore?
Who would not this sight desire,
  Though he thought to see no more?

Oh, fair eyes! yet let me see
  One good look and I am gone;
Look on me, for I am he,
  Thy poor silly Corydon.

Thou that art the shepherds' queen,
  Look upon the silly swain;
By thy comfort have been seen
  Dead men brought to life again.

N. Breton

LXXXVII A SWEET PASTORAL

Good Muse, rock me asleep
  With some sweet harmony;
The weary eye is not to keep
  Thy wary company.

Sweet Love, begone awhile,
  Thou knowest my heaviness;
Beauty is born but to beguile
  My heart of happiness.

See how my little flock,
  That loved to feed on high,
Do headlong tumble down the rock,
  And in the valley die.

The bushes and the trees
  That were so fresh and green,
Do all their dainty colour leese,
  And not a leaf is seen.

The blackbird and the thrush
  That made the woods to ring,
With all the rest are now at hush,
  And not a note they sing.

Sweet Philomel, the bird
  That hath the heavenly throat,
Doth now, alas! not once afford
  Recording of a note.

The flowers have had a frost,
  Each herb hath lost her savour,
And Phyllida the fair hath lost
  The comfort of her favour.

Now all these careful sights
  So kill me in conceit,
That how to hope upon delights,
  It is but mere deceit.

And therefore, my sweet Muse,
  Thou knowest what help is best;
Do now thy heavenly cunning use,
  To set my heart at rest.

And in a dream bewray
  What fate shall be my friend,
Whether my life shall still decay,
  Or when my sorrow end.

N. Breton

LXXXVIII THE JOLLY SHEPHERD

Jolly shepherd, shepherd on a hill,
    On a hill so merrily,
    On a hill so cheerily,
Fear not, shepherd, there to pipe thy fill,
Fill every dale, fill every plain:
  Both sing and say, "Love feels no pain."

Jolly shepherd, shepherd on a green,
    On a green so merrily
    On a green so cheerily,
Be thy voice shrill, be thy mirth seen,
Heard to each swain, seen to each trill:
    Both sing and say, "Love's joy is full."

Jolly shepherd, shepherd in the sun,
In the sun so merrily,
In the sun so cheerily,
Sing forth thy songs, and let thy rhymes run
Down to the dales from the hills above:
Both sing and say, "No life to love."

Jolly shepherd, shepherd in the shade
In the shade so merrily,
In the shade so cheerily,
Joy in thy life, life of shepherd's trade
Joy in thy love, love full of glee:
Both sing and say, "Sweet Love for me."

Jolly shepherd, shepherd here or there,
Here or there so merrily,
Here or there so cheerily,
Or in thy chat, either at thy cheer,
In every jig, in every lay
Both sing and say, "Love lasts for aye."

Jolly shepherd, shepherd Daphnis' love,
Daphnis' love so merrily,
Daphnis' love so cheerily,
Let thy fancy never more remove,
Fancy be fix'd, fix'd not to fleet
Still sing and say, "Love's yoke is sweet."

John Wootton

LXXXIX THE FAIR SHEPHERDESS

My Phyllis hath the morning Sun,
At first to look upon her;
And Phyllis hath morn-waking birds,
Her rising still to honour.
My Phyllis hath prime-feathered flowers,
That smile when she treads on them;
And Phyllis hath a gallant flock,
That leaps since she doth own them.
But Phyllis hath too hard a heart,
Alas, that she should have it!

It yields no mercy to desert,
Nor grace to those that crave it.
Sweet Sun, when thou look'st on,
Pray her regard my moan!

Sweet birds, when you sing to her,
  To yield some pity, woo her!
Sweet flowers, that she treads on,
  Tell her her beauty deads one.
And if in life her love she nill agree me,
  Pray her before I die, she will come see me.

THOMAS LODGE

XC THE SHEPHERD'S DUMP

Like desert woods, with darksome shades obscurèd,
Where dreadful beasts, where hateful horror reigneth,
  Such is my wounded heart, whom sorrow paineth.

The trees are fatal shafts, to death inurèd,
That cruel love within my heart maintaineth
  To whet my grief, whenas my sorrow waneth.

The ghastly beasts, my thoughts in cares assurèd,
Which wage me war, whilst heart no succour gaineth,
  With false suspect and fear that still remaineth.

The horrors, burning sighs, by cares procurèd,
Which forth I send, whilst weeping eye complaineth,
  To cool the heat the helpless heart containeth.

But shafts, but cares, sighs, horrors unrecurèd,
Were nought esteem'd if, for their pains awarded,
  Your shepherd's love might be by you regarded.

S. E. D.

XCI SWEET SUFFOLK OWL

Sweet Suffolk owl, so trimly dight
With feathers, like a lady bright,
Thou sing'st alone, sitting by night,
    Te whit, te whoo!

Thy note that forth so freely rolls,
With shrill command the mouse controls
And sings a dirge for dying souls,
    Te whit, te whoo!

XCII THE SHEPHERDS' CAROL

Sweet Music, sweeter far
Than any song is sweet;
Sweet Music, heavenly rare,
Mine ears (O peers!) doth greet.

You gentle flocks, whose fleeces, pearl'd with dew,
Resemble heaven, whom gólden drops make bright,
Listen, O listen! now, O not to you
Our pipes make sport to shorten weary night.
  But voices most divine,
  Make blissful harmony;
  Voices that seem to shine,
  For what else clears the sky?
Tunes can we hear, but not the singers see;
The tunes divine, and so the singers be.

  Lo! how the firmament
  Within an azure fold
  The flock of stars hath pent,
  That we might them behold.
Yet from their beams proceedeth not this light,
Nor can their crystals such reflection give.
What, then, doth make the element so bright?
The heavens are come down upon earth to live.
  But hearken to the song:
  "Glory to glory's King!
  And peace all men among!"
  These choristers do sing.
Angels they are, as also, shepherds, he
Whom in our fear we do admire to see.

  "Let not amazement blind
  Your souls," said he, "annoy;
  To you and all mankind,
  My message bringeth joy.
For, lo! the world's great Shepherd now is born,
A blessed babe, an infant full of power;
After long night uprisen is the morn,
Renowning Bethlem in the Saviour.
  Sprung is the perfect day,
  By prophets seen afar;
  Sprung is the mirthful May,
  Which Winter cannot mar."
In David's city doth this sun appear,
Clouded in flesh, yet, shepherds, sit we here?

E. B.

XCIII TO AMARYLLIS

Though Amaryllis dance in green,
Like fairy queen,
And sing full clear
With smiling cheer;
Yet since her eyes make heart so sore,
Heigho! chill love no more.

My sheep are lost for want of food,
And I so wood,
That all the day
I sit and watch a herdmaid gay,
Who laughs to see me sigh so sore;
Heigho! chill love no more.

Love ye who list, I force him not;
Sith God it wot
The more I wail,
The less my sighs and tears prevail.
What shall I do? but say therefore,
Heigho! chill love no more.

XCIV THE SHEPHERD'S SLUMBER

In peascod time, when hound to horn
Gives ear till buck be kill'd,
And little lads with pipes of corn
Sat keeping beasts a-field,
I went to gather strawberries tho,
By woods and groves full fair;
And parch'd my face with Phœbus so,
In walking in the air,
That down I laid me by a stream,
With boughs all over-clad;
And there I met the strangest dream
That ever shepherd had.
Methought I saw each Christmas game,
Each revel all and some,
And everything that I can name,
Or may in fancy come.

XCV A WOOING SONG OF A YEOMAN OF KENT'S SON

I have house and land in Kent,
And if you'll love me, love me now;
Twopence-halfpenny is my rent,
I cannot come every day to woo.
Chorus. Twopence-halfpenny is his rent,
And he cannot come every day to woo.

I am my vather's eldest zonne,
My mother eke doth love me well,
For I can bravely clout my shoone,
And I full well can ring a bell.
Chorus. For he can bravely clout his shoone,
And he full well can ring a bell.

My vather he gave me a hog,
My mouther she gave me a zow;
I have a God-vather dwells thereby,
And he on me bestowed a plow.
Chorus. He has a God-vather dwells thereby,
And he on him bestowed a plough.

One time I gave thee a paper of pins,
Another time a tawdry-lace;
And if thou wilt not grant me love,
In truth I die bevore thy vace.
Chorus. And if thou wilt not grant his love,
In truth he'll die bevore thy face.

I have been twice our Whitson-lord,
I have had ladies many vair,
And eke thou hast my heart in hold
And in my mind zeemes passing rare.
Chorus. And eke thou hadst his heart in hold
And in his mind zeemes passing rare.

I will put on my best white slops
And I will wear my yellow hose,
And on my head a good grey hat,
And in't I stick a lovely rose.
Chorus. And on his head a good grey hat,
And in't he'll stick a lovely rose.

Wherefore cease off, make no delay;
 And if you'll love me, love me now,
Or else I'll zeek zome oderwhere,
 For I cannot come every day to woo.

Chorus. Or else he'll zeek zome oderwhere,
 For he cannot come every day to woo.

XCVI THE MARRIAGE OF THE FROG AND THE MOUSE

It was the frog in the well,
 Humbledum, Humbledum,
And the merry mouse in the mill,
 Tweedle, tweedle, twino.

The frog would a-wooing ride
Sword and buckler by his side.

When he upon his high horse set,
His boots they shone as black as jet.

When he came to the merry mill-pin,—
"Lady Mouse, been you within?"

Then came out the dusty mouse:
"I am Lady of this house:

Hast thou any mind of me?"
"I have e'en great mind of thee."

"Who shall this marriage make?"
"Our Lord which is the rat."

"What shall we have to our supper?"
"Three beans in a pound of butter."

When supper they were at,
The frog, the mouse, and e'en the rat;

Then came in Gib our cat,
And catched the mouse e'en by the back.

Then did they separate,
And the frog leaped on the floor so flat.

Then came in Dick our drake,
And drew the frog e'en to the lake.

The rat ran up the wall,
  Humbledum, humbledum;
A goodly company, the Devil go with all!
  Tweedle, tweedle, twino.

IN MIDST OF WOODS OR PLEASANT GROVES

In midst of woods or pleasant groves,
  Where all sweet birds do sing,
Methought I heard so rare a sound
  Which made the heavens to ring.

The charm was good, the noise full sweet,
  Each bird did play his part;
And I admired to hear the same;
  Joy sprang into my heart.

The blackbird made the sweetest sound,
  Whose tunes did far excel;
Full pleasantly, and most profound
  Was all things placèd well.

Thy pretty tunes, mine own sweet bird,
  Done with so good a grace,
Extol thy name, prefer the same
  Abroad in every place.

Thy music grave, bedeckèd well
  With sundry points of skill,
Bewrays thy knowledge excellent
  Ingrafted in thy will.

My tongue shall speak, my pen shall write
  In praise of thee to tell;
The sweetest bird that ever was—
  In friendly sort farewell!

THE BELLMAN'S SONG

Maids to bed, and cover coal;
Let the mouse out of her hole;
Crickets in the chimney sing
Whilst the little bell doth ring:
If fast asleep, who can tell
When the clapper hits the bell?

XCIX SISTER, AWAKE!

Sister, awake! close not your eyes!
  The day her light discloses,
And the bright morning doth arise
  Out of her bed of roses.

See the clear sun, the world's bright eye,
  In at our window peeping,
Lo, how he blusheth to espy
  Us idle wenches sleeping.

Therefore awake! make haste, I say,
  And let us, without staying,
All in our gowns of green so gay
  Into the Park a-Maying.

C FAIN WOULD I CHANGE THAT NOTE

Fain would I change that note
To which fond Love hath charm'd me
Long, long to sing by rote,
Fancying that that harmed me:
Yet when this thought doth come
"Love is the perfect sum
    Of all delight,"
I have no other choice
Either for pen or voice
    To sing or write.

O Love! they wrong thee much
That say thy sweet is bitter,
When thy rich fruit is such
As nothing can be sweeter.
Fair house of joy and bliss,
Where truest pleasure is,
    I do adore thee:
I know thee what thou art,
I serve thee with my heart,
    And fall before thee!

CI WINTER, PLAGUE AND PESTILENCE

Autumn hath all the summer's fruitful treasure;
Gone is our sport, fled is our Croydon's pleasure!

ort days, sharp days, long nights come on apace:
h, who shall hide us from the winter's face?
old doth increase, the sickness will not cease,
nd here we lie, God knows, with little ease.
From winter, plague and pestilence, good Lord, deliver us!

ondon doth mourn, Lambeth is quite forlorn!
rades cry, woe worth that ever they were born!
he want of term is town and city's harm;
lose chambers we do want to keep us warm.
ong banishèd must we live from our friends;
his low-built house will bring us to our ends.
From winter, plague and pestilence, good Lord, deliver us!

II HAYMAKERS, RAKERS, REAPERS AND MOWERS

Haymakers, rakers, reapers and mowers,
Wait on your Summer-Queen!
Dress up with musk-rose her eglantine bowers,
Daffodils strew the green!
Sing, dance and play,
'Tis holiday!
The sun does bravely shine
On our ears of corn.
Rich as a pearl
Comes every girl.
This is mine, this is mine, this is mine.
Let us die ere away they be borne.

Bow to our Sun, to our Queen, and that fair one
Come to behold our sports;
Each bonny lass here is counted a rare one,
As those in princes' courts.
These and we
With country glee,
Will teach the woods to resound,
And the hills with echoes hollow.
Skipping lambs
Their bleating dams
'Mongst kids shall trip it round;
For joy thus our wenches we follow.

Wind jolly huntsmen, your neat bugles shrilly,
Hounds make a lusty cry;
Spring up, you falconers, partridges freely,
Then let your brave hawks fly!
Horses amain,
Over ridge, over plain,
The dogs have the stag in chase:
'Tis a sport to content a king.
So ho! ho! through the skies
How the proud bird flies,
And sousing, kills with a grace!
Now the deer falls; hark! how they ring.

DEKKER

CIII IN YOUTH IS PLEASURE

In an arbour green, asleep whereas I lay,
The birds sang sweet in the middes of the day;
I dreamèd fast of mirth and play:
In youth is pleasure, in youth is pleasure.

Methought I walked still to and fro,
And from her company I could not go;
But when I waked it was not so:
In youth is pleasure, in youth is pleasure.

Therefore my heart is surely pight
Of her alone to have a sight,
Which is my joy and heart's delight:
In youth is pleasure, in youth is pleasure.

R. WEVER

CIV THE BEGGAR

Love banish'd heaven, in earth was held in scorn,
Wand'ring abroad in need and beggary;
And wanting friends, though of a goddess born,
Yet crav'd the alms of such as passèd by:

I, like a man devout and charitable,
Clothèd the naked, lodg'd this wand'ring guest,
With sighs and tears still furnishing his table,
With what might make the miserable blest.

But this ungrateful, for my good desert,
 Entic'd my thoughts against me to conspire,
Who gave consent to steal away my heart,
 And set my breast, his lodging, on a fire.

Well, well, my friends, when beggars grow thus bold,
No marvel then though Charity grow cold.

DRAYTON

CV A SUMMER'S EVE

Clear had the day been from the dawn,
 All chequer'd was the sky,
Thin clouds, like scarfs of cobweb lawn,
 Veil'd heaven's most glorious eye.

The wind had no more strength than this,
 That leisurely it blew,
To make one leaf the next to kiss,
 That closely by it grew.

The flowers, like brave embroidered girls,
 Look'd as they most desired,
To see whose head with orient pearls
 Most curiously was tyred.

The rills, that on the pebbles played,
 Might now be heard at will;
This world the only music made,
 Else every thing was still.

And to itself the subtle air
 Such sovereignty assumes,
That it receive too large a share
 From nature's rich perfumes.

DRAYTON

CVI SIRENA

Neare to the silverre Trent Sirena dwelleth,
She to whom Nature lent all that excelleth,
By whom the Muses late and the neate Graces
Have for their greater state taken their places,
Twining an anademme wherewith to crowne her,
As it belonged to them most to renowne her.

Tagus and Pactolus are to the debtor,
Nor for their golde to us are they the better;
Henceforth of all the rest be thou the river,
Which, as the daintyest, puts them down ever;
For when my precious one o'er thee doth travelle
She to pearle paragonne turneth thy gravelle.

Our mournfulle Philomelle that rarest tuner,
Henceforth in April shall waken the sooner,
And to her shall complayne from the thicke cover,
Redoubling every strayne over and over;
For when my love too long her chamber keepeth,
As it had suffered wrong, the morning weepeth.

DRAYTON

CVII ETERNAL RHYME

Not marble, nor the gilded monuments
Of princes, shall outlive this powerful rhyme;
But you shall shine more bright in these contents
Than unswept stone, besmear'd with sluttish time.
When wasteful war shall statues overturn,
And broils root out the work of masonry,
Nor Mars his sword nor war's quick fire shall burn
The living record of your memory.
'Gainst death and all-oblivious enmity
Shall you pace forth; your praise shall still find room
Even in the eyes of all posterity
That wear this world out to the ending doom.
So, till the judgement that yourself arise,
You live in this, and dwell in lovers' eyes.

SHAKESPEARE

CVIII FULL MANY A GLORIOUS MORNING

Full many a glorious morning have I seen
Flatter the mountain-tops with sovereign eye,
Kissing with golden face the meadows green,
Gilding pale streams with heavenly alchemy;
Anon permit the basest clouds to ride
With ugly rack on his celestial face,
And from the forlorn world his visage hide,
Stealing unseen to west with this disgrace:

Even so my sun one early morn did shine
With all-triumphant splendour on my brow;
But, out, alack! he was but one hour mine,
The region cloud hath masked him from me now.
Yet him for this my love no whit disdaineth;
Suns of the world may stain when heaven's sun staineth.
SHAKESPEARE

CIX DEVOURING TIME

Devouring Time, blunt thou the lion's paws,
And make the earth devour her own sweet brood;
Pluck the keen teeth from the fierce tiger's jaws,
And burn the long-lived phœnix in her blood;
Make glad and sorry seasons as thou fleets,
And do whate'er thou wilt, swift-footed Time,
To the wide world and all her fading sweets;
But I forbid thee one most heinous crime:
O, carve not with thy hours my love's fair brow,
Nor draw no lines there with thine antique pen;
Him in thy course untainted do allow
For beauty's pattern to succeeding men.
Yet do thy worst, old Time: despite thy wrong,
My love shall in my verse ever live young.
SHAKESPEARE

CX WEALTH

Some glory in their birth, some in their skill,
Some in their wealth, some in their body's force;
Some in their garments, though new-fangled ill;
Some in their hawks and hounds, some in their horse;
And every humour hath his adjunct pleasure,
Wherein it finds a joy above the rest:
But these particulars are not my measure;
All these I better in one general best.
Thy love is better than high birth to me,
Richer than wealth, prouder than garments' cost,
Of more delight than hawks or horses be;
And having thee, of all men's pride I boast:
Wretched in this alone, that thou mayst take
All this away and me most wretched make.
SHAKESPEARE

CXI SELDOM PLEASURE.

So am I as the rich, whose blessed key
Can bring him to his sweet up-locked treasure,
The which he will not every hour survey,
For blunting the fine point of seldom pleasure.
Therefore are feasts so solemn and so rare,
Since, seldom coming, in the long year set,
Like stones of worth they thinly placed are,
Or captain jewels in the carcanet.
So is the time that keeps you as my chest,
Or as the wardrobe which the robe doth hide,
To make some special instant special blest,
By new unfolding his imprison'd pride.
Blessed are you, whose worthiness gives scope,
Being had, to triumph; being lack'd, to hope.

SHAKESPEARE

CXII SILVIA

Who is Silvia? what is she,
That all our swains commend her?
Holy, fair, and wise is she;
The heaven such grace did lend her,
That she might admired be.

Is she kind as she is fair?
For beauty lives with kindness.
Love doth to her eyes repair,
To help him of his blindness;
And, being helped, inhabits there.

Then to Silvia let us sing,
That Silvia is excelling;
She excels each mortal thing,
Upon the dull earth dwelling:
To her let us garlands bring.

SHAKESPEARE

CXIII PUCK

Over hill, over dale,
Thorough bush, thorough brier,
Over park, over pale,
Thorough flood, thorough fire,

I do wander everywhere,
Swifter than the moon's sphere;
And I serve the fairy queen,
To dew her orbs upon the green.
The cowslips tall her pensioners be;
In their gold coats spots you see,
Those be rubies, fairy favours,
In those freckles live their savours:
I must go seek some dewdrops here,
And hang a pearl in every cowslip's ear.

SHAKESPEARE

CXIV YOU SPOTTED SNAKES

You spotted snakes with double tongue,
Thorny hedge-hogs, be not seen;
Newts, and blind-worms, do no wrong;
Come not near our fairy queen:
Philomel, with melody,
Sing in our sweet lullaby;
Lulla, lulla, lullaby; lulla, lulla, lullaby;
Never harm,
Nor spell, nor charm,
Come our lovely lady nigh;
So, good-night, with lullaby.
Weaving spiders, come not here:
Hence, you long-legged spinners, hence!
Beetles black, approach not near;
Worm, nor snail, do no offence.

SHAKESPEARE

CXV THE OUSEL-COCK

The ousel-cock, so black of hue,
With orange-tawny bill,
The throstle with his note so true,
The wren with little quill;
The finch, the sparrow, and the lark,
The plain-song cuckoo gray,
Whose note full many a man doth mark,
And dares not answer nay.

SHAKESPEARE

CXVI HOW SHOULD I YOUR TRUE LOVE KNOW?

How should I your true love know
  From another one?
By his cockle hat and staff,
  And his sandal shoon.

He is dead and gone, lady,
  He is dead and gone;
At his head a grass-green turf,
  At his heels a stone.

White his shroud as the mountain snow,
  Larded all with sweet flowers,
Which bewept to the grave did go
  With true-love showers.

SHAKESPEARE

CXVII JOG ON! JOG ON!

Jog on, jog on, the footpath way,
  And merrily hent the stile-a:
A merry heart goes all the day,
  Your sad tires in a mile-a.

SHAKESPEARE

CXVIII YE LITTLE BIRDS THAT SIT AND SING

Ye little birds that sit and sing
  Amidst the shady valleys,
And see how Phillis sweetly walks
  Within her garden-alleys;
Go, pretty birds, about her bower;
Sing, pretty birds, she may not lower;
Ah, me, methinks I see her frown!
  Ye pretty wantons, warble.

Go, tell her through your chirping bills,
  As you by me are bidden,
To her is only known my love,
  Which from the world is hidden.
Go, pretty birds, and tell her so;
See that your notes strain not too low,
For still, methinks, I see her frown;
  Ye pretty wantons, warble.

Go, tune your voices' harmony,
  And sing, I am her lover;
Strain loud and sweet, that every note
  With sweet content may move her:
And she that hath the sweetest voice,
Tell her I will not change my choice;
Yet still, methinks, I see her frown!
  Ye pretty wantons, warble.

Oh, fly! make haste! see, see, she falls
  Into a pretty slumber.
Sing round about her rosy bed,
  That waking, she may wonder.
Say to her, 'tis her lover true
That sendeth love to you, to you;
And when you hear her kind reply,
  Return with pleasant warblings.

THOMAS HEYWOOD

ENVOI TO BOOK SECOND

PSYCHE

But Psyche lives, and on her breath attend
Delights that far surmount all earthly joy;
Music, sweet voices, and ambrosian fare;
Winds, and the light-winged creatures of the air;
Clear channeled rivers, springs, and flowery meads,
Are proud when Psyche wantons on their streams,
When Psyche on their rich embroidery treads,
When Psyche gilds their crystal with her beams.
We have but seen our sister, and, behold!
She sends us with our laps full brimmed with gold.

HEYWOOD

BOOK THIRD

CXIX SLOW, SLOW, FRESH FOUNT

Slow, slow, fresh fount, keep time with my salt tears;
Yet slower, yet; O faintly, gentle springs;
List to the heavy part the music bears,
Woe weeps out her division when she sings.
Droop herbs and flowers;
Fall grief in showers,
Our beauties are not ours;
O, I could still,
Like melting snow upon some craggy hill,
Drop, drop, drop, drop,
Since nature's pride is now a withered daffodil.

BEN JONSON

CXX STILL TO BE NEAT

Still to be neat, still to be drest,
As you were going to a feast;
Still to be powdered, still perfumed:
Lady, it is to be presumed,
Though art's hid causes are not found,
All is not sweet, all is not sound.

Give me a look, give me a face,
That makes simplicity a grace;
Robes loosely flowing, hair as free:
Such sweet neglect more taketh me
Than all the adulteries of art;
They strike mine eyes, but not my heart.

JONSON

CXXI WITCH'S CHARM

The owl is abroad, the bat and the toad,
And so is the cat-a-mountain;
The ant and the mole sit both in a hole,
And the frog peeps out o' the fountain.
The dogs they do bay, and the timbrels play,

The spindle is now a-turning;
The moon it is red, and the stars are fled,
But all the sky is a-burning:
The ditch is made, and our nails the spade,
With pictures full, of wax and of wool:
Their livers I stick with needles quick;
There lacks but the blood to make up the flood.
Quickly, dame, then bring your part in!
Spur, spur upon little Martin!
Merrily, merrily, make him sail,
A worm in his mouth and a thorn in his tail,
Fire above, and fire below,
With a whip in your hand to make him go!

JONSON

XXII BUZZ AND HUM

Buzz! quoth the Blue-Fly,
Hum! quoth the Bee;
Buzz and hum! they cry,
And so do we.
In his ear! in his nose!
Thus,—do you see?
He eat the Dormouse——
Else it was he.

JONSON

XXIII LOVE'S CHARIOT

See the chariot at hand here of Love,
Wherein my Lady rideth!
Each that draws is a swan or a dove,
And well the car Love guideth.
As she goes, all hearts do duty
Unto her beauty;
And enamoured do wish, so they might
But enjoy such a sight,
That they still were to run by her side,
Through swords, through seas, whither she would glide.

Do but look on her eyes, they do light
All that Love's world compriseth!
Do but look on her hair, it is bright
As Love's star when it riseth!

Do but mark, her forehead's smoother
Than words that soothe her;
And from her arched brows such a grace
Sheds itself through the face,
As alone there triumphs to the life
All the gain, all the good of the elements' strife.

Have you seen but a bright lily grow
Before rude hands have touched it?
Have you marked but the fall of the snow
Before the soil hath smutched it?
Have you felt the wool of the beaver,
Or swan's down ever?
Or have smelt o' the bud of the brier,
Or the nard in the fire?
Or have tasted the bag of the bee?
O so white, O so soft, O so sweet is she!

JONSON

CXXIV THOUGH I AM YOUNG AND CANNOT TELL

Though I am young and cannot tell
Either what Death or Love is well,
Yet I have heard they both bear darts,
And both do aim at human hearts;
And then again, I have been told,
Love wounds with heat, as Death with cold;
So that I fear they do but bring
Extremes to touch, and mean one thing.
As in a ruin we it call
One thing to be blown up, or fall;
Or to our end like way may have
By a flash of lightning, or a wave:
So Love's inflamed shaft or brand,
May kill as soon as Death's cold hand;
Except Love's fires the virtue have
To fright the frost out of the grave.

JONSON

CXXV SONG OF NIGHT

Break, Phant'sie, from thy cave of cloud,
And spread thy purple wings,
Now all thy figures are allowed
And various shapes of things;

Create of airy forms a stream,—
  It must have blood and nought of phlegm.
And though it be a waking dream,
Yet let it like an odour rise
  To all the senses here,
And fall like sleep upon their eyes,
  Or music on their ear.

JONSON

CXXVI ON MAY MORNING

Now the bright morning-star, day's harbinger,
Comes dancing from the east, and leads with her
The flowery May, who from her green lap throws
The yellow cowslip and the pale primrose.
Hail, bounteous May! that dost inspire
Mirth, and youth, and warm desire;
Woods and groves are of thy dressing,
Hill and dale doth boast thy blessing.
Thus we salute thee with our early song,
And welcome thee, and wish thee long.

MILTON

CXXVII SONG: "SWEET ECHO"

Sweet Echo, sweetest nymph, that liv'st unseen
    Within thy airy shell,
  By slow Meander's margent green,
And in the violet-embroidered vale,
  Where the love-lorn nightingale
Nightly to thee her sad song mourneth well;
Canst thou not tell me of a gentle pair
  That likest thy Narcissus are?
    O, if thou have
  Hid them in some flowery cave,
    Tell me but where,
 Sweet queen of parly, daughter of the sphere?
 So mayst thou be translated to the skies,
And give resounding grace to all heaven's harmonies.

MILTON

CXXVIII SONNETS

I

TO THE NIGHTINGALE

O Nightingale that on yon bloomy spray
Warblest at eve, when all the woods are still,
Thou with fresh hope the lover's heart dost fill,
While the jolly hours lead on propitious May.
Thy liquid notes that close the eye of day,
First heard before the shallow cuckoo's bill,
Portend success in love. O, if Jove's will
Have linked that amorous power to thy soft lay,
Now timely sing, ere the rude bird of hate
Foretell my hopeless doom, in some grove nigh;
As thou from year to year hast sung too late
For my relief, yet hadst no reason why.
Whether the Muse or Love call thee his mate,
Both them I serve, and of their train am I.

II

HOW SOON HATH TIME

How soon hath Time, the subtle thief of youth,
Stolen on his wing my three-and-twentieth year!
My hasting days fly on with full career,
But my late spring no bud or blossom shew'th.
Perhaps my semblance might deceive the truth
That I to manhood am arrived so near;
And inward ripeness doth much less appear,
That some more timely-happy spirits endu'th.
Yet, be it less or more, or soon or slow,
It shall be still in strictest measure even
To that same lot, however mean or high,
Toward which Time leads me, and the will of Heaven,
All is, if I have grace to use it so,
As ever in my great Task-Master's eye.

Milton

CXXIX COME, SLEEP

Come, Sleep, and with thy sweet deceiving,
Lock me in delight awhile;
Let some pleasing dreams beguile

All my fancies; that from thence
I may feel an influence,
All my powers of care bereaving!

Though but a shadow, but a sliding,
Let me know some little joy!
We that suffer long annoy
Are contented with a thought,
Through an idle fancy wrought:
Oh, let my joys have some abiding!

BEAUMONT and FLETCHER

ASPATIA'S SONG

Lay a garland on my hearse
Of the dismal yew;
Maidens, willow branches bear;
Say, I died true.

My love was false, but I was firm
From my hour of birth.
Upon my buried body lie
Lightly, gentle earth!

BEAUMONT and FLETCHER

MIRTH

'Tis mirth that fills the veins with blood,
More than wine, or sleep, or food;
Let each man keep his heart at ease;
No man dies of that disease.
He that would his body keep
From diseases, must not weep;
But whoever laughs and sings,
Never he his body brings
Into fevers, gouts, or rheums,
Or lingeringly his lungs consumes;
Or meets with achës in his bone,
Or catarrhs, or griping stone:
But contented lives for aye;
The more he laughs, the more he may.

BEAUMONT and FLETCHER

CXXXII A DIRGE

Come, you whose loves are dead,
    And, whiles I sing,
    Weep, and wring
Every hand, and every head
Bind with cypress and sad yew;
Ribbons black and candles blue
From him that was of men most true!

Come with heavy moaning,
    And on his grave
    Let him have
Sacrifice of sighs and groaning;
Let him have fair flowers enow,
White and purple, green and yellow,
For him that was of men most true!

BEAUMONT and FLETCHER

CXXXIII TELL ME, DEAREST, WHAT IS LOVE

Tell me, dearest, what is love?
'Tis a lightning from above;
  'Tis an arrow, 'tis a fire,
  'Tis a boy they call Desire.
      'Tis a grave,
      Gapes to have
Those poor fools that long to prove.

Tell me more are women true?
Yes, some are, and some as you.
  Some are willing, some are strange,
  Since you men first taught to change.
      And till troth
      Be in both,
All shall love, to love anew.

Tell me more yet, can they grieve?
Yes, and sicken sore, but live,
  And be wise, and delay,
  When you men are as wise as they.
      Then I see,
      Faith will be,
Never till they both believe.

FLETCHER

CXXXIV CARE-CHARMING SLEEP

Care-charming Sleep, thou easer of all woes,
Brother to Death, sweetly thyself dispose
On this afflicted prince; fall like a cloud,
In gentle showers; give nothing that is loud,
Or painful to his slumbers; easy, light,
And as a purling stream, thou son of Night
Pass by his troubled senses; sing his pain,
Like hollow murmuring wind or silver rain;
Into this prince gently, oh, gently slide,
And kiss him into slumbers like a bride.

FLETCHER

CXXXV SATYR'S SONG

From "The Faithful Shepherdess."

Here be berries for a queen,
Some be red, some be green;
These are of that luscious meat
The great god Pan himself doth eat:
All these, and what the woods can yield,
The hanging mountain or the field,
I freely offer, and ere long
Will bring you more, more sweet and strong;
Till when, humbly leave I take,
Lest the great Pan do awake,
That sleeping lies in a deep glade,
Under a broad beech's shade.
I must go, I must run,
Swifter than the fiery sun.

FLETCHER

CXXXVI A DIALOGUE BETWEEN THE RESOLVED SOUL AND CREATED PLEASURE

Courage, my soul! now learn to wield
The weight of thine immortal shield;
Close on thy head thy helmet bright;
Balance thy sword against the fight!

See where an army, strong as fair,
With silken banners spread the air!
Now, if thou be'st that thing divine,
In this day's combat let it shine,
And show that nature wants an art
To conquer one resolvèd heart.

Pleasure.

Welcome, the creation's guest,
Lord of earth, and heaven's heir!
Lay aside that warlike crest,
And of nature's banquet share,
Where the souls of fruits and flowers
Stand prepared to heighten yours.

Soul.

I sup above, and cannot stay
To bait so long upon the way.

Pleasure.

On these downy pillows lie,
Whose soft plumes will thither fly;
On these roses, strewed so plain
Lest one leaf thy side should strain.

Soul.

My gentle rest is on a thought,
Conscious of doing what I ought.

Pleasure.

If thou be'st with perfumes pleased
Such as oft the gods appeased,
Thou in fragrant clouds shalt show
Like another god below.

Soul.

A soul that knows not to presume
Is Heaven's and its own perfume.

Pleasure.

Every thing does seem to vie
Which should first attract thine eye;
But since none deserves that grace,
In this crystal view thy face.

Soul.

When the Creator's skill is p ized,
The rest is all but earth disguised.

Pleasure.

Hark how music then prepares
For thy stay these charming airs,
Which the posting winds recall,
And suspend the river's fall.

Soul.

Had I but any time to lose,
On this I would it all dispose.
Cease tempter! None can chain a mind
Whom this sweet cordage cannot bind.

Chorus.

Earth cannot show so brave a sight,
As when a single soul does fence
The battery of alluring Sense,
And Heaven views it with delight.
  Then persevere! for still new charges round:
  And if thou overcom'st thou shalt be crowned!

Pleasure.

All that's costly fair and sweet
  Which scatteringly doth shine,
Shall within one Beauty meet,
  And she be only thine.

Soul.

If things of sight such heavens be,
What heavens are those we cannot see!

Pleasure.

Wheresoe'er thy foot shall go
  The minted Gold shall lie,
Till thou purchase all below,
  And want new worlds to buy.

Soul.

Wer't not for price who'd value gold?
And that's worth naught that can be sold.

Pleasure.

Wilt thou all the Glory have
  That war or peace commend?
Half the world shall be thy slave,
  The other half thy friend.

Soul.

What friends, if to myself untrue?
What slaves, unless I captive you?

Pleasure.

Thou shalt Know each hidden cause
And see the future time;
Try what depth the centre draws,
And then to heaven climb.

Soul.

None thither mounts by the degree
Of knowledge, but humility.

Chorus.

Triumph, triumph, victorious soul!
The world has not one pleasure more:
The rest does lie beyond the pole,
And is thine everlasting store.

MARVELL

CXXXVII A DROP OF DEW

See how the orient dew,
Shed from the bosom of the morn
Into the blowing roses,
Yet careless of its mansion new,
For the clear region where 'twas born,
Round in itself incloses
And in its little globe's extent
Frames, as it can, its native element.
How it the purple flower does slight,
Scarce touching where it lies;
But gazing back upon the skies
Shines with a mournful light:
Likes its own tear,
Because so long divided from the sphere.
Restless it rolls and unsecure,
Trembling lest it grow impure;
Till the warm sun pities its pain,
And to the skies exhales it back again.
So the soul, that drop, that ray,
Of the clear fountain of eternal day,
Could it within the human flower be seen,
Remembering still its former height,
Shuns the sweet leaves and blossoms green;
And, recollecting its own light,
Does, in its pure and circling thoughts, express
The greater heaven in a heaven less.

In how coy a figure wound,
Every way it turns away,
So the world excluding round,
Yet receiving in the day;
Dark beneath, but bright above,
Here disdaining, there in love.
How loose and easy hence to go,
How girt and ready to ascend:
Moving but on a point below,
It all about does upward bend.
Such did the manna's sacred dew distil,
White and entire, although congealed and chill;
Congealed on earth; but does, dissolving, run
Into the glories of the almighty sun.

MARVELL

CXXXVIII THE OLD AND YOUNG COURTIER

An old song made by an aged old pate,
Of an old worshipful gentleman, who had a great estate,
That kept a brave old house at a bountiful rate,
And an old porter to relieve the poor at his gate;
Like an old courtier of the queen's,
And the queen's old courtier.

With an old lady, whose anger one word assuages;
They every quarter paid their old servants their wages,
And never knew what belonged to coachmen, footmen, nor pages,
But kept twenty old fellows with blue coats and badges;
Like an old courtier . . .

With an old study filled full of learned old books;
With an old reverend chaplain—you might know him by his looks;
With an old buttery hatch worn quite off the hooks;
And an old kitchen, that maintained half-a-dozen old cooks;
Like an old courtier . . .

With an old hall, hung about with pikes, guns, and bows,
With old swords and bucklers, that had borne many shrewd blows;
And an old frieze coat, to cover his worship's trunk hose;
A cup of old sherry, to comfort his copper nose;
Like an old courtier . . .

With a good old fashion, when Christmas was come,
To call in all his old neighbours with bagpipe and drum,
With good cheer enough to furnish every old room,
And old liquor able to make a cat speak, and man dumb;
  Like an old courtier . . .

With an old falconer, huntsmen, and a kennel of hounds,
That never hawked, nor hunted, but in his own grounds;
Who, like a wise man, kept himself within his own bounds,
And when he died, gave every child a thousand good pounds;
  Like an old courtier of the queen's,
  And the queen's old courtier.

CXXXIX THE MERRY MONTH OF MAY

O, the month of May, the merry month of May,
So frolic, so gay, and so green, so green, so green!
O, and then did I unto my true love say,
Sweet Peg, thou shalt be my Summer's Queen.

Now the nightingale, the pretty nightingale,
The sweetest singer in all the forest quire,
Entreats thee, sweet Peggy, to hear thy true love's tale:
Lo, yonder she sitteth, her breast against a brier.

But O, I spy the cuckoo, the cuckoo, the cuckoo;
See where she sitteth; come away, my joy:
Come away, I prithee, I do not like the cuckoo
Should sing where my Peggy and I kiss and toy.

O, the month of May, the merry month of May,
So frolic, so gay, and so green, so green, so green;
And then did I unto my true love say,
Sweet Peg, thou shalt be my Summer's Queen.

DEKKER

CXL COLD'S THE WIND

Cold's the wind, and wet's the rain,
  Saint Hugh be our good speed!
Ill is the weather that bringeth no gain,
  Nor helps good hearts in need.

Troll the bowl, the jolly nut-brown bowl,
  And here, kind mate, to thee!
Let's sing a dirge for Saint Hugh's soul,
  And down it merrily.

Down-a-down, hey, down-a-down!
Hey derry derry down-a-down!
Ho! well done, to me let come;
Ring compass, gentle joy!

DEKKER

LI FORTUNE SMILES

Fortune smiles, cry holyday!
Dimples on her cheeks do dwell.
Fortune frowns, cry well-a-day!
Her love is heaven, her hate is hell.
Since heaven and hell obey her power,
Tremble when her eyes do lower:
Since heaven and hell her power obey,
When she smiles cry holyday!
Holyday with joy we cry,
And bend, and bend, and merrily
Sing hymns to Fortune's deity,
Sing hymns to Fortune's deity.

Let us sing merrily, merrily, merrily!
With our song let heaven resound,
Fortune's hands our heads have crowned:
Let us sing merrily, merrily, merrily!

DEKKER

LII SIC VITA

Like to the falling of a star,
Or as the flights of eagles are;
Or like the fresh spring's gaudy hue,
Or silver drops of morning dew;
Or like a wind that chafes the flood,
Or bubbles which on water stood:
Ev'n such is man, whose borrowed light
Is straight called in, and paid to-night.
The wind blows out, the bubble dies;
The spring entombed in autumn lies;
The dew dries up, the star is shot;
The flight is past—and man forgot.

KING

CXLIII THE DOLE

Call for the robin red-breast and the wren,
Since o'er shady groves they hover,
And with leaves and flowers do cover
The friendless bodies of unburied men.
Call unto his funeral dole
The ant, the field-mouse and the mole,
To rear him hillocks that shall keep him warm.
And (when gay tombs are robbed) sustain no harm;
But keep the wolf far thence, that's foe to men,
For with his nails he'll dig them up again.

WEBSTER

CXLIV THE SHORTNESS OF LIFE

And what's a life?—a weary pilgrimage,
Whose glory in one day doth fill the stage
With childhood, manhood, and decrepit age.

And what's a life?—the flourishing array
ummer meadow, which to-day
Wears her green plush, and is to-morrow hay.

Read on this dial, how the shades devour
My short-lived winter's day! hour eats up hour;
Alas! the total's but from eight to four.

Behold these lilies, which thy hands have made,
Fair copies of my life, and open laid
To view, how soon they droop, how soon they fade!

Shade not that dial, night will blind too soon;
My non-aged day already points to noon;
How simple is my suit!—how small my boon!

Nor do I beg this slender inch to wile
The time away, or falsely to beguile
My thoughts with joy; here's nothing worth a smile.

QUARLES

CXLV ASK ME NO MORE

Ask me no more where Jove bestows,
When June is past, the fading rose;
For in your beauty's orient deep
These flowers, as in their causes, sleep.

Ask me no more whither do stray
The golden atoms of the day,
For in pure love did Heaven prepare
Those powders to enrich your hair.
Ask me no more whither dost haste
The nightingale when May is past,
For in your sweet dividing throat
She winters and keeps warm her note.
Ask me no more where those stars light
That downwards fall in dead of night,
For in your eyes they sit, and there
Fixèd become as in their sphere.
Ask me no more if east or west,
The phœnix builds her spicy nest,
For unto you at last she flies,
And in your fragrant bosom dies.

CAREW

CXLVI THE PRIMROSE

Ask me why I send you here
This firstling of the infant year;
Ask me why I send to you
This primrose all bepearled with dew:
I straight will whisper in your ears,
The sweets of love are washed with tears.
Ask me why this flower doth show
So yellow, green, and sickly too;
Ask me why the stalk is weak
And bending, yet it doth not break;
I must tell you, these discover
What doubts and fears are in a lover.

CAREW

CXLVII THE GOOD MORROW

I wonder, by my troth, what thou and I
Did till we loved! Were we not weaned till then,
But sucked on country pleasures childishly?
Or snorted we in the Seven Sleepers' den?
'Twas so; but thus all pleasures fancies be.
If ever any beauty I did see,
Which I desired and got,—'twas but a dream of thee.

And, now, good morrow to our waking souls,
  Which watch not one another out of fear;
For Love all love of other sights controls,
  And makes one little room an everywhere.
Let sea-discoverers to new worlds be gone;
Let maps to other worlds our world have shown;
Let us possess one world; each hath one, and is one.

My face in thine eye, thine in mine appears,
  And true plain hearts do in the faces rest.
Where can we find two fitter hemispheres,
  Without sharp North, without declining West?
Whatever dies was not mixed equally;
If our two loves be one, or thou and I
Love so alike that none do slacken, none can die.

JOHN DONNE

CXLVIII

A VALEDICTION FORBIDDING MOURNING

As virtuous men pass mildly away,
And whisper to their souls to go;
Whilst some of their sad friends do say,
The breath goes now—and some say, no;

So let us melt, and make no noise,
No tear-floods, nor sigh-tempests move;
'Twere profanation of our joys
To tell the laity our love.

Moving of th' earth brings harms and fears,
Men reckon what it did, and meant;
But trepidation of the spheres,
Though greater far, is innocent.

Dull, sublunary lovers' love—
Whose soul is sense—cannot admit
Absence, because it doth remove
Those things which alimented it.

But we're by love so much refined,
That ourselves know not what it is;
Inter-assured of the mind,
Careless eyes, lips, and hands to miss.

Our two souls, therefore—which are one—
Though I must go, endure not yet
A breach, but an expansion,
Like gold to airy thinness beat.

If they be two, they are two so
As stiff twin compasses are two;
Thy soul, the fixed foot, makes no shew
To move, but doth, if th' other do.

And though it in the centre sit,
Yet when the other far doth roam,
It leans, and hearkens after it,
And grows erect as that comes home.

Such wilt thou be to me, who must
Like th' other foot, obliquely run;
Thy firmness makes my circles just,
And makes me end where I begun.

DONNE

CXLIX THE LYRIC ARGUMENT

I sing of brooks, of blossoms, birds, and bowers,
Of April, May, of June, and July flowers;
I sing of May-poles, hock-carts, wassails, wakes,
Of bridegrooms, brides, and of their bridal cakes.
I write of Youth, of Love, and have access
By these, to sing of cleanly wantonness;
I sing of dews, of rains, and, piece by piece,
Of balm, of oil, of spice, and ambergris;
I sing of times trans-shifting; and I write
How roses first came red, and lilies white;
I write of groves, of twilights, and I sing
The court of Mab, and of the Fairy King.
I write of Hell; I sing and ever shall,
Of Heaven, and hope to have it after all.

HERRICK

CL THE MAD MAID'S SONG

Good morrow to the day so fair;
  Good morning, sir, to you;
Good morrow to mine own torn hair,
  Bedabbled with the dew.

Good morning to this primrose too;
  Good morrow to each maid
That will with flowers the tomb bestrew
  Wherein my love is laid.

Ah! woe is me, woe, woe is me,
  Alack, and well-a-day!
For pity, sir, find out that bee
  Which bore my love away.

I'll seek him in your bonnet brave;
  I'll seek him in your eyes;
Nay, now I think they've made his grave
  I'th' bed of strawberries.

I'll seek him there; I know, ere this,
  The cold, cold earth doth shake him;
But I will go, or send a kiss
  By you, sir, to awake him.

Pray hurt him not; though he be dead,
  He knows well who do love him;
And who with green turfs rear his head,
  And who do rudely move him.

He's soft and tender, pray take heed,
  With bands of cowslips bind him,
And bring him home; but 'tis decreed,
  That I shall never find him.

HERRICK

CLI

TO MEADOWS

Ye have been fresh and green,
  Ye have been fill'd with flowers;
And ye the walks have been
  Where maids have spent their hours.

You have beheld how they
  With wicker arks did come
To kiss and bear away
  The richer cowslips home.

Ye've heard them sweetly sing,
  And seen them in a round;
Each virgin, like a spring,
  With honeysuckles crowned.

But now, we see none here,
  Whose silv'ry feet did tread,
And with dishevelled hair
  Adorned this smoother mead.

Like unthrifts, having spent
  Your stock, and needy grown,
Ye're left here to lament
  Your poor estates, alone.

HERRICK

CHERRY RIPE

Cherry-ripe, ripe, ripe, I cry,
Full and fair ones, come and buy;
If so be you ask me where
They do grow? I answer—There,
Where my Julia's lips do smile,
There's the land of cherry isle,
Whose plantations fully show
All the year, where cherries grow.

HERRICK

WHENAS IN SILKS MY JULIA GOES

Whenas in silks my Julia goes,
Then, then, methinks, how sweetly flows
That liquefaction of her clothes.
Next, when I cast mine eyes, and see
That brave vibration each way free;
Oh, how that glittering taketh me!

HERRICK

CHEAT OF CUPID; OR, THE UNGENTLE GUEST

One silent night of late,
  When every creature rested,
Came one unto my gate,
  And knocking, me molested.

"Who's that," said I, "beats there,
  And troubles thus the sleepy?"
"Cast off," said he, "all fear,
  And let not locks thus keep ye.

"For I a boy am, who
  By moonless nights have swervèd;
And all with show'rs wet through,
  And e'en with cold half starvèd."

I pitiful arose,
  And soon a taper lighted;
And did myself disclose
  Unto the lad benighted.

I saw he had a bow,
  And wings too, which did shiver;
And looking down below,
  I spied he had a quiver.

I to my chimney's shine
  Brought him, as Love professes,
And chafed his hands with mine,
  And dried his dropping tresses.

But when he felt him warmed,
  "Let's try this bow of ours
And string, if they be harmed,"
  Said he, "with these late show'rs."

Forthwith his bow he bent,
  And wedded string and arrow,
And struck me that it went
  Quite through my heart and marrow.

Then laughing loud, he flew
  Away, and thus said flying,
"Adieu, mine host, adieu,
  I'll leave thy heart a-dying."

HERRICK

CLV TO BE MERRY

Let's now take our time,
While we're in our prime,
And old, old age is afar off:
For the evil, evil days
Will come on apace,
Before we can be aware of.

HERRICK

CLVI TO DAISIES, NOT TO SHUT SO SOON

Shut not so soon; the dull-eyed night
  Has not as yet begun
To make a seizure on the light,
  Or to seal up the sun.

No marigolds yet closèd are;
No shadows great appear;
Nor doth the early shepherd's star
Shine like a spangle here.

Stay but till my Julia close
Her life-begetting eye;
And let the whole world then dispose
Itself to live or die.

HERRICK

CLVII THE NIGHT-PIECE, TO JULIA

Her eyes the glow-worm lend thee,
The shooting stars attend thee;
And the elves also,
Whose little eyes glow,
Like the sparks of fire, befriend thee.

No Will-o'-th'-Wisp mislight thee,
Nor snake or slow-worm bite thee;
But on, on thy way,
Not making a stay,
Since ghost there's none to affright thee.

Let not the dark thee cumber;
What though the moon does slumber?
The stars of the night
Will lend thee their light,
Like tapers clear, without number.

Then, Julia, let me woo thee,
Thus, thus to come unto me;
And when I shall meet
Thy silv'ry feet,
My soul I'll pour into thee.

HERRICK

CLVIII AN EPITAPH UPON A VIRGIN

Here a solemn fast we keep,
While all beauty lies asleep:
Hushed be all things, no noise here
But the toning of a tear;
Or a sigh of such as bring
Cowslips for her covering.

HERRICK

CLIX THE MUSE

She doth tell me where to borrow
Comfort in the midst of sorrow:
Makes the desolatest place
To her presence be a grace;
And the blackest discontents
Be her fairest ornaments,
In my former days of bliss,
Her divine skill taught me this.
That from everything I saw,
I could some invention draw,
And raise pleasure to her height,
Through the meanest object's sight;
By the murmur of a spring,
Or the least bough's rustlëing.
By a daisy, whose leaves spread,
Shut when Titan goes to bed;
Or a shady bush or tree,
She could more infuse in me,
Than all Nature's beauties can
In some other wiser man.
By her help I also now
Make this churlish place allow
Some things that may sweeten gladness,
In the very gall of sadness.
The dull loneness, the black shade,
That these hanging vaults have made;
The strange music of the waves,
Beating on these hollow caves;
This black den which rocks emboss,
Overgrown with eldest moss:
The rude portals that give light
More to terror than delight;
This my chamber of neglect,
Walled about with disrespect.
From all these, and this dull air,
A fit object for despair,
She hath taught me by her might
To draw comfort and delight.
Therefore, thou best earthly bliss,
I will cherish thee for this.

Poesy, thou sweet'st content
That e'er heaven to mortals lent:
Though they as a trifle leave thee,
Whose dull thoughts cannot conceive thee,
Though thou be to them a scorn,
That to nought but earth are born,
Let my life no longer be
Than I am in love with thee,
Though our wise ones call thee madness,
Let me never taste of gladness,
If I love not thy madd'st fits
Above all their greatest wits.
And though some, too seeming holy,
Do account thy raptures folly,
Thou dost teach me to contemn
What makes knaves and fools of them.

WITHER

LX THE QUIP

The merry World did on a day
  With his train-bands and mates agree
To meet together, where I lay,
  And all in sport to jeer at me.

First, Beauty crept into a rose,
  Which when I plucked not, "Sir," said she,
"Tell me, I pray, whose hands are those?"—
  But Thou shalt answer, Lord, for me.

Then Money came, and chinking still,
  "What tune is this, poor man?" said he:
"I heard in Music you had skill."
  But Thou shalt answer, Lord, for me.

Then came brave Glory puffing by
  In silks that whistled—who but he?
He scarce allowed me half an eye—
  But Thou shalt answer, Lord, for me.

Then came quick Wit and Conversation,
  And he would needs a comfort be,
And, to be short, make an oration—
  But Thou shalt answer, Lord, for me.

Yet when the hour of Thy design
  To answer these fine things shall come,
Speak not at large, say, I am Thine,
  And then they have their answer home.

GEORGE HERBERT

CLXI VIRTUE

Sweet day, so cool, so calm, so bright—
The bridal of the earth and sky;
The dew shall weep thy fall to-night;
      For thou must die.

Sweet rose, whose hue angry and brave
Bids the rash gazer wipe his eye,
Thy root is ever in its grave,
      And thou must die.

Sweet spring, full of sweet days and roses,
A box where sweets compacted lie,
My music shows ye have your closes,
      And all must die.

Only a sweet and virtuous soul,
Like seasoned timber, never gives;
But though the whole world turn to coal,
      Then chiefly lives.

HERBERT

CLXII THE ELIXIR

  Teach me, my God and King,
  In all things Thee to see,
And what I do in anything,
  To do it as for Thee.

  Not rudely, as a beast,
  To run into an action;
But still to make Thee prepossest,
  And give it his perfection.

  A man that looks on glass,
  On it may stay his eye;
Or, if he pleaseth, through it pass,
  And then the Heaven espy.

All may of Thee partake:
Nothing can be so mean
Which with his tincture, for Thy sake,
Will not grow bright and clean.

A servant with this clause
Makes drudgery divine;
Who sweeps a room as for Thy laws,
Makes that and the action fine.

This is the famous stone
That turneth all to gold;
For that which God doth touch and own
Cannot for less be told.

HERBERT

CLXIII PEACE

My Soul, there is a Countrie
Afar beyond the stars,
Where stands a winged Sentrie
All skilful in the wars.
There, above noise and danger,
Sweet peace sits crown'd with smiles,
And one born in a Manger
Commands the Beauteous files.
He is thy gracious friend
And (O my Soul awake!)
Did in pure love descend,
To die here for thy sake.
If thou canst get but thither,
There grows the flowre of peace,
The Rose that cannot wither,
Thy fortress, and thy ease.
Leave then thy foolish ranges;
For none can thee secure,
But One, who never changes,
Thy God, thy Life, thy Cure.

HENRY VAUGHAN

CLXIV BEAUTEOUS DEATH

They are all gone into the world of light!
And I alone sit lingring here!
Their very memory is fair and bright,
And my sad thoughts doth clear.

It glows and glitters in my cloudy brest
Like stars upon some gloomy grove,
Or those faint beams in which this hill is drest
After the Sun's remove.

I see them walking in an Air of glory,
Whose light doth trample on my days;
My days, which are at best but dull and hoary,
Mere glimmering and decays.

O holy hope! and high humility!
High as the Heavens above!
These are your walks, and you have shew'd them me
To kindle my cold love.

Dear, beauteous death; the Jewel of the Just!
Shining no where but in the dark;
What mysteries do lie beyond thy dust,
Could man outlook that mark!

He that hath found some fledg'd birds nest may know
At first sight if the bird be flown;
But what fair Dell or Grove he sings in now,
That is to him unknown.

And yet, as Angels in some brighter dreams
Call to the soul when man doth sleep,
So some strange thoughts transcend our wonted themes,
And into glory peep.

If a star were confin'd into a Tomb,
Her captive flames must needs burn there;
But when the hand that lockt her up gives room,
She'll shine through all the sphere.

O Father of eternal life, and all
Created glories under thee!
Resume thy spirit from this world of thrall
Into true liberty!

Either disperse these mists, which blot and fill
My perspective still as they pass;
Or else remove me hence unto that hill,
Where I shall need no glass.

VAUGHAN

CLXV

THE WORLD

I

I saw eternity the other night
Like a great *Ring* of pure and endless light,
All calm, as it was bright;

And round beneath it, Time in hours, days, years,
Driv'n by the spheres
Like a vast shadow mov'd, in which the world
And all her train were hurl'd.
The doting Lover in his quaintest strain
Did there Complain;
Near him, his Lute, his fancy, and his flights,
Wit's sour delights;
With gloves, and knots the silly snares of pleasure,
Yet his dear Treasure
All scatter'd lay, while he his eyes did pour
Upon a flowr.

II

The darksome Statesman hung with weights and woe,
Like a thick midnight fog, mov'd there so slow,
He did not stay, nor go;
Condemning thoughts like sad Eclipses scowl
Upon his soul,
And Clouds of crying witnesses without
Pursued him with one shout.
Yet digg'd the Mole, and, lest his ways be found,
Workt under ground,
Where he did clutch his prey; but one did see
That policie;
Churches altars fed him; Perjuries
Were gnats and flies;
It rain'd about him blood and tears; but he
Drank them as free.

III

The fearfull miser on a heap of rust
Sate pining all his life there, did scarce trust
His own hands with the dust,
Yet would not place one piece above, but lives
In feare of thieves.
Thousands there were as frantick as himself,
And hugg'd each one his pelf;
The down-right Epicure plac'd heav'n in sense,
And scorn'd pretence;
While others, slipt into a wide Excess,
Said little less;
The weaker sort slight, trivial wares enslave,
Who think them brave,

And poor, despisèd truth sate counting by
Their victory.

IV

Yet some, who all this while did weep and sing,
And sing and weep, soar'd up into the *Ring*;
But most would use no wing.
O fools, said I, thus to prefer dark night
Before true light!
To live in grots and caves, and hate the day
Because it shews the way,
The way, which from this dead and dark abode
Leads up to God,
A way where you might tread the Sun, and be
More bright than he!
But as I did their madnes to discusse,
One whisper'd thus,
This Ring the Bridegroome did for none provide,
But for his bride.

VAUGHAN

CLXVI THE MORNING-WATCH

O joys! Infinite sweetness! with what flowers
And shoots of glory my soul breaks and buds!
All the long hours
Of night and Rest,
Through the still shrouds
Of sleep and Clouds,
This Dew fell on my Breast;
O how it *Bloods*,
And *Spirits* all my Earth! hark! In what Rings,
And *Hymning Circulations* the quick world
Awakes and sings!
The rising winds,
And falling springs,
Birds, beasts, all things
Adore him in their kinds.
Thus all is hurl'd
In sacred *Hymns* and *Order*, the great *Chime*
And *Symphony* of nature. Prayer is
The world in tune,
A spirit-voice,
And vocal joys,

Whose *Echo* is heav'ns bliss.
O let me climb
When I lie down! The Pious soul by night
Is like a clouded star, whose beams, though said
To shed their light
Under some Cloud,
Yet are above,
And shine and move
Beyond that misty shroud.
So in my Bed,
That Curtain'd grave, though sleep, like ashes, hide
My lamp and life, both shall in thee abide.

VAUGHAN

CLXVII ON THE GLORIOUS ASSUMPTION OF THE BLESSED VIRGIN

Hark! she is call'd, the parting hour is come;
Take thy farewell, poor world, Heaven must go home.
A piece of heavenly light, purer and brighter
Than the chaste stars, whose choice lamps come to light her,
While through the crystal orbs, clearer than they,
She climbs, and makes a far more milky way.
She's call'd again; hark! how th' immortal Dove
Sighs to his silver mate:—"Rise up, my love,
Rise up, my fair, my spotless one!
The winter 's past, the rain is gone:
The spring is come, the flowers appear,
No sweets, since thou are wanting here.
Come away, my love;
Come away, my dove;
Cast off delay:
The court of heav'n is come,
To wait upon thee home;
Come away, come away!"

She's call'd again, and will she go?
When Heav'n bids come, who can say no?
Heav'n calls her, and she must away;
Heav'n will not, and she cannot stay.
Go then, go, glorious, on the golden wings
Of the bright youth of heaven, that sings

Under so sweet a burden: go,
Since thy great Son will have it so:
And while thou go'st, our song and we
Will, as we may, reach after thee:—
"Hail! holy queen of humble hearts,
We in thy praise will have our parts;
And though thy dearest looks must now be light
To none but the blest heavens, whose bright
Beholders, lost in sweet delight,
Feed for ever their fair sight
With those divinest eyes, which we
And our dark world no more shall see;
Though our poor joys are parted so,
Yet shall our lips never let go
Thy gracious name, but to the last
Our loving song shall hold it fast.

Thy sacred name shall be
Thyself to us, and we
With holy cares will keep it by us;
We to the last
Will hold it fast,
And no assumption shall deny us.
All sweetest showers
Of fairest flowers
We'll strew upon it:
Though our sweetness cannot make
It sweeter, they may take
Themselves new sweetness from it.

Maria, men and angels sing,
Maria, mother of our king.
Live, rarest princess, and may the bright
Crown of a most incomparable light
Embrace thy radiant brows! O, may the best
Of everlasting joys bathe thy white breast!
Live our chaste love, the holy mirth
Of heaven, and humble pride of earth:
Live crown of women, queen of men:
Live mistress of our song; and when
Our weak desires have done their best,
Sweet angels come, and sing the rest!"

RICHARD CRASHAW

CLXVIII UPON THE DEATH OF THE MOST DESIRED MR. HERRYS

Death, what dost? O hold thy blow,
What thou dost thou dost not know.
Death, thou must not here be cruel,
This is Nature's choicest jewel:
This is he, in whose rare frame
Nature labour'd for a name:
And meant to leave his precious feature
The pattern of a perfect creature.
Joy of goodness, Love of Art,
Virtue wears him next her heart,
Him the Muses love to follow,
Him they call their vice-Apollo.
Apollo, golden though thou be,
Th' art not fairer than is he,
Nor more lovely lifted thy head,
(Blushing) from thine Eastern bed.
The glories of thy youth ne'er knew
Brighter hopes than he can shew,
Why then should it e'er be seen
That his should fade, while thine is green?
And wilt thou (O cruel boast!)
Put poor Nature to such a cost?
O, 'twill undo our common Mother,
To be at charge of such another:
What? think we to no other end,
Gracious heavens do use to send
Earth her best perfection,
But to vanish, and be gone?
Therefore only given to-day,
To-morrow to be snatch'd away?
 I've seen indeed the hopeful bud
Of a ruddy rose that stood
Blushing, to behold the ray
Of the new saluted Day;
(His tender top not fully spread)
The sweet dash of a shower new-shed
Invited him no more to hide
Within himself the purple pride
Of his forward flower, when lo,
While he sweetly 'gan to show

His swelling glories, Auster spied him,
Cruel Auster thither hied him,
And with the rush of one rude blast,
Shamed not spitefully to waste
All his leaves, so fresh, so sweet,
And lay them trembling at his feet.
I've seen the Morning's lovely ray
Hover o'er the new-born Day
With rosy wings so richly bright
As if he scorned to think of night;
When a rugged storm whose scowl
Made heaven's radiant face look foul,
Called for an untimely night
To blot the newly-blossomed light.
But were the rose's blush so rare,
Were the morning's smile so fair,
As is he, nor cloud, nor wind,
But would be courteous, would be kind.
Spare him, Death, O spare him then,
Spare the sweetest among men!
Let not pity, with her tears,
Keep such distance from thine ears;
But O! thou wilt not, can'st not spare,
Haste hath never time to hear.
Therefore if he needs must go,
And the Fates will have it so,
Softly may he be possessed
Of his monumental rest.
Safe, thou dark home of the dead
Safe, O hide his lovèd head.
For Pity's sake, O, hide him quite
From his mother Nature's sight;
Lest for grief his loss may move
All her births abortive prove.

CRASHAW

CLXIX FOLLOW YOUR SAINT

Follow your saint, follow with accents sweet!
Haste you, sad notes, fall at her flying feet!
There, wrapped in cloud of sorrow, pity move,
And tell the ravisher of my soul I perish for her love:
But, if she scorns my never-ceasing pain,
Then burst with sighing in her sight and ne'er return again.

ll that I sang still to her praise did tend,
till she was first, still she my songs did end;
et she my love and music both doth fly,
he music that her echo is and beauty's sympathy:
hen let my notes pursue her scornful flight!
t shall suffice that they were breathed and died for her delight.

CAMPION

LXX SONG FROM A MASQUE

"Tell me, gentle hour of night
Wherein dost thou most delight?"
"Not in sleep."
"Wherein then?"
"In the frolic view of men."
"Lovest thou music?"
"O 'tis sweet."
"What's dancing?"
"Ev'n the mirth of feet."

CAMPION

CLXXI GIVE BEAUTY ALL HER RIGHT

Give beauty all her right!
She's not to one form tied;
Each shape yields fair delight
Where her perfections bide:
Helen, I grant, might pleasing be,
And Ros'mond was as sweet as she.

Some the quick eye commends,
Some swelling lips and red;
Pale looks have many friends,
Through sacred sweetness bred:
Meadows have flowers that pleasures move,
Though roses are the flowers of love.

Free beauty is not bound
To one unmoved clime;
She visits every ground
And favours every time.
Let the old loves with mine compare,
My sovereign is as sweet and fair.

CAMPION

CLXXII SHALL I COME, SWEET LOVE?

Shall I come, sweet Love, to thee
When the evening beams are set?
Shall I not excluded be,
Will you find no feignèd let?
Let me not, for pity, more
Tell the long hours at your door.

Who can tell what thief or foe,
In the covert of the night,
For his prey will work my woe,
Or through wicked foul despite?
So may I die unredrest
Ere my long love be possest.

But to let such dangers pass,
Which a lover's thoughts disdain,
'Tis enough in such a place
To attend love's joys in vain:
Do not mock me in thy bed,
While these cold nights freeze me dead.

CAMPION.

CLXXIII FOLLOW THY FAIR SUN

Follow thy fair sun, unhappy shadow!
Though thou be black as night,
And she made all of light,
Yet follow thy fair sun, unhappy shadow!

Follow her, whose light thy light depriveth!
Though here thou liv'st disgraced,
And she in heaven is placed,
Yet follow her whose light the world reviveth!

Follow those pure beams, whose beauty burneth!
That so have scorched thee
As thou still black must be
Till her kind beams thy black to brightness turneth.

Follow her, while yet her glory shineth!
There comes a luckless night
That will dim all her light;
And this the black unhappy shade divineth.

Follow still, since so thy fates ordained!
The sun must have his shade,
Till both at once do fade,
The sun still proved, the shadow still disdained.

Campion

CLXXIV THOU ART NOT FAIR

Thou art not fair, for all thy red and white,
For all those rosy ornaments in thee;
Thou art not sweet, tho' made of mere delight,
Nor fair, nor sweet—unless thou pity me.
I will not soothe thy fancies, thou shalt prove
That beauty is no beauty without love.

Yet love not me, nor seek not to allure
My thoughts with beauty were it more divine;
Thy smiles and kisses I cannot endure,
I'll not be wrapped up in those arms of thine:
Now show it, if thou be a woman right,—
Embrace and kiss and love me in despite.

Campion

CLXXV CORINNA

When to her lute Corinna sings,
Her voice revives the leaden strings,
And doth in highest notes appear
As any challenged echo clear;
But when she doth of mourning speak,
E'en with her sighs the strings do break.

And as her lute doth live or die,
Led by her passion, so must I:
For when of pleasure she doth sing,
My thoughts enjoy a sudden spring;
But if she doth of sorrow speak,
E'en from my heart the strings do break.

Campion

CLXXVI COME, CHEERFUL DAY

Come, cheerful day, part of my life to me;
For while thou view'st me with thy fading light,
Part of my life doth still depart with thee,
And I still onward haste to my last night:
Time's fatal wings do ever forward fly,
So every day we live a day we die.

But, O ye nights, ordained for barren rest,
  How are my days deprived of life in you,
When heavy sleep my soul hath dispossest,
  By feigned death life sweetly to renew!
Part of my life in that, you life deny:
So every day we live a day we die.

CAMPION

CLXXVII JACK AND JOAN

Jack and Joan, they think no ill,
But loving live, and merry still;
Do their week-days' work, and pray
Devoutly on the holy day:
Skip and trip it on the green,
And help to choose the Summer Queen;
Lash out at a country feast
Their silver penny with the best.

Well can they judge of nappy ale,
And tell at large a winter tale;
Climb up to the apple loft,
And turn the crabs till they be soft.
Tib is all the father's joy,
And little Tom the mother's boy.
All their pleasure is Content;
And care, to pay their yearly rent.

Joan can call by name her cows
And deck her windows with green boughs;
She can wreaths and tutties make,
And trim with plums a bridal cake.
Jack knows what brings gain or loss;
And his long flail can stoutly toss:
Makes the hedge which others break,
And ever thinks what he doth speak.

Now, you courtly dames and knights,
That study only strange delights;
Though you scorn the homespun gray
And revel in your rich array;
Though your tongues dissemble deep,
And can your heads from danger keep;
Yet, for all your pomp and train,
Securer lives the silly swain.

CAMPION

CLXXVIII WINTER NIGHTS

Now winter nights enlarge
The number of their hours,
And clouds their storms discharge
Upon the airy towers.
Let now the chimneys blaze,
And cups o'erflow with wine;
Let well-tuned words amaze
With harmony divine.
Now yellow waxen lights
Shall wait on honey love,
While youthful revels, masques, and courtly sights
Sleep's leaden spells remove.
This time doth well dispense
With lovers' long discourse;
Much speech hath some defence
Though beauty no remorse.
All do not all things well;
Some measures comely tread,
Some knotted riddles tell,
Some poems smoothly read.
The summer hath his joys
And winter his delights;
Though love and all his pleasures are but toys,
They shorten tedious nights.

CAMPION

CLXXIX DIRGE

Glories, pleasures, pomps, delights and ease,
Can but please
Outward senses, when the mind
's untroubled, or by peace refined.
Crowns may flourish and decay,
Beauties shine, but fade away.
Youth may revel, yet it must
Lie down in a bed of dust.
Earthly honours flow and waste,
Time alone doth change and last.
Sorrows mingled with contents, prepare
Rest for care;
Love only reigns in death; though art
Can find no comfort for a broken heart.

FORD

CLXXX SORROW

Here full of April, veil'd with Sorrow's wing,
For lovely lays, I dreary dirges sing.
Whoso hath seen young lads (to sport themselves)
Run in a low ebb to the sandy shelves;
Where seriously they work in digging wells,
Or building childish sorts of cockle-shells;
Or liquid water each to other bandy;
Or with the pebbles play at handy-dandy,
Till unawares the tide hath clos'd them round,
And they must wade it through or else be drown'd:
May (if unto my pipe he listen well)
My Muse' distress with theirs soon parallel.

For where I whilom sung the loves of swains,
And woo'd the crystal currents of the plains,
Teaching the birds to love, whilst every tree
Gave his attention to my melody:
Fate now (as envying my too-happy theme)
Hath round begirt my song with Sorrow's stream,
Which till my Muse wade through and get on shore,
My grief-swoll'n soul can sing of love no more.

William Browne

CLXXXI THOUGHTS, HOPES AND LOVE

My Thoughts are winged with Hopes, my Hopes with Love:
Mount Love unto the moon in clearest night,
And say, as she doth in the heavens move,
In earth so wanes and waxeth my delight:
And whisper this, but softly, in her ears,
"Hope oft doth hang the head and Trust shed tears."

And you, my Thoughts, that some mistrust do carry,
If for mistrust my mistress do you blame,
Say, though you alter, yet you do not vary,
As she doth change and yet remain the same;
Distrust doth enter hearts, but not infect,
And Love is sweetest seasoned with Suspect.

If she for this with clouds do mask her eyes
And make the heavens dark with her disdain,
With windy sighs disperse them in the skies
Or with thy tears dissolve them into rain.
Thoughts, Hopes, and Love, return to me no more
Till Cynthia shine as she hath done before.

CLXXXII SORROW AND TEARS

I saw my Lady weep,
And Sorrow proud to be advanced so
In those fair eyes where all perfections keep.
Her face was full of woe,
But such a woe (believe me) as wins more hearts
Than Mirth can do with her enticing parts.

Sorrow was there made fair,
And Passion wise; Tears a delightful thing;
Silence beyond all speech, a wisdom rare;
She made her sighs to sing,
And all things with so sweet a sadness move
As made my heart at once both grieve and love.

O fairer than aught else
The world can show, leave off in time to grieve.
Enough, enough: your joyful look excels:
Tears kill the heart, believe.
O strive not to be excellent in woe,
Which only breeds your beauty's overthrow.

CLXXXIII THE HAWKER

Fine knacks for ladies, cheap, choice, brave and new,
Good pennyworths,—but money cannot move:
I keep a fair but for the Fair to view,—
A beggar may be liberal of love.
Though all my wares be trash, the heart is true,
The heart is true.

Great gifts are guiles and look for gifts again,
My trifles come as treasures from my mind;
It is a precious jewel to be plain;
Sometimes in shell the orient'st pearls we find:
Of others take a sheaf, of me a grain!
Of me a grain!

Within this pack pins, points, laces, and gloves,
And divers toys fitting a country fair,
But my heart, wherein duty serves and loves,
Turtles and twins, court's brood, a heavenly pair—
Happy the heart that thinks of no removes!
Of no removes!

CLXXXIV CARE'S CONFESSOR

The sea hath many thousand sands,
The sun hath motes as many;
The sky is full of stars, and love
As full of woes as any:
Believe me, that do know the elf,
And make no trial by thyself.

It is in truth a pretty toy
For babes to play withal;
But O the honies of our youth
Are oft our age's gall!
Self-proof in time will make thee know
He was a prophet told thee so:

A prophet that, Cassandra-like,
Tells truth without belief;
For headstrong youth will run his race,
Although his goal be grief:
Love's martyr, when his heat is past,
Proves Care's confessor at the last.

CLXXXV THE SLEEPER

Weep you no more, sad fountains;
  What need you flow so fast?
Look how the snowy mountains
  Heaven's sun doth gently waste!
But my sun's heavenly eyes,
  View not your weeping,
  That now lies sleeping
Softly, now softly lies
                Sleeping.

Sleep is a reconciling,
  A rest that peace begets;
Doth not the sun rise smiling
  When fair at ev'n he sets?
Rest you then, rest, sad eyes
  Melt not in weeping,
  While she lies sleeping,
Softly, now softly lies
                Sleeping.

CLXXXVI HOB'S LOVE

1. Who made thee, Hob, forsake the plough
   And fall in Love?
2. Sweet beauty, which hath power to bow
   The gods above.
1. What dost thou serve? 2. A shepherdess;
   One such as hath no peer, I guess.
1. What is her name who bears thy heart
   Within her breast?
2. Silvana fair, of high desert,
   Whom I love best.
1. O, Hob, I fear she looks too high.
2. Yet love I must, or else I die.

CLXXXVII FA, LA, LA!

Now is the month of maying,
When merry lads are playing
Each with his bonny lass
Upon the greeny grass.
Fa la la!

The spring clad all in gladness
Doth laugh at winter's sadness,
And to the bagpipe's sound
The nymphs tread out their ground.
Fa la la!

Fie then, why sit we musing,
Youth's sweet delight refusing?
Say, dainty nymphs, and speak,
Shall we play barley-break.
Fa la la!

CLXXXVIII GREAT GIFTS

See, see, mine own sweet jewel,
What I have for my darling:
A robin red-breast and a starling.
These I give both in hope to move thee;
Yet thou say'st I do not love thee.

CLXXXIX LOVE'S FOOL

Once did my thoughts both ebb and flow,
  As passion did them move;
Once did I hope, straight fear again,—
  And then I was in love.

Once did I waking spend the night,
  And tell how many minutes move.
Once did I wishing waste the day,—
  And then I was in love.

Once, by my carving true love's knot,
  The weeping trees did prove
That wounds and tears were both our lot,—
  And then I was in love.

Once did I breathe another's breath
  And in my mistress move,
Once was I not mine own at all,—
  And then I was in love.

Once wore I bracelets made of hair,
  And collars did approve,
Once were my clothes made out of wax,—
  And then I was in love.

Once did I sonnet to my saint,
  My soul in numbers move,
Once did I tell a thousand lies,—
  And then I was in love.

Once in my ear did dangling hang
  A little turtle-dove,
Once, in a word, I was a fool,—
  And then I was in love.

CXC THE MORRICE DANCE

Ho! who comes here along with bagpiping and drumming?
O! the Morrice 'tis I see, the morrice dance a-coming.
  Come, lasses, come, come quickly!
  See how trim they dance and trickly.
  Hey, there again! ho, there again!
    How the bells they shake it!
    Now for our town; there, and take it.

Soft awhile, not away so fast; they melt them:
Piper, piper, piper! be hanged awhile, knave, the dancers
swelt them!
Out there, out awhile! you come too far, I say, in:
Give the hobby horse more room to play in.

CXCI DIAPHENIA

Diaphenia, like the daffadown dilly,
White as the sun, fair as the lily,
Heigho, how I do love thee!
I do love thee as my lambs
Are belovèd of their dams:
How blest were I if thou wouldst prove me!

Diaphenia, like the spreading roses,
That in thy sweets all sweets encloses,
Fair sweet, how do I love thee!
I do love thee as each flower
Loves the sun's life-giving power;
For dead, thy breath to life might move me.

Diaphenia, like to all things blessèd,
When all thy praises are expressèd,
Dear joy, how I do love thee!
As the birds do love the spring,
Or the bees their careful king:
Then in requite, sweet virgin, love me!

CXCII FAREWELL TO THE FAIRIES

Farewell rewards and fairies,
Good housewives now may say,
For now foul sluts in dairies
Do fare as well as they.
And though they sweep their hearths no less
Than maids were wont to do,
Yet who of late, for cleanliness,
Finds sixpence in her shoe?

Lament, lament, old Abbeys,
The fairies lost command;
They did but change priests' babies,
But some have changed your land;

And all your children sprung from thence
  Are now grown Puritans;
Who live as changelings ever since,
  For love of your domains.

At morning and at evening both,
  You merry were and glad,
So little care of sleep or sloth
  These pretty ladies had;
When Tom came home from labour,
  Or Cis to milking rose,
Then merrily went their tabor,
  And nimbly went their toes.

Witness those rings and roundelays
  Of theirs, which yet remain,
Were footed in Queen Mary's days
  On many a grassy plain;
But since of late Elizabeth,
  And later, James came in,
They never danced on any heath
  As when the time hath been.

By which we note the fairies
  Were of the old profession,
Their songs were Ave-Maries,
  Their dances were procession:
But now, alas! they all are dead,
  Or gone beyond the seas;
Or farther for religion fled,
  Or else they take their ease.

A tell-tale in their company
  They never could endure,
And whoso kept not secretly
  Their mirth, was punished sure;
It was a just and Christian deed,
  To pinch such black and blue:
O how the commonwealth doth need
  Such justices as you!

CORBET

CXCIII OLD AGE AND DEATH

The seas are quiet when the winds give o'er;
So calm are we when passions are no more.

For then we know how vain it was to boast
Of fleeting things, too certain to be lost.
Clouds of affection from our younger eyes
Conceal that emptiness which age descries.

The soul's dark cottage, battered and decayed,
Lets in new light through chinks that time has made:
Stronger by weakness, wiser men become,
As they draw near to their eternal home.
Leaving the old, both worlds at once they view,
That stand upon the threshold of the new.

EDMUND WALLER

ENVOI TO BOOK THIRD

OF ENGLISH VERSE

Poets may boast, as safely vain,
Their works shall with the world remain;
Both bound together, live or die,
The verses and the prophecy.

But who can hope his line should long
Last in a daily changing tongue?
While they are new, envy prevails;
And, as that dies, our language fails.

When architects have done their part,
The matter may betray their art:
Time, if we use ill-chosen stone,
Soon brings a well-built palace down.

Poets, that lasting marble seek,
Must carve in Latin or in Greek:
We write in sand: our language grows,
And, like the tide, our work o'erflows.

WALLER

BOOK FOURTH

CXCIV ORINDA UPON LITTLE HECTOR PHILIPS

What on earth deserves our trust?
Youth and beauty both are dust;
Long we gathering are with pain.
What one moment calls again.
Seven years childless marriage past,
A son, a son is born at last:
So exactly limb'd and fair,
Full of good spirits, mien, and air,
As a long life promisèd—
Yet, in less than six weeks dead.
Too promising, too great a mind
In so small room to be confin'd,
Therefore, as fit in heaven to dwell,
He quickly broke the prison shell.
So the subtle alchymist
Can't with Hermes' seal resist
The powerful spirit's subtler flight,
But 'twill bid him long good night.
And so the sun, if it arise
Half so glorious as his eyes,
Like this infant, takes a shroud,
Buried in a morning cloud.

"ORINDA" (Katherine Philips)

CXCV SONG

I prithee send me back my heart,
  Since I can not have thine,
For if from yours you will not part,
  Why then should'st thou have mine?

Yet now I think on't, let it lie,
  To find it were in vain;
For thou'st a thief in either eye
  Would steal it back again.

Why should two hearts in one breast lie,
  And yet not lodge together?
Oh love! where is thy sympathy,
  If thus our breasts thou sever?

But love is such a mystery,
  I cannot find it out;
For when I think I'm best resolved,
  I then am in most doubt.

Then farewell care, and farewell wo,
  I will no longer pine;
For I'll believe I have her heart
  As much as she has mine.

Sir John Suckling

CXCVI CONSTANCY

Out upon it, I have loved
  Three whole days together;
And am like to love three more,
  If it prove fair weather.

Time shall moult away his wings,
  Ere he shall discover
In the whole wide world again
  Such a constant lover.

But the spite on 't is, no praise
  Is due at all to me;
Love with me had made no stays,
  Had it any been but she.

Had it any been but she,
  And that very face,
There had been at least ere this
  A dozen in her place.

Suckling

CXCVII SONG

Love still has something of the sea,
  From whence his mother rose;
No time his slaves from doubt can free,
  Nor give their thoughts repose.

They are becalmed in clearest days,
  And in rough weather tossed;
They wither under cold delays,
  Or are in tempests lost.

One while they seem to touch the port,
  Then straight into the main
Some angry wind, in cruel sport,
  The vessel drives again.

At first disdain and pride they fear,
  Which, if they chance to 'scape,
Rivals and falsehood soon appear
  In a more cruel shape.

By such degrees to joy they come,
  And are so long withstood;
So slowly they receive the sun,
  It hardly does them good.

'Tis cruel to prolong the pain;
  And to defer a joy,
Believe me, gentle Celemene,
  Offends the winged boy.

A hundred thousand oaths your fears
  Perhaps would not remove;
And if I gazed a thousand years,
  I could not deeper love.

Sir Charles Sedley

CXCVIII TO HIS MISTRESS

Why dost thou shade thy lovely face? O, why
Does that eclipsing hand of thine deny
The sunshine of the Sun's enlivening eye?

Without thy light, what light remains in me?
Thou art my life: my way, my light's in thee;
I live, I move, and by thy beams I see.

Thou art my life: if thou but turn away,
My life's a thousand deaths. Thou art my way:
Without thee, Love, I travel not, but stray.

My light thou art: without thy glorious sight,
My eyes are darkened with eternal night.
My Love, thou art my way, my life, my light.

Thou art my way: I wander if thou fly.
Thou art my light: if hid, how blind am I!
Thou art my life: if thou withdraw'st, I die.

My eyes are dark and blind, I cannot see:
To whom, or whither should my darkness flee,
But to that light? and who's that light but thee?

If I have lost my path, dear lover, say,
Shall I still wander in a doubtful way?
Love, shall a lamb of Israel's sheep-fold stray?

My path is lost, my wandering steps do stray,
I cannot go, nor can I safely stay:
Whom should I seek, but thee, my path, my way?

And yet thou turn'st thy face away, and fly'st me!
And yet I sue for grace, and thou deny'st me!
Speak, art thou angry, love, or only try'st me? . . .

Thou art the pilgrim's path, the blind man's eye,
The dead man's life: on thee my hopes rely:
If I but them remove, I surely die.

Dissolve thy sunbeams, close thy wings, and stay!
See, see how I am blind, and dead, and stray,
O thou that art my life, my light, my way!

Then work thy will! If passion bid me flee,
My reason shall obey, my wings shall be
Stretched out no farther than from me to thee.

JOHN WILMOT, EARL OF ROCHESTER

CXCIX ABSENCE

With leaden foot Time creeps along,
  While Delia is away.
With her, nor plaintive was the song,
  Nor tedious was the day.

Ah! envious power! reverse my doom,
  Now double thy career;
Strain every nerve, stretch every plume,
  And rest them when she's here.

RICHARD JAGO

CC THE REGRATE OF A TRUE LOVER

I wish I were those gloves, dear heart,
  Which could thy hands inshrine;
Then should no sorrow, grief or smart
  Molest this heart of mine.

CCI WINIFREDA

Away; let nought to love displeasing,
  My Winifreda, move your care;
Let nought delay the heavenly blessing,
  Nor squeamish pride, nor gloomy fear.

What tho' no grants of royal donors
  With pompous titles grace our blood;
We'll shine in more substantial honours
  And to be noble we'll be good.

Our name, while virtue thus we tender,
  Will sweetly sound where'er 'tis spoke:
And all the great ones, they shall wonder
  How they respect such little folk.

What though from fortune's lavish bounty
  No mighty treasures we possess;
We'll find within our pittance plenty,
  And be content without excess.

Still shall each returning season
  Sufficient for our wishes give;
For we will live a life of reason,
  And that's the only life to live.

Through youth and age in love excelling
  We'll hand in hand together tread;
Sweet smiling peace shall crown our dwelling,
  And babes, sweet-smiling babes, our bed.

How should I love the pretty creatures,
  While round my knees they fondly clung:
To see them look their mother's features,
  To hear them lisp their mother's tongue.

And when with envy time transported
  Shall think to rob us of our joys,
You'll in your girls again be courted,
  And I'll go a wooing in my boys.

CCII CHLOE

What I speak, my fair Chloe, and what I write, shews
  The difference there is betwixt nature and art;
I court others in verse, but I love thee in prose;
  And they have my whimsies, but thou hast my heart.

The god of us verse-men—you know, child—the Sun,
  How after his journey he sets up his rest;
If at morning o'er earth 'tis his fancy to run,
  At night he reclines on his Thetis's breast.

So when I am wearied with wandering all day,
  To thee, my delight, in the evening I come;
No matter what beauties I saw in my way,
  They were but my visits, but thou art my home.

MATTHEW PRIOR

CCIII CHLOE HUNTING

Behind her neck her comely tresses tied,
Her ivory quiver graceful by her side,
A-hunting Chloe went: she lost her way,
And through the woods uncertain chanc'd to stray.

Apollo, passing by, beheld the maid;
And, "Sister dear, bright Cynthia, turn, (he said)
The hunted hind lies close in yonder brake."
Loud Cupid laugh'd to see the god's mistake;

And, laughing, cried, "Learn better, great divine,
To know thy kindred, and to honour mine.
Rightly advis'd, far hence thy sister seek,
Or on Meander's bank or Latmus' peak;

But in this nymph, my friend, my sister, know;
She draws my arrows, and she bends my bow:
Fair Thames she haunts, and every neighbouring grove.
Sacred to soft recess and gentle love.

Go, with thy Cynthia hurl the pointed spear
At the rough boar, or chase the flying deer:
I and my Chloe take a nobler aim;
At human hearts we fling, nor ever miss the game."

PRIOR

CCIV THE TWO ROSES

As in the cool of early day
A poet sought the sweets of May,
The garden's fragrant breath ascends,
And every stalk with odour bends;
A rose he plucked, he gazed, admired,
Thus singing, as the muse inspired:

"Go, Rose, my Chloe's bosom grace;
How happy should I prove,
Might I supply that envied place
With never-fading love!
There, Phœnix-like, beneath her eye,
Involved in fragrance, burn and die.
Know, hapless flower! that thou shalt find
More fragrant roses there:
I see thy withering head reclined
With envy and despair!
One common fate we both must prove;
You die with envy, I with love."
"Spare your comparisons," replied
An angry Rose, who grew beside.
"Of all mankind, you should not flout us;
What can a poet do without us?
In every love-song roses bloom;
We lend you colour and perfume.
Does it to Chloe's charms conduce,
To found her praise on our abuse?
Must we, to flatter her, be made
To wither, envy, pine, and fade?"

JOHN GAY

CCV THE WHITE ROSE

SENT BY A YORKIST GENTLEMAN TO HIS LANCASTRIAN LOVE

If this fair rose offend thy sight,
Placed in thy bosom bare,
'Twill blush to find itself less white,
And turn Lancastrian there.

But if thy ruby lip it spy,—
As kiss it thou mayst deign,—
With envy pale 'twill lose its dye,
And Yorkist turn again.

JAMES SOMERVILLE (?)

CCVI ON A CERTAIN LADY AT COURT

I know the thing that's most uncommon;
(Envy be silent, and attend!)
I know a reasonable woman,
Handsome and witty, yet a friend.

Not warped by passion, awed by rumour,
  Not grave through pride, or gay through folly;
An equal mixture of good-humour,
  And sensible soft melancholy.

"Has she no faults then, (Envy says,) sir?"
  Yes, she has one, I must aver;
When all the world conspires to praise her,—
  The woman's deaf, and does not hear.

ALEX. POPE

CCVII SONNET

ON THE DEATH OF MR. RICHARD WEST

In vain to me the smiling Mornings shine,
  And redd'ning Phœbus lifts his golden fire:
The birds in vain their amorous descant join;
  Or cheerful fields resume their green attire:
These ears, alas! for other notes repine,
  A different object do these eyes require:
My lonely anguish melts no heart but mine;
  And in my breast the imperfect joys expire.
Yet Morning smiles the busy race to cheer,
  And new-born pleasure brings to happier men:
The fields to all their wonted tribute bear:
  To warm their little loves the birds complain:
I fruitless mourn to him, that cannot hear,
  And weep the more, because I weep in vain.

THOMAS GRAY

CCVIII SONG TO AN OLD AIR

Thyrsis, when he left me, swore
  Ere the Spring he would return—
Ah! what means the op'ning flower?
  And the bud that decks the thorn?
'Twas the nightingale that sung!
'Twas the lark that upward sprung!

Idle notes! untimely green!
  Why such unavailing haste?
Gentle gales and skies serene
  Prove not always Winter past.
Cease, my doubts, my fears to move—
Spare the honour of my love.

GRAY

CCIX FIDELE'S DIRGE

To fair Fidele's grassy tomb
  Soft maids and village hinds shall bring
Each opening sweet, of earliest bloom,
  And rifle all the breathing spring.

No wailing ghost shall dare appear
  To vex with shrieks this quiet grove,
But shepherd lads assemble here,
  And melting virgins own their love.

No withered witch shall here be seen,
  No goblins lead their nightly crew;
The female fays shall haunt the green,
  And dress thy grave with pearly dew;

The redbreast oft, at evening hours,
  Shall kindly lend his little aid,
With hoary moss, and gathered flowers,
  To deck the ground where thou art laid.

When howling winds, and beating rain,
  In tempests shake the sylvan cell,
Or midst the chase, on every plain,
  The tender thought on thee shall dwell.

Each lonely scene shall thee restore,
  For thee the tear be duly shed;
Beloved till life can charm no more;
  And mourned till Pity's self be dead.

WILLIAM COLLINS

CCX ODE TO PITY

O thou, the friend of man assigned
With balmy hands his wounds to bind,
  And charm his frantic woe:
When first distress, with dagger keen,
Broke forth to waste his destined scene,
  His wild, unsated foe!

But Pella's bard, a magic name,
By all the griefs his thought could frame,
  Receive my humble rite:
Long, pity, let the nations view
Thy sky-worn robes of tenderest blue,
  And eyes of dewy light!

But wherefore need I wander wide
To old Ilissus' distant side,
  Deserted stream, and mute?
Wild Arun, too, has heard thy strains,
And echo, 'midst thy native plains,
  Been soothed by pity's lute.

There first the wren thy myrtles shed
On gentlest Otway's infant head,
  To him thy cell was shown;
And while he sung the female heart,
With youth's soft notes unspoiled by art,
  Thy turtles mixed their own.

Come, pity, come, by fancy's aid,
Ev'n now my thoughts, relenting maid,
  Thy temple's pride design:
Its southern site, its truth complete,
Shall raise a wild enthusiast heat
  In all who view the shrine.

There picture's toils shall well relate
How chance, or hard involving fate,
  O'er mortal bliss prevail:
The buskined muse shall near her stand,
And sighing, prompt her tender hand,
  With each disastrous tale.

There let me oft, retired by day,
In dreams of passion melt away,
  Allowed with thee to dwell:
There waste the mournful lamp of night,
Till, virgin, thou again delight
  To hear a British shell!

COLLINS

CXI ODE TO FEAR

Thou, to whom the world unknown
With all its shadowy shapes, is shown;
Who seest, appalled, the unreal scene,
While fancy lifts the veil between:
  Ah fear! ah frantic fear!
  I see, I see thee near.
I know thy hurried step, thy haggard eye!
Like thee I start; like thee disordered fly.

For, lo, what monsters in thy train appear!
Danger, whose limbs of giant mould
What mortal eye can fixed behold?
Who stalks his round, an hideous form,
Howling amidst the midnight storm;
Or throws him on the ridgy steep
Of some loose hanging rock to sleep:
And with him thousand phantoms joined,
Who prompt to deeds accursed the mind:
And those, the fiends, who, near allied,
O'er nature's wounds, and wrecks, preside;
Whilst vengeance, in the lurid air,
Lifts her red arm, exposed and bare:
On whom that ravening brood of fate,
Who lap the blood of sorrow, wait:
Who, fear, this ghastly train can see,
And look not madly wild, like thee?

EPODE

In earliest Greece, to thee, with partial choice,
The grief-full muse addrest her infant tongue;
The maids and matrons, on her awful voice,
Silent and pale, in wild amazement hung.

Yet he, the bard who first invoked thy name,
Disdained in Marathon its power to feel:
For not alone he nursed the poet's flame,
But reached from virtue's hand the patriot's steel.

But who is he whom later garlands grace,
Who left awhile o'er Hybla's dews to rove,
With trembling eyes thy dreary steps to trace,
Where thou and furies shared the baleful grove?

Wrapt in thy cloudy veil, the incestuous queen
Sighed the sad call her son and husband heard,
When once alone it broke the silent scene,
And he, the wretch of Thebes, no more appeared.

O fear, I know thee by my throbbing heart:
Thy withering power inspired each mournful line:
Though gentle pity claim her mingled part,
Yet all the thunders of the scene are thine!

ANTISTROPHE

Thou who such weary lengths hast past,
Where wilt thou rest, mad nymph, at last?

Say, wilt thou shroud in haunted cell,
Where gloomy rape and murder dwell?
  Or, in some hollowed seat,
  'Gainst which the big waves beat,
Hear drowning seamen's cries, in tempests brought?
Dark power, with shuddering meek submitted thought,
Be mine to read the visions old
Which thy awakening bards have told:
And, lest thou meet my blasted view,
Hold each strange tale devoutly true;
Ne'er be I found, by thee o'erawed,
In that thrice hallowed eve, abroad,
When ghosts, as cottage maids believe,
Their pebbled beds permitted leave;
And goblins haunt, from fire, or fen,
Or mine, or flood, the walks of men!

  O thou, whose spirit most possest
The sacred seat of Shakespeare's breast!
By all that from thy prophet broke,
In thy divine emotions spoke;
Hither again thy fury deal,
Teach me but once like him to feel:
His cypress wreath my meed decree,
And I, O fear, will dwell with thee!

COLLINS

CXII ODE TO A SCHOOLMASTER

TO THE MUCH HONOURED MR. THOMAS ROWE, ON FREE PHILOSOPHY

I

Custom, that Tyranness of Fools
  That leads the Learned round the Schools
In magic Chains of Forms and Rules!
  My Genius storms her Throne:
No more, ye Slaves, with Awe profound
Beat the dull Track, nor dance the Round;
Loose Hands, and quit th' inchanted Ground.
Knowledge invites us each alone.

II

I hate these Shacklers of the mind
  Forg'd by the haughty wise;

Souls were not born to be confin'd,
And led like *Sampson* blind and bound;
But when his native Strength he found
  He well aveng'd his Eyes.
I love thy gentle Influence, Rowe,
Thy gentle Influence like the Sun
Only dissolves the frozen Snow,
Then bids our Thoughts like Rivers flow,
And chuse the Channels where they run.

III

Thoughts should be free as Fire or Wind
The Pinions of a single Mind
  Will thro' all Nature fly:
But who can drag up to the Poles
Long fetter'd Ranks of Leaden Souls?
My Genius which no Chain controuls
Roves with Delight, or deep or high:
Swift I survey the Globe around,
Dive to the Centre thro' the solid Ground,
  Or travel o'er the Sky.

Isaac Watts

CCXIII ON THE DEATH OF MATZEL, A FAVOURITE BULLFINCH

Matzel's no more! ye Graces, Loves,
Ye linnets, nightingales, and doves,
  Attend th' untimely bier;
Let every sorrow be express'd,
Beat with your wings each mournful breast,
  And drop the natural tear.

For thee, my bird, the sacred Nine,
Who loved thy tuneful notes, shall join
  In thy funereal verse;
My painful task shall be to write
Th' eternal dirge which they indite,
  And hang it on thy hearse.

In height of song, in beauty's pride,
By fell Grimalkin's claws he died—
  But vengeance shall have way.
On pains and tortures I'll refine;
Yet, Matzel, that one death of thine
  His nine will ill repay.

In vain I loved, in vain I mourn
My bird, who never to return,
  Is fled to happier shades,
Where Lesbia shall for him prepare
The place most charming and most fair
  Of all the Elysian glades.

There shall thy notes in cypress grove
Soothe wretched ghosts that died for love,
  There shall thy plaintive strain
Lull impious Phædra's endless grief,
To Procris yield some short relief,
  And soften Dido's pain.

Till Proserpine by chance shall hear
Thy notes, and make thee all her care,
  And love thee with my love;
While each attendant's soul shall praise
The matchless Matzel's tuneful lays,
  And all his songs approve.

Sir Ch. Hanbury Williams

CCXIV LOCHABER NO MORE

Farewell to Lochaber, farewell to my Jean,
Where heartsome wi' her I ha'e mony a day been;
To Lochaber no more, to Lochaber no more,
We'll maybe return to Lochaber no more!
These tears that I shed, they're a' for my dear,
And no for the dangers attending on weir;
Though borne on rough seas to a far bloody shore,
Maybe to return to Lochaber no more;

Though hurricanes rise, though rise every wind,
No tempest can equal the storm in my mind;
Though loudest of thunders on louder waves roar,
That's naething like leavin' my love on the shore.
To leave thee behind me my heart is sair pain'd;
But by ease that's inglorious no fame can be gain'd;
And beauty and love's the reward of the brave,
And I maun deserve it before I can crave.

Then glory, my Jeanie, maun plead my excuse;
Since honour commands me, how can I refuse?
Without it, I ne'er can have merit for thee;
And losing thy favour, I'd better not be.

I gae then, my lass, to win honour and fame;
And if I should chance to come glorious hame,
I'll bring a heart to thee with love running o'er,
And then I'll leave thee and Lochaber no more.

ALLAN RAMSAY

CCXV THE BUSH ABOON TRAQUAIR

Hear me, ye nymphs, and every swain,
  I'll tell how Peggy grieves me;
Tho' thus I languish, thus complain,
  Alas! she ne'er believes me.
My vows and sighs, like silent air,
  Unheeded never move her;
At the bonny bush aboon Traquair,
  'Twas there I first did love her.

That day she smiled, and made me glad,
  No maid seem'd ever kinder;
I thought myself the luckiest lad,
  So sweetly there to find her.
I tried to soothe my amorous flame
  In words that I thought tender;
If more there pass'd, I'm not to blame,
  I meant not to offend her.

Yet now she scornful flees the plain,
  The fields we then frequented;
If e'er we meet, she shows disdain,
  She looks as ne'er acquainted.
The bonny bush bloom'd fair in May,
  Its sweets I'll aye remember;
But now her frowns make it decay,
  Its fades as in December.

Ye rural powers, who hear my strains,
  Why thus should Peggy grieve me?
Oh! make her partner in my pains,
  Then let her smiles relieve me.
If not, my love will turn despair,
  My passion no more tender,
I'll leave the bush aboon Traquair,
  To lonely wilds I'll wander.

CRAWFORD

CCXVI THE FLOWERS OF THE FOREST

I've seen the smiling
Of Fortune beguiling—
I've tasted her favours,
  And felt her decay:
Sweet is her blessing,
And kind her caressing—
But soon it is fled—
  It is fled far away.

I've seen the Forest,
Adorn'd of the foremost
With flowers of the fairest,
  Both pleasant and gay:
Full sweet was their blooming,
Their scent the air perfuming,
But now they are wither'd,
  And a' wede away.

I've seen the morning
With gold the hills adorning;
And the red storm roaring,
  Before the parting day:
I've seen Tweed's silver streams,
Glittering in the sunny beams,
Turn drumlie and dark
  As they roll'd on their way.

Oh, fickle Fortune!
Why this cruel sporting?
Why thus perplex us,
  Poor sons of a day?
Thy frowns cannot fear me,
Thy smiles cannot cheer me,
Since the Flowers of the Forest
  Are a' wede away.

MRS. COCKBURN

CCXVII STRADA'S NIGHTINGALE

The shepherd touched his reed: sweet Philomel
  Essay'd, and oft essay'd to catch the strain;
And treasuring, as on her ear they fell,
  The numbers, echoed note for note again.

The peevish youth, who ne'er had found before
  A rival of his skill, indignant heard,
And soon (for various was his tuneful store)
  In loftier tones defied the simple bird.

She dared the task, and, rising as he rose,
  With all the force that passion gives inspired,
Returned the sounds awhile, but in the close
  Exhausted fell and at his feet expired.

Thus strength, not skill prevailed: O fatal strife,
  By thee, poor songstress, playfully begun!
And, O sad victory, which cost thy life,
  And he may wish that he had never won.

William Cowper

CCXVIII THE JACKDAW

There is a bird, who by his coat,
And by the hoarseness of his note,
  Might be supposed a crow;
A great frequenter of the church,
Where bishop-like he finds a perch,
  And dormitory too.

Above the steeple shines a plate,
That turns and turns, to indicate
  From what point blows the weather:
Look up—your brains begin to swim,
'Tis in the clouds—that pleases him,
  He chooses it the rather.

Fond of the speculative height,
Thither he wings his airy flight,
  And thence securely sees
The bustle and the rareeshow
That occupy mankind below,
  Secure and at his ease.

You think, no doubt, he sits and muses
On future broken bones and bruises,
  If he should chance to fall.
No; not a single thought like that
Employs his philosophic pate,
  Or troubles it at all.

He sees that this great roundabout,
The world, with all its motley rout,
Church, army, physic, law,
Its customs, and its businesses,
Is no concern at all of his,
And says—what says he?—Caw.

Thrice happy bird! I too have seen
Much of the vanities of men;
And, sick of having seen 'em,
Would cheerfully these limbs resign
For such a pair of wings as thine,
And such a head between 'em.

COWPER

CCXIX MINSTREL'S SONG IN ELLA

Oh! sing unto my roundelay;
Oh! drop the briny tear with me;
Dance no more at holiday,
Like a running river be;
My love is dead,
Gone to his death-bed,
All under the willow-tree.

Black his hair as the winter night,
White his neck as summer snow,
Ruddy his face as the morning light,
Cold he lies in the grave below:
My love is dead,
Gone to his death-bed,
All under the willow-tree.

Sweet his tongue as throstle's note,
Quick in dance as thought was he;
Deft his tabor, cudgel stout;
Oh! he lies by the willow-tree.
My love is dead,
Gone to his death-bed,
All under the willow-tree.

Hark! the raven flaps his wing,
In the briered dell below;
Hark! the death-owl loud doth sing,
To the nightmares as they go.

My love is dead,
Gone to his death-bed,
All under the willow-tree.

See! the white moon shines on high;
Whiter is my true-love's shroud;
Whiter than the morning sky,
Whiter than the evening cloud.
My love is dead,
Gone to his death-bed,
All under the willow-tree.

Here, upon my true-love's grave,
Shall the garish flowers be laid,
Nor one holy saint to save
All the sorrows of a maid.
My love is dead,
Gone to his death-bed,
All under the willow-tree.

With my hands I'll bind the briers,
Round his holy corse to gre;
fairy, light your fires,
Here my body still shall be.
My love is dead,
Gone to his death-bed,
All under the willow-tree.

Come with acorn cup and thorn,
Drain my heart's blood all away;
Life and all its good I scorn,
Dance by night, and feast by day.
My love is dead,
Gone to his death-bed,
All under the willow-tree.

Water-witches, crowned with reytes,
Bear me to your deadly tide.
I die—I come—my true-love waits.
Thus the damsel spake, and died.

CHATTERTON

BOOK FIFTH

CCXX A SONG OF SINGING

Piping down the valleys wild,
Piping songs of pleasant glee,
On a cloud I saw a child,
And he laughing said to me:—

"Pipe a song about a Lamb!"
So I piped with merry cheer.
"Piper, pipe that song again."
So I piped: he wept to hear.

"Drop thy pipe, thy happy pipe;
Sing thy songs of happy cheer!"
So I sang the same again,
While he wept with joy to hear.

"Piper, sit thee down and write
In a book, that all may read."
So he vanished from my sight;
And I plucked a hollow reed,

And I made a rural pen,
And I stained the water clear,
And I wrote my happy songs
Every child may joy to hear.

William Blake

CCXXI SONG

How sweet I roamed from field to field,
And tasted all the summer's pride!
Till I the Prince of Love beheld,
Who in the sunny beams did glide!

He show'd me lilies for my hair,
And blushing roses for my brow;
He led me through his gardens fair,
Where all his golden pleasures grow.

With sweet May dews my wings were wet,
And Phœbus fired my vocal rage,
He caught me in his silken net,
And shut me in his golden cage.

He loves to sit and hear me sing,
  Then, laughing, sports and plays with me;
Then stretches out my golden wing,
  And mocks my loss of liberty.

BLAKE

CCXXII MY SILKS AND FINE ARRAY

My silks and fine array,
  My smiles and languished air;
By love are driven away.
  And mournful lean Despair
Brings me yew to deck my grave:
Such end true lovers have.

His face is fair as heaven
  When springing buds unfold;
Oh, why to him was't given,
  Whose heart is wintry cold?
His breast is Love's all-worshipped tomb
Where all love's pilgrims come.

Bring me an axe and spade,
  Bring me a winding sheet;
When I my grave have made,
  Let winds and tempests beat:
Then down I'll lie, as cold as clay,
True love doth pass away.

BLAKE

CCXXIII THE TIGER

Tiger, tiger, burning bright
In the forests of the night,
What immortal hand or eye
Could frame thy fearful symmetry?

In what distant deeps or skies
Burnt the fire of thine eyes?
On what wings dare he aspire?
What the hand dare seize the fire?

And what shoulder, and what art,
Could twist the sinews of thy heart?
And when thy heart began to beat,
What dread hand? and what dread feet?

What the hammer? what the chain?
In what furnace was thy brain?
What the anvil? what dread grasp
Dare its deadly terrors clasp?

When the stars threw down their spears,
And water'd heaven with their tears,
Did he smile his work to see?
Did he who made the lamb make thee?

Tiger, tiger, burning bright
In the forests of the night,
What immortal hand or eye
Dare frame thy fearful symmetry?

BLAKE

CCXXIV LOGIE O' BUCHAN

O Logie o' Buchan, O Logie the laird!
They ha'e ta'en awa' Jamie, that delved in the yard,
Wha play'd on the pipe and the viol sae sma',
They ha'e ta'en awa' Jamie, the flower o' them a'.
He said, Think na lang, lassie, though I gang awa';
He said, Think na lang, lassie, though I gang awa';
For simmer is coming, cauld winter's awa',
And I'll come and see thee in spite o' them a'.

Though Sandy has ousen, has gear, and has kye,
A house and a hadden, and siller forbye;
Yet I'd tak' mine ain lad wi' his staff in his hand,
Before I'd ha'e him wi' the houses and land.
He said, Think na lang, etc.
My daddie looks sulky, my minnie looks sour,
They frown upon Jamie because he is poor:
Though I lo'e them as weel as a daughter should do,
They're na haef sae dear to me, Jamie, as you.

I sit on my creepie, I spin at my wheel,
And think on the laddie that lo'ed me sae weel;
He had but ae saxpence, he brak' it in twa,
And gi'ed me the haef o't when he gade awa'.
Then haste ye back, Jamie, and bide na awa';
Then haste ye back, Jamie, and bide na awa';
The simmer is coming, cauld winter's awa',
And ye'll come back and see me in spite o' them a'.

GEORGE HALKET

CCXXV O'ER THE MOOR AMANG THE HEATHER

Comin' through the craigs o' Kyle,
  Amang the bonnie bloomin' heather,
There I met a bonnie lassie,
  Keepin' a' her ewes thegither.
    O'er the moor amang the heather,
      O'er the moor amang the heather;
    There I met a bonnie lassie,
      Keeping a' her ewes thegither.

Says I, my dear, where is thy hame,—
  In moor or dale, pray tell me whether?
She says, I tend the fleecy flocks
  That feed amang the blooming heather.

We laid us down upon a bank,
  Sae warm and sunnie was the weather:
She left her flocks at large to rove
  Amang the bonnie blooming heather.

While thus we lay, she sang a sang,
  Till echo rang a mile and farther;
And aye the burden of the sang
  Was, O'er the moor amang the heather.

She charm'd my heart, and aye sinsyne
  I couldna think on ony other:—
By sea and sky, she shall be mine,
  The bonnie lass amang the heather!
    O'er the moor amang the heather,
      Down amang the blooming heather,—
    By sea and sky, she shall be mine,
      The bonnie lass amang the heather!

JEAN GLOVER

CCXXVI THE WAYWARD WIFE

Alas! my son, you little know,
The sorrows which from wedlock flow:
Farewell sweet hours of mirth and ease,
When you have gotten a wife to please.
    Sae bide ye yet, and bide ye yet,
    Ye little ken what's to betide ye yet,
    The half o' that will gane you yet
    If a wayward wife obtain you yet.

Your hopes are high, your wisdom small,
Woe has not had you in its thrall;
The black cow on your foot ne'er trod,
Which makes you sing along the road.

When I, like you, was young and free,
I valued not the proudest she;
Like you, my boast was bold and vain,
That men alone were born to reign.

Great Hercules and Sampson too
Were stronger far than I or you,
Yet they were baffled by their dears,
And felt the distaff and the shears.

Stout gates of brass, and well-built walls,
Are proof 'gainst swords and cannon-balls;
But nought is found, by sea or land,
That can a wayward wife withstand.

Jenny Grahame

CXXVII BRAID CLAITH

Ye wha are fain to hae your name
Wrote i' the bonny book o' Fame,
Let Merit nae pretension claim
To laurel'd wreath,
But hap ye weel, baith back an' wame,
In gude Braid Claith.

He that some ells of this may fa'
An' slae-black hat on pow like snaw,
Bids bauld to bear the gree awa'
Wi' a' this graith,
When bienly clad wi' shell fu' braw
O' gude Braid Claith.

Weasuck for him wha has nae feck o't!
For he's a gowk they're sure to geck at,
A chiel that ne'er will be respeckit
While he draws breath,
Till his four quarters are bedeckit
Wi' gude Braid Claith.

On Sabbath-days, the barber spark,
Whan he has done wi' scrapin' wark,

Wi' siller broachie in his sark,
Gangs trigly, faith!
Or to the Meadows, or the Park,
In gude Braid Claith.

Weel might ye trow, to see them there,
That they to shave your haffits bare,
Or curl an' sleek a pickle hair,
Would be right laith,
Whan pacing wi' a gawsy air
In gude Braid Claith.

If ony mettl'd stirrah green
For favour frae a lady's een,
He maunna care for bein' seen
Before he sheath
His body in a scabbard clean
O' gude Braid Claith.

For gin he come wi' coat thread-bare,
A feg for him she winna care,
But crook her bonny mou' fu' sair,
An' scauld him baith:
Wooers shou'd ay their travel spare
Without Braid Claith.

Braid Claith lends fouk an unco heeze,
Maks mony kail-worms butterflies,
Gies mony a doctor his degrees
For little skaith;
In short, you may be what you please
Wi' gude Braid Claith.

For tho' ye had as wise a snout on
As Shakespeare or Sir Isaac Newton,
Your judgment fouk wou'd hae a doubt on,
I'll tak my aith,
Till they cou'd see ye wi' a suit on
O' gude Braid Claith.

FERGUSON

CCXXVIII IN SILK ATTIRE

And ye shall walk in silk attire,
And siller hae to spare,
Gin ye'll consent to be his bride,
Nor think o' Donald mair.

O wha wad buy a silken gown,
  Wi' a poor broken heart?
Or what's to me a siller crown
  Gin frae my love I part?

The mind whose meanest wish is pure
  Far dearest is to me,
And ere I'm forced to break my faith,
  I'll lay me down and die:
For I have vowed a virgin's vow,
  My lover's fate to share,
And he has gi'en to me his heart,
  And what can man do mair?

His mind and manners wan my heart,
  He gratefu' took the gift,
And did I wish to seek it back,
  It wad be waur than theft.
For langest life can ne'er repay
  The love he bears to me—
And ere I'm forced to break my faith,
  I'll lay me down and die.

SUSANNA BLAMIRE

CXXIX O GIN MY LOVE WERE YON RED ROSE

O gin my love were yon red rose,
  That grows upon the castle wa',
And I mysell a drap of dew,
  Down on that red rose I wad fa':
    O my love's bonny, bonny, bonny;
      My love's bonny, and fair to see;
    Whene'er I look on her weel-far'd face,
      She looks and smiles again to me.
O gin my love were a pickle of wheat,
  And growing upon yon lily lee,
And I mysell a bonny wee bird
  Awa' wi' that pickle o' wheat I wad flee.

O gin my love were a coffer o' gowd,
  And I the keeper of the key,
I wad open the kist whene'er I list,
  And in that coffer I wad be.

CCXXX MACPHERSON'S FAREWELL

Farewell, ye dungeons dark and strong:
  The wretch's destinie!
Macpherson's time will not be long
  On yonder gallows-tree.
    Sae rantingly, sae wantonly,
      Sae dauntingly gaed he;
    He play'd a spring, and danc'd it round,
      Below the gallows-tree.

Oh! What is death but parting breath?—
  On mony a bloody plain
I've dar'd his face, and in this place
  I scorn him yet again!

Untie these bands from off my hands,
  And bring to me my sword!
And there's no a man in all Scotland
  But I'll brave him at a word.

I've liv'd a life of sturt and strife;
  I die by treacherie;
It burns my heart I must depart,
  And not avengèd be.

Now farewell light—thou sunshine bright,
  And all beneath the sky!
May coward shame disdain his name,
  The wretch that dares not die!
    Sae rantingly, sae wantonly,
      Sae dauntingly gaed he;
    He play'd a spring, and danc'd it round,
      Below the gallows-tree.

Burns

CCXXXI THE BIRKS OF ABERFELDY

Bonnie lassie, will ye go,
Will ye go, will ye go;
Bonnie lassie, will ye go
  To the birks of Aberfeldy?

Now simmer blinks on flowery braes,
And o'er the crystal streamlet plays;
Come, let us spend the lightsome days
  In the birks of Aberfeldy.

While o'er their heads the hazels hing,
The little birdies blithely sing,
Or lightly flit on wanton wing
In the birks of Aberfeldy.

The braes ascend, like lofty wa's,
The foaming stream deep-roaring fa's,
O'erhung wi' fragrant spreading shaws
The birks of Aberfeldy.

The hoary cliffs are crown'd wi' flowers,
White o'er the linns the burnie pours,
And rising, weets wi' misty showers
The birks of Aberfeldy.

Let fortune's gifts at random flee,
They ne'er shall draw a wish frae me,
Supremely blest wi' love and thee,
In the birks of Aberfeldy.
Bonnie lassie, will ye go,
Will ye go, will ye go;
Bonnie lassie, will ye go
To the birks of Aberfeldy?

BURNS

CCXXXII THE HIGHLAND WIDOW'S LAMENT

Oh! I am come to the low countrie,
Och-on, och-on, och-rie!
Without a penny in my purse,
To buy a meal to me.

It was na sae in the Highland hills,
Och-on, och-on, och-rie!
Nae woman in the country wide
Sae happy was as me.

For then I had a score o' kye,
Och-on, och-on, och-rie!
Feeding on yon hills so high,
And giving milk to me.

And there I had three score o' yowes,
Och-on, och-on, och-rie!
Skipping on yon bonnie knowes,
And casting woo' to me.

I was the happiest of a' the clan,
  Sair, sair may I repine;
For Donald was the brawest man,
  And Donald he was mine.

Till Charlie Steuart cam' at last,
  Sae far to set us free;
My Donald's arm was wanted then
  For Scotland and for me.

Their waefu' fate what need I tell,
  Right to the wrang did yield:
My Donald and his Country fell
  Upon Culloden-field.

Ochon, O, Donald, Oh!
  Och-on, och-on, och-rie!
Nae woman in the warld wide
  Sae wretched now as me.

BURNS

CCXXXIII OH, WERT THOU IN THE CAULD BLAST

Oh, wert thou in the cauld blast
  On yonder lea, on yonder lea,
My plaidie to the angry airt,
  I'd shelter thee, I'd shelter thee:
Or did misfortune's bitter storms
  Around thee blaw, around thee blaw,
Thy bield should be my bosom,
  To share it a', to share it a'.

Or were I in the wildest waste,
  Sae bleak and bare, sae bleak and bare,
The desert were a paradise,
  If thou wert there, if thou wert there:
Or were I monarch o' the globe,
  Wi' thee to reign, wi' thee to reign,
The brightest jewel in my crown
  Wad be my queen, wad be my queen.

BURNS

CCXXXIV UP IN THE MORNING EARLY

Cold blaws the wind frae east to west,
  The drift is driving sairly;

Sae loud and shrill I hear the blast,
I'm sure it's winter fairly.
The birds sit chittering in the thorn
A' day they fare but sparely!
And lang's the night frae e'en to morn—
I'm sure it's winter fairly.
Up in the morning's no for me,
Up in the morning early;
When a' the hills are cover'd wi' snaw
I'm sure it's winter fairly.

Burns

CCXXXV SIMMER'S A PLEASANT TIME

Simmer's a pleasant time,
Flow'rs of ev'ry colour;
The water rins o'er the heugh,
And I long for my true lover.
Ay waukin O,
Waukin still and wearie:
Sleep I can get nane
For thinking on my dearie.

When I sleep I dream,
When I wauk I'm eerie;
Sleep I can get nane
For thinking on my dearie.

Lanely night comes on,
A' the lave are sleepin';
I think on my bonnie lad,
And I bleer my een with greetin'.
Ay waukin O,
Waukin still and wearie;
Sleep I can get nane
For thinking on my dearie.

Burns

CCXXXVI COMING THROUGH THE RYE

Coming through the rye, poor body,
Coming through the rye,
She draiglet a' her petticoatie,
Coming through the rye.

Oh Jenny's a' wat, poor body,
Jenny's seldom dry;
She draiglet a' her petticoatie,
Coming through the rye.

Gin a body meet a body—
Coming through the rye,
Gin a body kiss a body—
Need a body cry?

Gin a body meet a body
Coming through the glen,
Gin a body kiss a body—
Need the warld ken?
Oh Jenny's a' wat, poor body;
Jenny's seldom dry;
She draiglet a' her petticoatie,
Coming through the rye.

Burns

CCXXXVII THE CARLES OF DYSART

Up wi' the carles o' Dysart
And lads o' Buckhaven,
And the kimmers o' Largo,
And the lasses o' Leven.
Hey, ca' thro', ca' thro',
For we hae mickle ado;
Hey, ca' thro', ca' thro',
For we hae mickle ado.

We hae tales to tell,
And we hae sangs to sing;
We hae pennies to spend,
And we hae pints to bring.

We'll live a' our days,
And them that come behin',
Let them do the like,
And spend the gear they win.

Burns

CCXXXVIII WHEN THE KYE COME HAME

Come all ye jolly shepherds
That whistle through the glen,

I'll tell ye of a secret
  That courtiers dinna ken:
What is the greatest bliss
  That the tongue o' man can name?
'Tis to woo a bonnie lass
  When the kye come hame.
      When the kye come hame,
        When the kye come hame,
      'Tween the gloamin' and the mirk,
        When the kye come hame.

'Tis not beneath the burgonet,
  Nor yet beneath the crown,
'Tis not on couch of velvet
  Nor yet on bed of down;
'Tis beneath the spreading birch,
  In the dell without a name,
Wi' a bonnie, bonnie lassie,
  When the kye come hame.

There the blackbird bigs his nest
  For the mate he loves to see,
And up upon the tapmost bough,
  Oh, a happy bird is he!
Then he pours his melting ditty,
  And love 'tis a' the theme,
And he'll woo his bonnie lassie
  When the kye come hame.

When the bluart bears a pearl,
  And the daisy turns a pea,
And the bonny lucken gowan
  Has fauldit up his e'e,
Then the laverock frae the blue lift
  Draps down, and thinks nae shame
To woo his bonnie lassie
  When the kye come hame.

Then the eye shines sae bright,
  The haill soul to beguile,
There's love in every whisper,
  And joy in every smile;
Oh, who would choose a crown,
  Wi' its perils and its fame,
And miss a bonnie lassie
  When the kye come hame?

See yonder pawky shepherd
That lingers on the hill—
His yowes are in the fauld,
And his lambs are lying still;
Yet he downa gang to rest,
For his heart is in a flame
To meet his bonnie lassie
When the kye come hame.

Awa' wi' fame and fortune—
What comfort can they gie?
And a' the airts that prey
On man's life and libertie!
Gi'e me the highest joy
That the heart o' man can frame—
My bonnie, bonnie lassie,
When the kye come hame.

CCXXXIX JEANIE MORRISON

I've wandered east, I've wandered west,
Through mony a weary way;
But never, never can forget
The luve o' life's young day!
The fire that's blawn on Beltane e'en,
May weel be black gin Yule;
But blacker fa' awaits the heart
Where first fond luve grows cule.

O dear, dear Jeanie Morrison,
The thochts o' bygane years
Still fling their shadows ower my path,
And blind my een wi' tears:
They blind my een wi' saut, saut tears,
And sair and sick I pine,
As memory idly summons up
The blithe blinks o' langsyne.

'Twas then we luvit ilk ither weel,
'Twas then we twa did part;
Sweet time—sad time! twa bairns at scule,
Twa bairns, and but ae heart!
'Twas then we sat on ae laigh bink,
To leir ilk ither lear;
And tones, and looks, and smiles were shed,
Remembered evermair.

I wonder, Jeanie, aften yet,
  When sitting on that bink,
Cheek touchin' cheek, loof lock'd in loof,
  What our wee heads could think?
When baith bent doun ower ae braid page,
  Wi' ae buik on our knee,
Thy lips were on thy lesson, but
  My lesson was in thee.

Oh, mind ye how we hung our heads,
  How cheeks brent red wi' shame,
Whene'er the scule-weans laughin' said,
  We cleek'd thegither hame?
And mind ye o' the Saturdays,
  (The scule then skail't at noon),
When we ran aff to speed the braes—
  The broomy braes o' June?

My head rins round and round about,
  My heart flows like a sea,
As ane by ane the thochts rush back
  O' scule-time and o' thee.
Oh, mornin' life! oh, mornin' luve!
  Oh, lichtsome days and lang,
When hinnied hopes around our hearts
  Like simmer blossoms sprang!

Oh mind ye, luve, how aft we left
  The deavin' dinsome toun,
To wander by the green burnside,
  And hear its waters croon?
The simmer leaves hung ower our head,
  The flowers burst round our feet,
And in the gloamin' o' the wood
  The throssil whusslit sweet.

The throssil whusslit in the wood,
  The burn sang to the trees,
And we with Nature's heart in tune,
  Concerted harmonies;
And on the knowe abune the burn,
  For hours thegither sat
In the silentness o' joy, till baith
  Wi' very gladness grat.

Ay, ay, dear Jeanie Morrison,
  Tears trinkled doun your cheek,
Like dew-beads on a rose, yet nane
  Had ony power to speak!
That was a time, a blessèd time,
  When hearts were fresh and young,
When freely gushed all feelings forth,
  Unsyllabled—unsung!

I marvel, Jeanie Morrison,
  Gin I hae been to thee
As closely twined wi' earliest thochts,
  As ye hae been to me?
Oh! tell me gin their music fills
  Thine ear as it does mine;
Oh! say gin e'er your heart grows grit
  Wi' dreamings o' langsyne?

I've wandered east, I've wandered west,
  I've borne a weary lot;
But in my wanderings, far or near,
  Ye never were forgot.
The fount that first burst frae this heart,
  Still travels on its way;
And channels deeper as it rins,
  The luve o' life's young day.

O dear, dear Jeanie Morrison,
  Since we were sindered young,
I've never seen your face, nor heard
  The music o' your tongue;
But I could hug all wretchedness,
  And happy could I dee,
Did I but ken your heart still dreamed
  O' bygane days and me!

MOTHERWELL

CCXL BONNIE GEORGE CAMPBELL

Hie upon Hielands
  And low upon Tay,
Bonny George Campbell
  Rode out on a day.
Saddled and bridled
  And gallant rade he;

Hame came his gude horse,
  But never came he!

Out cam his auld mither
  Greeting fu' sair,
And out cam his bonnie bride
  Rivin' her hair.
Saddled and bridled
  And booted rade he;
Toom hame cam the saddle,
  But never cam he!

"My meadow lies green,
  And my corn is unshorn;
My barn is to big,
  And my babie's unborn."
Saddled and bridled
  And booted rade he;
Toom hame cam the saddle,
  But never cam he!

MOTHERWELL

CXLI MY AIN COUNTREE

The sun rises bright in France,
  And fair sets he;
But he has tint the blithe blink he had
  In my ain countree.
Oh! gladness comes to many,
  But sorrow comes to me
As I look o'er the wide ocean
  To my ain countree.

Oh! it's not my ain ruin
  That saddens aye my e'e,
But the love I left in Galloway
  Wi' bonnie bairnies three.
My hamely hearth burned bonnie,
  And smiled my fair Marie;
I've left my heart behind me
  In my ain countree.

The bird comes back to summer
  And the blossom to the tree;
But I win back, oh! never,
  To my ain countree.

I'm leal to the high Heaven,
Which will be leal to me,
And there I'll meet ye a' sune
In my ain countree.

ALLAN CUNNINGHAM

CCXLII HAME, HAME, HAME

Hame, hame, hame, hame fain wad I be,
O hame, hame, hame, to my ain countrie!
When the flower is i' the bud, and the leaf is on the tree,
The larks shall sing me hame in my ain countrie;
Hame, hame, hame, hame fain wad I be,
O hame, hame, hame, to my ain countrie!

The green leaf o' loyalty's begun for to fa',
The bonny white rose it is withering an' a';
But I'll water 't wi' the blude of usurping tyrannie,
An' green it will grow in my ain countrie.
Hame, hame, hame, hame fain wad I be,
O hame, hame, hame, to my ain countrie!

O there's naught frae ruin my country can save,
But the keys o' kind heaven to open the grave,
That a' the noble martyrs wha died for loyaltie,
May rise again and fight for their ain countrie.
Hame, hame, hame, hame fain wad I be,
O hame, hame, hame, to my ain countrie!

The great are now gane, a' wha ventured to save,
The new grass is springing on the tap o' their graves;
But the sun through the mirk blinks blithe in my e'e,
"I'll shine on ye yet in yer ain countrie."
Hame, hame, hame, hame lain wad I be,
Hame, hame, hame, to my ain countrie!

ALLAN CUNNINGHAM

CCXLIII GOOD NIGHT, AND JOY BE WI' YOU A'

Good night, and joy be wi' ye a';
Your harmless mirth has cheer'd my heart:
May life's fell blasts out o'er ye blaw!
In sorrow may ye never part!

My spirit lives, but strength is gone;
  The mountain-fires now blaze in vain:
Remember, sons, the deeds I've done,
  And in your deeds I'll live again!

When on yon muir our gallant clan
  Frae boasting foes their banners tore,
Wha show'd himself a better man,
  Or fiercer wav'd the red claymore?
But when in peace—then mark me there—
  When through the glen the wand'rer came,
I gave him of our lordly fare,
  I gave him here a welcome hame.

The auld will speak, the young maun hear;
  Be cantie, but be good and leal;
Your ain ills, aye hae heart to bear;
  Anither's aye hae heart to feel.
So, ere I set, I'll see you shine,
  I'll see you triumph ere I fa';
My parting breath shall boast you mine—
  Good night, and joy be wi' ye a'.

SIR ALEXANDER BOSWELL

CCXLIV CLAUD HALCRO'S SONG

Farewell to Northmaven,
  Grey Hillswicke, farewell!
To the calms of thy haven,
  The storms on thy fell—
To each breeze that can vary
  The mood of thy main,
And to thee, bonny Mary!
  We meet not again!

Farewell the wild ferry,
  Which Hacon could brave,
When the peaks of the Skerry
  Were white in the wave.
There's a maid may look over
  These wild waves in vain,—
For the skiff of her lover—
  He comes not again!

The vows thou hast broke,
  On the wild currents fling them;
On the quicksand and rock
  Let the mermaidens sing them.
New sweetness they'll give her
  Bewildering strain;
But there's one who will never
  Believe them again.

O were there an island,
  Though ever so wild,
Where woman could smile, and
  No man be beguiled—
Too tempting a snare
  To poor mortals were given;
And the hope would fix there,
  That should anchor in heaven.

SIR WALTER SCOTT

CCXLV MACGREGORS' GATHERING

The moon's on the lake, and the mist's on the brae,
And the clan has a name that is nameless by day,
  Then gather, gather, gather, Grigalach!

Our signal for fight, that from monarchs we drew,
Must be heard but by night in our vengeful haloo!
  Then haloo, Grigalach! haloo, Grigalach!

Glen Orchy's proud mountains, Coalchuirn and her towers,
Glenstrae and Glenlyon no longer are ours;
  We're landless, landless, landless, Grigalach!

But doom'd and devoted by vassal and lord,
MacGregor has still both his heart and his sword!
  Then courage, courage, courage, Grigalach!

If they rob us of name, and pursue us with beagles,
Give their roofs to the flame, and their flesh to the eagles:
  Then vengeance, vengeance, vengeance, Grigalach!

While there's leaves in the forest, and foam on the river,
MacGregor, despite them, shall flourish for ever!
  Come then, Grigalach, come then, Grigalach.

Through the depths of Loch Katrine the steed shall career,
O'er the peak of Ben Lomond the galley shall steer,
And the rocks of Craig Royston like icicles melt,
Ere our wrongs be forgot, or our vengeance unfelt!
  Then gather, gather, gather, Grigalach!

Sir W. Scott

CCXLVI THE DOLE

And you shall deal the funeral dole;
  Ay, deal it, mother mine,
To weary body, and to heavy soul,
  The white bread and the wine.

And you shall deal my horses of pride;
  Ay, deal them, mother mine!
And you shall deal my lands so wide,
  And deal my castles nine.

But deal not vengeance for the deed,
  And deal not for the crime;
The body to its place, and the soul to Heaven's grace,
  And the rest in God's own time.

Sir W. Scott

CCXLVII NOVEMBER

I

The sheep, before the pinching heaven,
To sheltered dale and down are driven,
Where yet some faded herbage pines,
And yet a watery sun-beam shines:
In meek despondency they eye
The withered sward and wintry sky,
The shepherd shifts his mantle's fold,
And wraps him closer from the cold;
His dogs no merry circles wheel,
But, shivering, follow at his heel;
A cowering glance they often cast,
As deeper moans the gathering blast.

II

My imps, though hardy, bold, and wild,
As best befits the mountain child,
Feel the sad influence of the hour,
And wail the daisy's vanished flower;

Their summer gambols tell, and mourn,
And anxious ask,—Will spring return,
And birds and lambs again be gay,
And blossoms clothe the hawthorn spray?

SIR W. SCOTT

CCXLVIII THE CAMERONIAN'S DREAM

In a dream of the night I was wafted away,
To the muirland of mist where the martyrs lay;
Where Cameron's sword and his Bible are seen,
Engraved on the stone where the heather grows green.

'Twas a dream of those ages of darkness and blood,
When the minister's home was the mountain and wood;
When in Wellwood's dark valley the standard of Zion,
All bloody and torn 'mong the heather was lying.

'Twas morning; and summer's young sun from the east
Lay in loving repose on the green mountain's breast;
On Wardlaw and Cairntable the clear shining dew,
Glistened there 'mong the heath-bells and mountain flowers
blue.

And far up in heaven near the white sunny cloud,
The song of the lark was melodious and loud,
And in Glenmuir's wild solitude, lengthened and deep,
Were the whistling of plovers and bleating of sheep.

And Wellwood's sweet valleys breathed music and gladness,
The fresh meadow blooms hung in beauty and redness;
Its daughters were happy to hail the returning,
And drink the delights of July's sweet morning.

But, oh! there were hearts cherished far other feelings,
Illumed by the light of prophetic revealings,
Who drank from the scenery of beauty but sorrow,
For they knew that their blood would bedew it to-morrow.

'Twas the few faithful ones who with Cameron were lying,
Concealed 'mong the mist where the heath-fowl was crying,
For the horsemen of Earlshall around them were hovering,
And their bridle reins rung through the thin misty covering.

Their faces grew pale, and their swords were unsheathed,
But the vengeance that darkened their brow was unbreathed;
With eyes turned to heaven in calm resignation,
They sung their last song to the God of Salvation.

The hills with the deep mournful music were ringing,
The curlew and plover in concert were singing;
But the melody died 'mid derision and laughter,
As the host of ungodly rushed on to the slaughter.

Though in mist and in darkness and fire they were shrouded,
Yet the souls of the righteous were calm and unclouded.
Their dark eyes flashed lightning, as, firm and unbending,
They stood like the rock which the thunder is rending.

The muskets were flashing, the blue swords were gleaming,
The helmets were cleft, and the red blood was streaming,
The heavens grew dark, and the thunder was rolling,
When in Wellwood's dark muirlands the mighty were falling.

When the righteous had fallen, and the combat was ended,
A chariot of fire through the dark cloud descended;
Its drivers were angels on horses of whiteness,
And its burning wheels turned on axles of brightness.

A seraph unfolded its doors bright and shining,
All dazzling like gold of the seventh refining,
And the souls that came forth out of great tribulation,
Have mounted the chariots and steeds of salvation.

On the arch of the rainbow the chariot is gliding,
Through the path of the thunder the horsemen are riding;
Glide swiftly, bright spirits! the prize is before ye,
A crown never fading, a kingdom of glory!

HISLOP

CCXLIX THE HERB ROSEMARY

Sweet-scented flower! who art wont to bloom
On January's front severe,
And o'er the wintry desert drear
To waft thy waste perfume!
Come, thou shalt form my nosegay now,
And I will bind thee round my brow;
And as I twine the mournful wreath,
I'll weave a melancholy song,
And sweet the strain shall be, and long,
The melody of death.

Come funeral flower! who lov'st to dwell
With the pale corse in lonely tomb,
And throw across the desert gloom
A sweet decaying smell.

Come, press my lips, and lie with me
Beneath the lowly alder-tree;
  And we will sleep a pleasant sleep,
And not a care shall dare intrude
To break the marble solitude
  So peaceful and so deep.

And hark! the wind-god, as he flies,
  Moans hollow in the forest trees,
  And sailing on the gusty breeze,
    Mysteriously dies.
Sweet flower! that requiem wild is mine,
It warns me to the lonely shrine,
  The cold turf altar of the dead;
    My grave shall be in yon lone spot,
    Where as I lie, by all forgot,
A dying fragrance thou wilt o'er my ashes shed.

H. Kirke White

CCL

THE STATE

    What constitutes a State?
Not high rais'd battlement or labor'd mound,
    Thick wall or moated gate;
Not cities proud with spires and turrets crown'd;
    Not bays and broad arm'd ports,
Where, laughing at the storm, rich navies ride,
    Not starr'd and spangled courts,
Where low-brow'd baseness wafts perfume to pride,
    No:—Men, high-minded Men,
With pow'rs as far above dull brutes endued
    In forest, brake, or den,
As beasts excel cold rocks and brambles rude;
    Men, who their *duties* know,
But know their *rights*, and knowing, dare maintain,
    Prevent the long-aim'd blow,
And crush the tyrant while they rend the chain:
    These constitute a State,
And sov'reign Law, that State's collected will,
    O'er thrones and globes elate
Sits Empress, crowning good, repressing ill;
    Smit by her sacred frown
The fiend, Discretion, like a vapour sinks,
    And e'en th' all-dazzling Crown

Hides his faint rays, and at her bidding shrinks.
Such *was* this heav'n-lov'd isle,
Than Lesbos fairer and the Cretan shore!
No more shall freedom smile?
Shall Britons languish, and be Men no more?
Since all must life resign,
Those sweet rewards, which decorate the brave,
'Tis folly to decline,
And steal inglorious to the silent grave.

Sir W. Jones

WEEL MAY THE KEEL ROWE

As I came down the Cannongate
The Cannongate, the Cannongate,
As I came down the Cannongate,
I heard a lassie sing,
Weel may the keel rowe,
The keel rowe, the keel rowe,
Weel may the keel rowe,
The ship that my lad's in.

My love has breath o' roses,
O' roses, o' roses,
Wi' arms o' lilie posies,
To fauld a lassie in.
Weel may the keel rowe,
The keel rowe, the keel rowe,
Weel may the keel rowe,
The ship that my lad's in.

My love he wears a bonnet,
A bonnet, a bonnet,
A snawy rose upon it,
A dimple on his chin.
Weel may the keel rowe,
The keel rowe, the keel rowe,
Weel may the keel rowe,
The ship that my lad's in.

MUTABILITY

From low to high doth dissolution climb,
And sink from high to low, along a scale
Of awful notes, whose concord shall not fail;
A musical but melancholy chime,

Which they can hear who meddle not with crime,
Nor avarice, nor over-anxious care.
Truth fails not; but her outward forms that bear
The longest date, do melt like frosty rime,
That in the morning whitened hill and plain,
And is no more; drop like the tower sublime
Of yesterday, which royally did wear
His crown of weeds, but could not even sustain
Some casual shout that broke the silent air,
Or the unimaginable touch of Time.

WORDSWORTH

CCLIII STEPPING WESTWARD

"What, you are stepping westward?"—"Yea."
—'Twould be a wildish destiny,
If we, who thus together roam
In a strange Land, and far from home,
Were in this place the guests of Chance:
Yet who would stop, or fear to advance,
Though home or shelter he had none,
With such a sky to lead him on?

The dewy ground was dark and cold;
Behind, all gloomy to behold;
And stepping westward seemed to be
A kind of heavenly destiny:
I liked the greeting; 'twas a sound
Of something without place or bound
And seemed to give me spiritual right
To travel through that region bright.

The voice was soft, and she who spake
Was walking by her native lake:
The salutation had to me
The very sound of courtesy:
Its power was felt; and while my eye
Was fixed upon the glowing Sky,
The echo of the voice enwrought
A human sweetness with the thought
Of travelling through the world that lay
Before me in my endless way.

WORDSWORTH

CCLIV HELVELLYN

"FIDELITY"

A barking sound the Shepherd hears,
A cry as of a dog or fox;
He halts—and searches with his eyes
Among the scattered rocks:
And now at distance can discern
A stirring in a brake of fern;
And instantly a dog is seen,
Glancing through that covert green.

The Dog is not of mountain breed;
Its motions, too, are wild and shy;
With something, as the Shepherd thinks,
Unusual in its cry:
Nor is there any one in sight
All round, in hollow or on height;
No shout, nor whistle strikes his ear;
What is the creature doing here?

It was a cove, a huge recess,
That keeps, till June, December's snow;
A lofty precipice in front,
A silent tarn below!
Far in the bosom of Helvellyn,
Remote from public road or dwelling,
Pathway, or cultivated land;
From trace of human foot or hand.

There sometimes doth a leaping fish
Send through the tarn a lonely cheer;
The crags repeat the raven's croak,
In symphony austere;
Thither the rainbow comes—the cloud—
And mists that spread the flying shroud
And sunbeams; and the sounding blast,
That, if it could, would hurry past;
But that enormous barrier holds it fast.

Not free from brooding thoughts, a while
The Shepherd stood; then makes his way
O'er rocks and stones, following the Dog
As quickly as he may;

Not far had gone before he found
A human skeleton on the ground;
The appalled Discoverer with a sigh
Looks round, to learn the history.

From those abrupt and perilous rocks
The Man had fallen, that place of fear!
At length upon the Shepherd's mind
It breaks, and all is clear:
He instantly recalled the name,
And who he was, and whence he came;
Remembered, too, the very day
On which the Traveller passed this way.

But here a wonder, for whose sake
This lamentable tale I tell!
A lasting monument of words
This wonder merits well.
The Dog, which still was hovering nigh,
Repeating the same timid cry,
This Dog had been through three months' space
A dweller in that savage place.

Yes, proof was plain that, since the day
When this ill-fated Traveller died,
The dog had watched about the spot,
Or by his master's side:
How nourished here through such long time
He knows, who gave that love sublime;
And gave that strength of feeling, great
Above all human estimate!

WORDSWORTH

CCLV TO A SKYLARK

Up with me; up with me into the clouds!
  For thy song, Lark, is strong;
Up with me, up with me into the clouds;
      Singing, singing.
With clouds and sky about thee ringing,
  Lift me, guide me till I find
That spot which seems so to thy mind!

I have walked through wildernesses dreary
And to-day my heart is weary;

Had I now the wings of a Faery,
Up to thee would I fly.
There is madness about thee, and joy divine
In that song of thine;
Lift me, guide me high and high
To thy banqueting place in the sky.

Joyous as morning
Thou art laughing and scorning;
Thou hast a nest for thy love and thy rest,
And, though little troubled with sloth,
Drunken Lark! thou would'st be loth
To be such a traveller as I.
Happy, happy Liver,
With a soul as strong as a mountain river
Pouring out praise to the Almighty Giver,
Joy and jollity be with us both!

Alas! my journey, rugged and uneven,
Through prickly moors or dusty ways must wind;
But hearing thee, or others of thy kind,
As full of gladness and as free of heaven,
I, with my fate contented, will plod on.
And hope for higher raptures, when life's day is done.

WORDSWORTH

CCLVI THE NIGHTINGALE AND THE STOCK-DOVE

O Nightingale! thou surely art
A creature of a "fiery heart":—
These notes of thine—they pierce and pierce;
Tumultuous harmony and fierce!
Thou sing'st as if the God of wine
Had helped thee to a Valentine;
A song in mockery and despite
Of shades, and dews, and silent night;
And steady bliss, and all the loves
Now sleeping in these peaceful groves.
I heard a Stock-dove sing or say
His homely tale, this very day;
His voice was buried among trees,
Yet to be come at by the breeze:

He did not cease; but cooed—and cooed;
And somewhat pensively he wooed:
He sang of love, with quiet blending,
Slow to begin and never ending;
Of serious faith and inward glee;
That was the song—the song for me!

WORDSWORTH

CCLVII THE CHILD OF NATURE

Dear Child of Nature, let them rail!
—There is a nest in a green dale,
A harbour and a hold;
Where thou, a Wife and Friend, shalt see
Thy own heart-stirring days, and be
A light to young and old.

There, healthy as a shepherd boy,
And treading among flowers of joy
Which at no season fade,
Thou, while thy babes around thee cling,
Shalt show us how divine a thing
A Woman may be made.

Thy thoughts and feelings shall not die,
Nor leave thee, when grey hairs are nigh,
A melancholy slave;
But an old age serene and bright,
And lovely as a Lapland night,
Shall lead thee to thy grave.

WORDSWORTH

CCLVIII THE SHIPS

I

With Ships the sea was sprinkled far and nigh,
Like stars in heaven, and joyously it showed;
Some lying fast at anchor in the road,
Some veering up and down, one knew not why.
A goodly Vessel did I then espy
Come like a giant from a haven broad;
And lustily along the bay she strode,
Her tackling rich, and of apparel high.
The Ship was nought to me, nor I to her,
Yet I pursued her with a Lover's look;

This Ship to all the rest did I prefer:
When will she turn, and whither? She will brook
No tarrying; where She comes the winds must stir:
On went She, and due north her journey took.

II

Where lies the Land to which yon Ship must go?
Fresh as a lark mounting at break of day,
Festively she puts forth in trim array;
Is she for tropic suns, or polar snow?
What boots the inquiry?—Neither friend nor foe
She cares for; let her travel where she may,
She finds familiar names, a beaten way
Ever before her, and a wind to blow,
Yet still I ask, what haven is her mark?
And, almost as it was when ships were rare,
(From time to time, like Pilgrims, here and there
Crossing the waters) doubt, and something dark,
Of the old Sea some reverential fear,
Is with me at thy farewell, joyous Bark!

WORDSWORTH

CCLIX SIR WALTER SCOTT'S FAREWELL

A trouble, not of clouds, or weeping rain,
Nor of the setting sun's pathetic light
Engendered, hangs o'er Eildon's triple height:
Spirits of Power, assembled there, complain
For kindred Power departing from their sight;
While Tweed, best pleased in chanting a blithe strain,
Saddens his voice again, and yet again.
Lift up your hearts, ye Mourners! for the might
Of the whole world's good wishes with him goes.
Blessings and prayers, in nobler retinue
Than sceptred king or laurelled conqueror knows
Follow this wondrous Potentate. Be true,
Ye winds of ocean, and the midland sea,
Wafting your Charge in soft Parthenope!

WORDSWORTH

CCLX THE HOME-COMING

Farewell, thou little Nook of mountain-ground,
Thou rocky corner in the lowest stair

Of that magnificent temple which doth bound
One side of our whole vale with grandeur rare;
Sweet garden-orchard, eminently fair,
The loveliest spot that man hath ever found,
Farewell!—we leave thee to Heaven's peaceful care,
Thee, and the Cottage which thou dost surround.

Our boat is safely anchored by the shore,
And there will safely ride when we are gone;
The flowering shrubs that deck our humble door
Will prosper, though untended and alone:
Fields, goods, and far-off chattels we have none:
These narrow bounds contain our private store
Of things earth makes, and sun doth shine upon;
Here are they in our sight—we have no more.

Sunshine and shower be with you, bud and bell!
For two months now in vain we shall be sought:
We leave you here in solitude to dwell
With these our latest gifts of tender thoughts;
Thou, like the morning, in thy saffron coat,
Bright gowan, and marsh-marigold, farewell!
Whom from the borders of the Lake we brought,
And placed together near our rocky Well.

We go for One to whom ye will be dear;
And she will prize this Bower, this Indian shed,
Our old contrivance, Building without peer!

—A gentle Maid, whose heart is lowly bred,
Whose pleasures are in wild fields gatherèd,
With joyousness, and with a thoughtful cheer,
Will come to you; to you herself will wed;
And love the blessed life that we lead here.

Dear Spot! which we have watched with tender heed,
Bringing thee chosen plants and blossoms blown
Among the distant mountains, flower and weed,
Which thou hast taken to thee as thy own,
Making all kindness registered and known;
Thou for our sakes, though Nature's child indeed,
Fair in thyself and beautiful alone,
Hast taken gifts which thou dost little need.

And O most constant, yet most fickle Place,
Thou hast thy wayward moods, as thou dost show

To them who look not daily on thy face;
Who, being loved, in love no bounds dost know,
And say'st when we forsake thee, "Let them go!"
Thou easy-hearted Thing, with thy wild race
Of weeds and flowers, till we return be slow,
And travel with the year at a soft pace.

Help us to tell Her tales of years gone by,
And this sweet spring, the best beloved and best;
Joy will be flown in its mortality;
Something must stay to tell us of the rest.
Here, thronged with primroses, the steep rock's breast
Glittered at evening like a starry sky;
And in this bush our sparrow built her nest,
Of which I sang one song that will not die.

O happy Garden! whose seclusion deep
Hath been so friendly to industrious hours;
And to soft slumbers, that did gently steep
Our spirits, carrying with them dreams of flowers,
And wild notes warbled among leafy bowers;
Two burning months let summer overleap,
And, coming back with Her who will be ours,
Into thy bosom we again shall creep.

WORDSWORTH

CCLXI THE SCHOOLMASTER

Long time his pulse hath ceased to beat
But benefits, his gift, we trace—
Expressed in every eye we meet
Round this dear Vale, his native place.

To stately Hall and Cottage rude
Flowed from his life what still they hold,
Light pleasures, every day, renewed;
And blessings half a century old.

Oh true of heart, of spirit gay,
Thy faults, where not already gone
From memory, prolong their stay
For charity's sweet sake alone.

Such solace find we for our loss;
And what beyond this thought we crave
Comes in the promise from the Cross,
Shining upon thy happy grave. WORDSWORTH

CCLXII MATTHEW

If Nature, for a favourite child,
In thee hath tempered so her clay,
That every hour thy heart runs wild,
Yet never once doth go astray,

Read o'er these lines; and then review
This tablet, that thus humbly rears
In such diversity of hue
Its history of two hundred years.

—When through this little wreck of fame,
Cipher and syllable! thine eye
Has travelled down to Matthew's name,
Pause with no common sympathy.

And if a sleeping tear should wake,
Then be it neither checked nor stayed:
For Matthew a request I make
Which for himself he had not made.

Poor Matthew, all his frolics o'er,
Is silent as a standing pool;
Far from the chimney's merry roar,
And murmur of the village school.

The sighs which Matthew heaved were sighs
Of one tired out with fun and madness;
The tears which came to Matthew's eyes
Were tears of light, the dew of gladness.

Yet, sometimes, when the secret cup
Of still and serious thought went round,
It seemed as if he drank it up—
He felt with spirit so profound.

—Thou soul of God's best earthly mould!
Thou happy Soul! and can it be
That these two words of glittering gold
Are all that must remain of thee?

WORDSWORTH

CCLXIII COME, YE LITTLE NOISY CREW

I come, ye little noisy Crew,
Not long your pastime to prevent;
I heard the blessing which to you
Our common Friend and Father sent.

I kissed his cheek before he died;
And when his breath was fled,
I raised, while kneeling by his side,
His hand:—it dropped like lead.
Your hands, dear Little-ones do all
That can be done, will never fall
Like his till they are dead.
By night or day blow foul or fair,
Ne'er will the best of all your train
Play with the locks of his white hair,
Or stand between his knees again.
  Here did he sit confined for hours;
But he could see the woods and plains,
Could hear the wind and mark the showers
Come streaming down the streaming panes.
Now stretched beneath his grass-green mound
He rests a prisoner of the ground.
He loved the breathing air,
He loved the sun; but if it rise
Or set, to him where now he lies,
Brings not a moment's care.
Alas! what idle words; but take
The Dirge which for our Master's sake
And yours, love prompted me to make.
The rhymes so homely in attire
With learned ears may ill agree,
But chanted by your orphan quire
Will make a touching melody.

DIRGE

Mourn, Shepherd, near thy old grey stone;
Thou Angler, by the silent flood;
And mourn when thou art all alone;
Thou Woodman, in the distant wood!

Thou one blind Sailor, rich in joy
Though blind, thy tunes in sadness hum;
And mourn, thou poor half-witted Boy!
Born deaf, and living deaf and dumb.

Thou drooping sick Man, bless the Guide
Who checked or turned thy headstrong youth,
As he before had sanctified
Thy infancy with heavenly truth.

Ye Striplings, light of heart and gay,
Bold settlers on some foreign shore,
Give, when your thoughts are turned this way,
A sigh to him whom we deplore.

For us who here in funeral strain
With one accord our voices raise,
Let sorrow overcharged with pain
Be lost in thankfulness and praise.

WORDSWORTH

CCLXIV TO JOHN DYER

Bard of the Fleece, whose skilful genius made
That work a living landscape fair and bright;
Nor hallowed less with musical delight
Than those soft scenes through which thy childhood strayed,
Those southern tracks of Cambria, "deep embayed,
With green hills fenced, with ocean's murmur lulled;"
Though hasty Fame hath many a chaplet culled
For worthless brows, while in the pensive shade
Of cold neglect she leaves thy head ungraced,
Yet pure and powerful minds, hearts meek and still,
A grateful few, shall love thy modest Lay,
Long as the shepherd's bleating flock shall stray
O'er naked Snowdon's wide aërial waste;
Long as the thrush shall pipe on Grongar Hill!

WORDSWORTH

CCLXV HESPERUS

It is no Spirit who from Heaven hath flown,
And is descending on his embassy;
Nor Traveller gone from earth the heavens to espy!
'Tis Hesperus—there he stands with glittering crown,
First admonition that the sun is down!
For yet it is broad day-light: clouds pass by;
A few are near him still—and now the sky,
He hath it to himself—'tis all his own.
O most ambitious Star! an inquest wrought
Within me when I recognised thy light;
A moment I was startled at the sight:
And, while I gazed, there came to me a thought
That I might step beyond my natural race

As thou seem'st now to do; might one day trace
Some ground not mine; and, strong her strength above,
My Soul, an Apparition in the place,
Tread there with steps that no one shall reprove!

WORDSWORTH

CCLXVI THE RIVER DUDDON

Child of the clouds! remote from every taint
Of sordid industry thy lot is cast;
Thine are the honours of the lofty waste;
Not seldom, when with heat the valleys faint,
Thy handmaid Frost with spangled tissue quaint
Thy cradle decks;—to chant thy birth, thou hast
No meaner Poet than the whistling Blast,
And Desolation is thy Patron-saint!
She guards thee, ruthless Power! who would not spare
Those mighty forests, once the bison's screen,
Where stalked the huge deer to his shaggy lair
Through paths and alleys roofed with darkest green;
Thousands of years before the silent air
Was pierced by whizzing shaft of hunter keen!

WORDSWORTH

CCLXVII THE GLOW-WORM

Among all lovely things my Love had been;
Had noted well the stars, all flowers that grew
About her home; but she had never seen
A glow-worm, never one, and this I knew.

While riding near her home one stormy night
A single glow-worm did I chance to espy;
I gave a fervent welcome to the sight,
And from my horse I leapt; great joy had I.

Upon a leaf the glow-worm did I lay,
To bear it with me through the stormy night:
And, as before, it shone without dismay;
Albeit putting forth a fainter light.

When to the dwelling of my love I came,
I went into the orchard quietly;
And left the glow-worm, blessing it by name,
Laid safely by itself, beneath a tree.

The whole next day, I hoped, and hoped with fear;
At night the glow-worm shone beneath the tree;
I led my Lucy to the spot, "Look here,"
O! joy it was for her, and joy for me!

WORDSWORTH

CCLXVIII THE SMALL CELANDINE

Pleasures newly found are sweet
When they lie about our feet:
February last, my heart
First at sight of thee was glad
All unheard of as thou art,
Thou must needs, I think, have had,
Celandine! and long ago,
Praise of which I nothing know.

I have not a doubt but he,
Whosoe'er the man might be,
Who the first with pointed rays
(Workman worthy to be sainted)
Set the sign-board in a blaze
When the rising sun be painted,
Took the fancy from a glance
At thy glittering countenance.

Soon as gentle breezes bring
News of winter's vanishing,
And the children build their bowers,
Sticking 'kerchief-plots of mould
All about with full-blown flowers,
Thick as sheep in shepherd's fold!
With the proudest thou art there,
Mantling in the tiny square.

Often have I sighed to measure
By myself a lonely pleasure,
Sighed to think, I read a book
Only read, perhaps, by me;
Yet I long could overlook
Thy bright coronet and Thee,
And thy arch and wily ways,
And thy store of other praise.

Blithe of heart, from week to week
Thou dost play at hide-and-seek;

While the patient primrose sits
Like a beggar in the cold,
Thou, a flower of wiser wits,
Slipp'st into thy sheltering hold;
Liveliest of the vernal train
When ye all are out again.

Drawn by that peculiar spell,
By what charm of sight or smell,
Does the dim-eyed curious Bee,
Labouring for her waxen cells,
Fondly settle upon Thee
Prized above all buds and bells
Opening daily at thy side,
By the season multiplied?

Thou art not beyond the moon,
But a thing beneath our shoon:
Let the bold Discoverer thrid
In his bark the polar sea;
Rear who will a pyramid;
Praise it is enough for me,
If there be but three or four
Who will love my little Flower.

WORDSWORTH

CCLXIX GLYCINE'S SONG

A sunny shaft did I behold,
From sky to earth it slanted:
And poised therein a bird so bold—
Sweet bird, thou wert enchanted!

He sunk, he rose, he twinkled, he trolled
Within that shaft of sunny mist;
His eyes of fire, his beak of gold,
All else of amethyst!

And thus he sang: "Adieu! adieu!
Love's dreams prove seldom true.
The blossoms they make no delay:
The sparkling dew-drops will not stay:
Sweet month of May, we must away;
Far, far away! to-day! to-day!"

S. T. COLERIDGE

CCLXX THE KNIGHT'S TOMB

Where is the grave of Sir Arthur O'Kellyn?
Where may the grave of that good man be?—
By the side of a spring, on the breast of Helvellyn,
Under the twigs of a young birch tree!
The oak that in summer was sweet to hear,
And rustled its leaves in the fall of the year,
And whistled and roar'd in the winter alone,
Is gone,—and the birch in its stead is grown.—
The Knight's bones are dust,
And his good sword rust;—
His soul is with the saints, I trust.

COLERIDGE

CCLXXI TIME, REAL AND IMAGINARY

On the wide level of a mountain's head,
(I knew not where, but 'twas some faery place)
Their pinions, ostrich-like, for sails outspread,
Two lovely children run an endless race,
A sister and a brother!
This far outstript the other;
Yet ever runs she with reverted face,
And looks and listens for the boy behind:
For he, alas! is blind!
O'er rough and smooth with even step he passed,
And knows not whether he be first or last.

COLERIDGE

CCLXXII WORK WITHOUT HOPE

All Nature seems at work. Slugs leave their lair—
The bees are stirring—birds are on the wing—
And Winter slumbering in the open air,
Wears on his smiling face a dream of Spring!
And I the while, the sole unbusy thing,
Nor honey make, nor pair, nor build, nor sing.

Yet well I ken the banks where amaranths blew,
Have traced the fount whence streams of nectar flow.
Bloom, O ye amaranths! bloom for whom ye may,
For me ye bloom not! Glide, rich streams, away!

With lips unbrightened, wreathless brow, I stroll:
And would you learn the spells that drowse my soul?
Work without Hope draws nectar in a sieve,
And Hope without an object cannot live.

COLERIDGE

CCLXXIII POPPIES

We are slumberous Poppies,
  Lords of Lethe downs;
Some asleep and some awake;
  Sleeping in our crowns.
What perchance our dreams may know
Let our serious beauty show.

Central depth of purple,
  Leaves more bright than rose;
Who shall tell what brightest thought
  Out of darkness grows?
Who, through what funereal pain
Souls to love and peace attain?

Visions aye are on us,
  Unto eyes of power;
Pluto's always setting sun
  And Proserpine's bower,
There, like bees, the pale souls come
For our drink with drowsy hum.

Taste, ye mortals, also,
  Milky-hearted we;
Taste, but with a rev'rent care,—
  Active, patient be,
Too much gladness brings to gloom
Those who on the gods presume.

LEIGH HUNT

CCLXXIV LILIES

We are Lilies fair,
  The flower of virgin light;
Nature held us forth, and said,
  "Lo! my thoughts of white!"

Ever since then, angels
  Hold us in their hands;
You may see them where they take
  In pictures their sweet stands.

Like the garden's angels
  Also do we seem,
And not the less for being crowned
  With a golden dream.

Could you see around us
  The enamoured air,
You would see it pale with bliss
  To hold a thing so fair.

LEIGH HUNT

CCLXXV JENNY KISS'D ME

Jenny kiss'd me when we met,
  Jumping from the chair she sat in;
Time, you thief! who love to get
  Sweets into your list, put that in.
Say I'm weary, say I'm sad;
  Say that health and wealth have miss'd me;
Say I'm growing old, but add—
  Jenny kiss'd me!

LEIGH HUNT

CCLXXVI TO THE GRASSHOPPER AND THE CRICKET

Green little vaulter in the sunny grass,
  Catching your heart up at the feel of June,
  Sole voice that's heard amidst the lazy noon,
When even the bees lag at the summoning brass;
And you, warm little housekeeper, who class
  With those who think the candles come too soon,
  Loving the fire, and with your tricksome tune
Nick the glad silent moments as they pass;
Oh, sweet and tiny cousins, that belong,
  One to the fields, the other to the hearth,
Both have your sunshine; both, though small, are strong
  At your clear hearts; and both were sent on earth
To sing in thoughtful ears this natural song—
  Indoors and out, summer and winter, mirth.

LEIGH HUNT

CCLXXVII ABOU BEN ADHEM

Abou Ben Adhem—may his tribe increase !—
Awoke one night from a deep dream of peace,
And saw, within the moonlight in his room,
Making it rich and like a lily in bloom,
An angel writing in a book of gold.
Exceeding peace had made Ben Adhem bold,
And to the presence in the room he said :
"What writest thou ?" The vision raised its head,
And with a look made of all sweet accord,
Answered : "The names of those who love the Lord."
"And is mine one ?" said Abou. "Nay, not so,"
Replied the angel. Abou spoke more low,
But cheerly still ; and said : "I pray thee, then,
Write me as one that loves his fellow-men."
The angel wrote, and vanished. The next night
It came again with a great wakening light,
And shewed the names whom love of God had blessed,
And lo ! Ben Adhem's name led all the rest.

LEIGH HUNT

CCLXXVIII A SONNET ON CHRISTIAN NAMES

In Christian world Mary the garland wears !
Rebecca sweetens on a Hebrew's ear ;
Quakers for pure Priscilla are more clear ;
And the light Gaul by amorous Ninon swears.
Among the lesser lights how Lucy shines !
What air of fragrance Rosamond throws around !
How like a hymn doth sweet Cecilia sound !
Of Marthas, and of Abigails, few lines
Have bragged in verse. Of coarsest household stuff
Should homely Joan be fashioned. But can
You Barbara resist, or Marian ?
And is not Clare for love excuse enough ?
Yet, by my faith in numbers, I profess,
These all, than Saxon Edith, please me less.

CHARLES LAMB

CCLXXIX ROSE AYLMER

Ah ! what avails the sceptred race !
Ah ! what the form divine !
What every virtue, every grace !
Rose Aylmer, all were thine.

Rose Aylmer, whom these wakeful eyes
  May weep, but never see,
A night of memories and of sighs
  I consecrate to thee.

WALTER SAVAGE LANDOR

CCLXXX SIXTEEN

In Clementina's artless mien,
  Lucilla asks me what I see,
And are the roses of sixteen
          Enough for me?

Lucilla asks, if that be all,
  Have I not cull'd as sweet before—
Ah, yes, Lucilla! and their fall
          I still deplore.

I now behold another scene,
  Where Pleasure beams with heaven's own light,
More pure, more constant, more serene,
          And not less bright.

Faith on whose breast the Loves repose,
  Whose chain of flowers no force can sever,
And Modesty, who when she goes,
          Is gone for ever.

LANDOR

CCLXXXI I STROVE WITH NONE

I strove with none, for none was worth my strife;
  Nature I loved, and, next to nature, art;
I warm'd both hands before the fire of life;
  It sinks, and I am ready to depart.

LANDOR

CCLXXXII SYMPATHY

The maid I love ne'er thought of me
Amid the scenes of gaiety;
But when her heart or mine sank low,
Ah, then it was no longer so.

From the slant palm she raised her head,
And kiss'd the cheek whence youth had fled,
Angels! some future day for this,
Give her as sweet and pure a kiss.

LANDOR

CCLXXXIII TWENTY YEARS HENCE

Twenty years hence my eyes may grow,
If not quite dim, yet rather so,
Yet yours from others they shall know
Twenty years hence.

Twenty years hence, tho' it may hap
That I be call'd to take a nap
In a cool cell where thunder clap
Was never heard.

There breathe but o'er my arch of grass
A not too-sadly sigh'd *Alas;*
And I shall catch, ere you can pass,
That wingèd word.

LANDOR

CCLXXXIV ROSES AND THORNS

Why do our joys depart
For cares to seize the heart?
I know not. Nature says,
Obey; and man obeys,
I see, and know not why
Thorns live and roses die.

LANDOR

CCLXXXV TARA

The harp that once through Tara's halls
The soul of music shed,
Now hangs as mute on Tara's walls
As if that soul were fled.
So sleeps the pride of former days,
So glory's thrill is o'er,
And hearts that once beat high for praise
Now feel that pulse no more.

No more to chiefs and ladies bright
  The harp of Tara swells;
The chord alone that breaks at night
  Its tale of ruin tells.
Thus Freedom now so seldom wakes,—
  The only throb she gives
Is when some heart indignant breaks
  To show that still she lives.

Tom Moore

CCLXXXVI THE LIGHT OF OTHER DAYS

Oft, in the stilly night,
  Ere slumber's chain has bound me,
Fond Memory brings the light
  Of other days around me:
    The smiles, the tears
    Of boyhood's years,
  The words of love then spoken;
    The eyes that shone,
    Now dimm'd and gone,
  The cheerful hearts now broken!
Thus, in the stilly night,
  Ere slumber's chain has bound me,
Sad Memory brings the light
  Of other days around me.

When I remember all
  The friends, so linked together,
I've seen around me fall
  Like leaves in wintry weather,
    I feel like one
    Who treads alone
  Some banquet-hall deserted,
    Whose lights are fled,
    Whose garlands dead,
  And all but he departed!
Thus, in the stilly night,
  Ere slumber's chain has bound me,
Sad Memory brings the light
  Of other days around me.

Moore

CCLXXXVII THE LAST ROSE OF SUMMER

'Tis the last rose of summer
  Left blooming alone;
All her lovely companions
  Are faded and gone;
No flower of her kindred,
  No rosebud is nigh,
To reflect back her blushes,
  To give sigh for sigh.

I'll not leave thee, thou lone one,
  To pine on the stem;
Since the lovely are sleeping,
  Go sleep thou with them.
Thus kindly I scatter
  Thy leaves o'er the bed,
Where thy mates of the garden
  Lie scentless and dead.

So soon may I follow,
  When friendships decay,
And from Love's shining circle
  The gems drop away!
When true hearts lie wither'd
  And fond ones are flown,
Oh! who would inhabit
  This bleak world alone!

MOORE

CCLXXXVIII AT THE MID HOUR OF NIGHT

At the mid hour of night, when stars are weeping, I fly
To the lone vale we loved, when life shone warm in thine eye;
  And I think oft, if spirits can steal from the regions of air
  To revisit past scenes of delight, thou wilt come to me there.
And tell me our love is remembered even in the sky!

Then I'll sing the wild song 'twas once such pleasure to hear,
When our voices commingling, breathed, like one, on the ear;
  And as Echo far off through the vale my sad orison rolls,
  I think, O my love! 'tis thy voice from the Kingdom of Souls
Faintly answering still the notes that once were so dear.

MOORE

CCLXXXIX SO, WE'LL GO NO MORE A ROVING

So, we'll go no more a roving
  So late into the night,
Though the heart be still as loving,
  And the moon be still as bright.

For the sword outwears its sheath,
  And the soul wears out the breast,
And the heart must pause to breathe,
  And love itself have rest

Though the night was made for loving,
  And the day returns too soon,
Yet we'll go no more a roving
  By the light of the moon.

LORD BYRON

CCXC STANZAS TO AUGUSTA

Though the day of my destiny's over,
  And the star of my fate hath declined,
Thy soft heart refused to discover
  The faults which so many could find ;
Though thy soul with my grief was acquainted,
  It shrunk not to share it with me,
And the love, which my spirit hath painted,
  It never hath found but in thee.

Then, when nature around me is smiling
  The last smile which answers to mine,
I do not believe it beguiling,
  Because it reminds me of thine ;
And when winds are at war with the ocean,
  As the breasts I believed in with me,
If their billows excite an emotion,
  It is that they bear me from thee.

Though the rock of my last hope is shiver'd,
  And its fragments are sunk in the wave,
Though I feel that my soul is deliver'd
  To pain—it shall not be its slave !
There is many a pang to pursue me :
  They may crush, but they shall not contemn,
They may torture, but shall not subdue me—
  'Tis of thee that I think—not of them !

Though human, thou didst not deceive me,
  Though woman, thou didst not forsake,
Though loved, thou forborest to grieve me,
  Though slander'd, thou never couldst shake:
Though trusted, thou didst not disclaim me,
  Though parted, it was not to fly,
Though watchful, 'twas not to defame me,
  Nor, mute, that the world might belie.

Yet I blame not the world, nor despise it,
  Nor the war of the many with one—
If my soul was not fitted to prize it,
  'Twas folly not sooner to shun:
And if dearly that error hath cost me,
  And more than I once could foresee,
I have found that, whatever it lost me,
  It could not deprive me of thee.

From the wreck of the past, which hath perish'd,
  Thus much I at least may recall:
It hath taught me that what I most cherish'd
  Deserved to be dearest of all:
In the desert a fountain is springing,
  In the wide waste there still is a tree,
And a bird in the solitude singing
  Which speaks to my spirit of thee.

BYRON

CCXCI THE CASTLED CRAG OF DRACHENFELS

The castled crag of Drachenfels
Frowns o'er the wide and winding Rhine,
Whose breast of waters broadly swells
Between the banks which bear the vine,
And hills all rich with blossom'd trees,
And fields which promise corn and wine,
And scatter'd cities crowning these,
Whose far white walls along them shine,
Have strew'd a scene, which I should see
With double joy wert thou with me.

And peasant girls, with deep blue eyes,
And hands which offer early flowers,
Walk smiling o'er this paradise;
Above, the frequent feudal towers

Through green leaves lift their walls of gray,
And many a rock which steeply lowers,
And noble arch in proud decay,
Look o'er this vale of vintage-bowers;
But one thing want these banks of Rhine,—
Thy gentle hand to clasp in mine!

I send the lilies given to me;
Though long before thy hand they touch,
I know that they must wither'd be,
But yet reject them not as such;
For I have cherish'd them as dear,
Because they yet may meet thine eye,
And guide thy soul to mine even here,
When thou behold'st them drooping nigh,
And know'st them gather'd by the Rhine,
And offer'd from my heart to thine!

The river nobly foams and flows,
The charm of this enchanted ground,
And all its thousand turns disclose
Some fresher beauty varying round:
The haughtiest breast its wish might bound
Through life to dwell delighted here;
Nor could on earth a spot be found
To nature and to me so dear,
Could thy dear eyes in following mine
Still sweeten more these banks of Rhine!

BYRON

CCXCII MY BOAT IS ON THE SHORE

My boat is on the shore,
  And my bark is on the sea:
But, before I go, Tom Moore,
  Here's a double health to thee!

Here's a sigh to those that love me,
  And a smile to those who hate;
And, whatever sky's above me,
  Here's a heart for every fate.

Though the ocean roar around me,
  Yet it shall yet bear me on;
Though a desert should surround me,
  It hath springs that may be won.

Were't the last drop in the well,
  As I gasped upon the brink,
Ere my fainting spirit fell,
  'Tis to thee that I would drink.

With that water as this wine,
  The libation I would pour
Should be:—"Peace with thine and mine,
  And a health to thee, Tom Moore!"

BYRON

CCXCIII THE ISLES OF GREECE

The isles of Greece, the isles of Greece!
  Where burning Sappho loved and sung,
Where grew the arts of war and peace,
  Where Delos rose, and Phœbus sprung!
Eternal summer gilds them yet,
But all, except their sun, is set.

The Scian and the Teian muse,
  The hero's harp, the lover's lute,
Have found the fame your shores refuse;
  Their place of birth alone is mute
To sounds which echo further west
Than your sires' "Islands of the Blest."

The mountains look on Marathon—
  And Marathon looks on the sea;
And musing there an hour alone,
  I dream'd that Greece might still be free;
For, standing on the Persian's grave,
I could not deem myself a slave.

A king sate on the rocky brow
  Which looks o'er sea-born Salamis;
And ships, by thousands, lay below,
  And men in nations—all were his!
He counted them at break of day—
And when the sun set, where were they?

And where are they? and where art thou,
  My country? On thy voiceless shore
The heroic lay is tuneless now—
  The heroic bosom beats no more!
And must thy lyre, so long divine,
Degenerate into hands like mine?

'Tis something, in the dearth of fame,
  Though link'd among a fetter'd race,
To feel at least a patriot's shame,
  Even as I sing, suffuse my face;
For what is left the poet here?
For Greeks a blush—for Greece a tear.

Must we but weep o'er days more blest?
  Must we but blush? Our fathers bled.
Earth! render back from out thy breast
  A remnant of our Spartan dead!
Of the three hundred grant but three
To make a new Thermopylæ!

What, silent still? and silent all?
  Ah! no;—the voices of the dead
Sound like a distant torrent's fall,
  And answer:—"Let one living head,
But one, arise—we come, we come!"
'Tis but the living who are dumb.

In vain—in vain! Strike other chords,
  Fill high the cup with Samian wine!
Leave battles to the Turkish hordes,
  And shed the blood of Scio's vine!
Hark! rising to the ignoble call—
How answers each bold Bacchanal!

You have the Pyrrhic dance as yet—
  Where is the Pyrrhic phalanx gone?
Of two such lessons, why forget
  The nobler and the manlier one?
You have the letters Cadmus gave—
Think ye, he meant them for a slave?

Fill high the bowl with Samian wine!
  We will not think of themes like these!
It made Anacreon's song divine:
  He served—but served Polycrates—
A tyrant; but our masters then
Were still, at least, our countrymen.

The tyrant of the Chersonese
  Was freedom's best and bravest friend;
That tyrant was Miltiades!
  O! that the present hour would lend

Another despot of the kind!
Such chains as his were sure to bind.

Fill high the bowl with Samian wine!
  On Suli's rock and Parga's shore
Exists the remnant of a line
  Such as the Doric mothers bore;
And there, perhaps, some seed is sown,
The Heracleidan blood might own.

Trust not for freedom to the Franks—
  They have a king who buys and sells!
In native swords, and native ranks,
  The only hope of courage dwells:
But Turkish force and Latin fraud
Would break your shield, however broad.

Fill high the bowl with Samian wine!
  Our virgins dance beneath the shade—
I see their glorious black eyes shine;
  But, gazing on each glowing maid,
My own the burning tear-drop laves,
To think such breasts must suckle slaves.

Place me on Sunium's marbled steep,
  Where nothing, save the waves and I,
May hear our mutual murmurs sweep:
  There, swan-like, let me sing and die.
A land of slaves shall ne'er be mine—
Dash down yon cup of Samian wine!

BYRON

CCXCIV BYRON'S FAREWELL

'Tis time this heart should be unmoved,
  Since others it hath ceased to move:
Yet, though I cannot be beloved,
    Still let me love!

My days are in the yellow leaf;
  The flowers and fruits of love are gone;
The worm, the canker, and the grief
    Are mine alone!

The fire that on my bosom preys
  Is lone as some volcanic isle;
No torch is kindled at its blaze—
    A funeral pile.

The hope, the fear, the jealous care,
  The exalted portion of the pain
And power of love, I cannot share,
    But wear the chain.

But 'tis not thus— and 'tis not here—
  Such thoughts should shake my soul, nor now,
Where glory decks the hero's bier,
    Or binds his brow.

The sword, the banner, and the field,
  Glory and Greece, around me see!
The Spartan, borne upon his shield,
    Was not more free.

Awake! (not Greece—she is awake!)
  Awake my spirit! Think through whom
Thy life-blood tracks its parent lake,
    And then strike home!

Tread those reviving passions down,
  Unworthy manhood!—Unto thee
Indifferent should the smile or frown
    Of beauty be.

If thou regret'st thy youth, why live?
  The land of honourable death
Is here:—up to the field, and give
    Away thy breath!

Seek out—less often sought than found—
  A soldier's grave, for thee the best;
Then look around and choose thy ground,
    And take thy rest.

BYRON

CCXCV IN THE GREAT MORNING OF THE WORLD

In the great morning of the world,
The spirit of God with might unfurled
The flag of Freedom over Chaos,
  And all its banded anarchs fled,
Like vultures frighted from Imaus,
  Before an earthquake's tread.—
So from Time's tempestuous dawn

Freedom's splendour burst and shone:—
Thermopylæ and Marathon
Caught, like mountains beacon-lighted,
  The springing Fire.—The wingèd glory
On Phillippi half-lighted,
  Like an eagle on a promontory.
Its unwearied wings could fan
The quenchless ashes of Milan.
From age to age, from man to man,
  It lived; and lit from land to land
  Florence, Albion, Switzerland.

Then night fell; and, as from night,
Reassuming fiery flight,
From the West swift Freedom came,
  Against the course of Heaven and doom,
A second sun arrayed in flame,
  To burn, to kindle, to illume.
From far Atlantis its young beams
Chased the shadows and the dreams.
France, with all her sanguine steams,
  Hid, but quenched it not; again
  Through clouds its shafts of glory rain
  From utmost Germany to Spain.

As an eagle fed with morning
Scorns the embattled tempests' warning,
When she seeks her aërie hanging
In the mountain-cedar's hair,
And her brood expect the clanging
Of her wings through the wild air,
Sick with famine:—Freedom, so
To what of Greece remaineth now
Returns; her hoary ruins glow
Like Orient mountains lost in day;
  Beneath the safety of her wings
Her renovated nurslings prey,
  And in the naked lightnings
Of truth they purge their dazzled eyes.
Let Freedom leave—where'er she flies,
A Desert, or a Paradise:
  Let the beautiful and the brave
  Share her glory, or a grave.

PERCY BYSSHE SHELLEY

CCXCVI HYMN OF APOLLO

I

The sleepless Hours who watch me as I lie,
  Curtained with star-inwoven tapestries,
From the broad moonlight of the sky,
  Fanning the busy dreams from my dim eyes,—
Waken me when their Mother, the gray Dawn,
Tells them that dreams and that the moon is gone.

II

Then I arise, and climbing Heaven's blue dome,
  I walk over the mountains and the waves,
Leaving my robe upon the ocean foam;
  My footsteps pave the clouds with fire; the caves
Are filled with my bright presence, and the air
Leaves the green earth to my embraces bare.

III

The sunbeams are my shafts, with which I kill
  Deceit, that loves the night and fears the day;
All men who do or even imagine ill
  Fly me, and from the glory of my ray
Good minds and open actions take new might,
Until diminished by the reign of night.

IV

I feed the clouds, the rainbows and the flowers
  With their ethereal colours; the Moon's globe
And the pure stars in their eternal bowers
  Are cinctured with my power as with a robe;
Whatever lamps on Earth or Heaven may shine,
Are portions of one power, which is mine.

V

I stand at noon upon the peak of Heaven,
  Then with unwilling steps I wander down
Into the clouds of the Atlantic even;
  For grief that I depart they weep and frown:
What look is more delightful than the smile
With which I soothe them from the western isle?

VI

I am the eye with which the Universe
  Beholds itself and knows itself divine;

All harmony of instrument or verse,
 All prophecy, all medicine are mine,
All light of art or nature ;—to my song,
Victory and praise in their own right belong.

SHELLEY

CCXCVII THE COURSERS

My coursers are fed with the lightning,
 They drink of the whirlwind's stream,
And when the red morning is brightning
 They bathe in the fresh sunbeam ;
 They have strength for their swiftness I deem,
Then ascend with me, daughter of Ocean.

I desire: and their speed makes night kindle;
 I fear: they outstrip the Typhoon;
Ere the cloud piled on Atlas can dwindle
 We encircle the earth and the moon:
 We shall rest from long labours at noon:
Then ascend with me, daughter of Ocean.

On the brink of the night and the morning
 My coursers are wont to respire;
But the Earth has just whispered a warning
 That their flight must be swifter than fire:
 They shall drink the hot speed of desire!

SHELLEY

CCXCVIII LIFE OF LIFE!

Life of life! thy lips enkindle
 With their love the breath between them;
And thy smiles before they dwindle
 Make the cold air fire; then screen them
In those looks, where whoso gazes
Faints, entangled in their mazes.

Child of Light! thy limbs are burning
 Thro' the vest which seems to hide them;
As the radiant lines of morning
 Thro' the clouds ere they divide them;
And this atmosphere divinest
Shrouds thee wheresoe'er thou shinest.

Fair are others; none beholds thee,
  But thy voice sounds low and tender
Like the fairest, for it folds thee
  From the sight, that liquid splendour,
And all feel, yet see thee never,
As I feel now, lost for ever!

Lamp of Earth! where'er thou movest
  Its dim shapes are clad with brightness,
And the souls of whom thou lovest
  Walk upon the winds with lightness,
Till they fail, as I am failing,
Dizzy, lost, yet unbewailing!

SHELLEY

CCXCIX

LIBERTY

Life may change, but it may fly not;
Hope may vanish, but can die not;
Truth be veiled, but still it burneth;
Love repulsed, but it returneth!

Yet were life a charnel where
Hope lay coffined with Despair;
Yet were truth a sacred lie,
Love were lust—If Liberty

Lent not life its soul of light,
Hope its iris of delight,
Truth its prophet's robe to wear,
Love its power to give and bear.

SHELLEY

CCC

O SLAVERY!

Let there be light! said Liberty,
And like sunrise from the sea,
Athens arose!—Around her born,
Shone like mountains in the morn
Glorious states;—and are they now
Ashes, wrecks, oblivion? Go,

Where Thermæ and Asopus swallowed
  Persia, as the sand does foam,
Deluge upon deluge followed,
  Discord, Macedon, and Rome:
And lastly thou!

Temples and towers,
   Citadels and marts, and they
Who live and die there, have been ours,
   And may be thine, and must decay;
But Greece and her foundations are
Built below the tide of war,
Based on the crystàlline sea
Of thought and its eternity;
Her citizens, imperial spirits,
   Rule the present from the past,
On all this world of men inherits
Their seal is set.

SHELLEY

CCCI THE WORLD'S GREAT AGE

The world's great age begins anew,
   The golden years return,
The earth doth like a snake renew
   Her winter weeds outworn:
Heaven smiles, and faiths and empires gleam,
Like wrecks of a dissolving dream.

A brighter Hellas rears its mountains
   From waves serener far;
A new Peneus rolls his fountains
   Against the morning star.
Where fairer Tempes bloom, there sleep
Young Cyclads on a sunnier deep.

A loftier Argo cleaves the main,
   Fraught with a later prize;
Another Orpheus sings again,
   And loves, and weeps, and dies.
A new Ulysses leaves once more
Calypso for his native shore.

Oh, write no more the tale of Troy,
   If earth Death's scroll must be!
Nor mix with Laian rage the joy
   Which dawns upon the free:
Although a subtler Sphinx renew
Riddles of death Thebes never knew.

Another Athens shall arise,
  And to remoter time
Bequeath, like sunset to the skies,
  The splendour of its prime;
And leave, if nought so bright may live,
All earth can take or Heaven can give.

Saturn and Love their long repose
  Shall burst, more bright and good
Than all who fell, than One who rose,
  Than many unsubdued:
Not gold, not blood, their altar dowers,
But votive tears and symbol flowers.

Oh, cease! must hate and death return?
  Cease! must men kill and die?
Cease! drain not to its dregs the urn
  Of bitter prophecy.
The world is weary of the past,
Oh, might it die or rest at last!

SHELLEY

CCCII

MEN OF ENGLAND

I

Men of England, wherefore plough
For the lords who lay ye low?
Wherefore weave with toil and care
The rich robes your tyrants wear?

II

Wherefore feed, and clothe, and save,
From the cradle to the grave,
Those ungrateful drones who would
Drain your sweat—nay, drink your blood?

III

Wherefore, Bees of England, forge
Many a weapon, chain, and scourge,
That these stingless drones may spoil
The forced produce of your toil?

IV

Have ye leisure, comfort, calm,
Shelter, food, love's gentle balm?
Or what is it ye buy so dear
With your pain and with your fear?

V

The seed ye sow, another reaps;
The wealth ye find, another keeps;
The robes ye weave, another wears;
The arms ye forge, another bears.

VI

Sow seed,—but let no tyrant reap;
Find wealth,—let no impostor heap;
Weave robes,—let not the idle wear;
Forge arms,—in your defence to bear.

VII

Shrink to your cellars, holes, and cells;
In halls ye deck another dwells.
Why shake the chains ye wrought? Ye see
The steel ye tempered glance on ye.

VIII

With plough and spade, and hoe and loom,
Trace your grave, and build your tomb,
And weave your winding-sheet, till fair
England be your sepulchre.

SHELLEY

CCCIII MUSIC

I pant for the music which is divine,
My heart in its thirst is a dying flower;
Pour forth the sound like enchanted wine,
Loosen the notes in a silver shower;
Like a herbless plain, for the gentle rain,
I gasp, I faint, till they wake again.
Let me drink of the spirit of that sweet sound,
More, oh more,—I am thirsting yet,
It loosens the serpent which care has bound
Upon my heart to stifle it;
The dissolving strain, through every vein,
Passes into my heart and brain.

SHELLEY

CCCIV THE AZIOLA

I

"Do you not hear the Aziola cry?
Methinks she must be nigh,"
Said Mary, as we sate

In dusk, ere stars were lit, or candles brought;
And I, who thought
This Aziola was some tedious woman,
Asked, "Who is Aziola?" How elate
I felt to know that it was nothing human,
No mockery of myself to fear or hate:
And Mary saw my soul,
And laughed, and said, "Disquiet yourself not;
'Tis nothing but a little downy owl."

II

Sad Aziola! many an eventide
Thy music I had heard
By wood and stream, meadow and mountain side,
And fields and marshes wide,
Such as nor voice, nor lute, nor wind, nor bird,
The soul ever stirred;
Unlike and far sweeter than them all.
Sad Aziola! from that moment I
Loved thee and thy sad cry.

SHELLEY

CCCV ON THE SEA

It keeps eternal whisperings around
Desolate shores, and with its mighty swell
Gluts twice ten thousand caverns, till the spell
Of Hecate leaves them their old shadowy sound.
Often 'tis in such gentle temper found,
That scarcely will the very smallest shell
Be moved for days from whence it sometime fell,
When last the winds of heaven were unbound.
Oh ye! who have your eye-balls vex'd and tired,
Feast them upon the wideness of the Sea;
Oh ye! whose ears are dinn'd with uproar rude,
Or fed too much with cloying melody,—
Sit ye near some old cavern's mouth, and brood
Until ye start, as if the sea-nymphs quired!

JOHN KEATS

CCCVI TO HOMER

Standing aloof in giant ignorance,
Of thee I hear and of the Cyclades,
As one who sits ashore and longs perchance
To visit dolphin-coral in deep seas.

So thou wast blind!—but then the veil was rent;
  For Jove uncurtain'd Heaven to let thee live,
And Neptune made for thee a spermy tent,
  And Pan made sing for thee his forest-hive;
Ay, on the shores of darkness there is light,
  And precipices show untrodden green;
There is a budding morrow in midnight;
  There is a triple sight in blindness keen:
Such seeing hadst thou, as it once befel,
  To Dian, Queen of Earth, and Heaven and Hell.

KEATS

CCCVII ON MELANCHOLY

No, no, go not to Lethe, neither twist
  Wolf's-bane, tight-rooted, for its poisonous wine;
Nor suffer thy pale forehead to be kiss'd
  By nightshade, ruby grape of Proserpine;
Make not your rosary of yew-berries,
  Nor let the beetle nor the death-moth be
    Your mournful Psyche, nor the downy owl
A partner in your sorrow's mysteries;
  For shade to shade will come too drowsily,
    And drown the wakeful anguish of the soul.

But when the melancholy fit shall fall
  Sudden from heaven like a weeping cloud,
That fosters the droop-headed flowers all,
  And hides the green hill in an April shroud;
Then glut thy sorrow on a morning rose,
  Or on the rainbow of the salt sand-wave,
    Or on the wealth of globed peonies;
Or if thy mistress some rich anger shows,
  Emprison her soft hand, and let her rave,
    And feed deep, deep upon her peerless eyes.

She dwells with Beauty—Beauty that must die;
  And Joy, whose hand is ever at his lips
Bidding adieu; and aching Pleasure nigh,
  Turning to poison while the bee-mouth sips:
Ay, in the very temple of Delight
  Veil'd Melancholy has her sovran shrine,
    Though seen of none save him whose strenuous
      tongue

Can burst Joy's grape against his palate fine:
His soul shall taste the sadness of her might,
And be among her cloudy trophies hung.

Keats

CCCVIII MEG MERRILIES

Old Meg she was a gipsy;
And lived upon the moors,
Her bed it was the brown heath turf,
And her house was out of doors.
Her apples were swart blackberries,
Her currants, pods o' broom;
Her wine was dew of the wild white rose,
Her book a churchyard tomb.

Her brothers were the craggy hills,
Her sisters larchen trees;
Alone with her great family
She lived as she did please.
No breakfast had she many a morn,
No dinner many a noon,
And, 'stead of supper, she would stare
Full hard against the moon.

But every morn, of woodbine fresh
She made her garlanding,
And, every night, the dark glen yew
She wove, and she would sing.
And with her fingers, old and brown,
She plaited mats of rushes,
And gave them to the cottagers
She met among the bushes.

Old Meg was as brave as Margaret Queen,
And tall as Amazon;
An old red blanket cloak she wore,
A ship-hat had she on:
God rest her aged bones somewhere!
She died full long agone!

Keats

CCCIX SONG OF SORROW

"O Sorrow!
Why dost borrow
The natural hue of health, from vermeil lips?—

To give maiden blushes
To the white rose bushes?
Or is it thy dewy hand the daisy tips?

"O Sorrow!
Why dost borrow
The lustrous passion from a falcon-eye?
To give the glow-worm light?
Or, on a moonless night,
To tinge, on syren shores, the salt sea-spry?

"O Sorrow!
Why dost borrow
The mellow ditties from a mourning tongue?
To give at evening pale
Unto the nightingale,
That thou mayst listen the cold dews among?

"O Sorrow!
Why dost borrow
Heart's lightness from the merriment of May?
A lover who could tread
A cowslip on the head,
Though he should dance from eve till peep of day.
Nor any drooping flower
Held sacred for thy bower,
Wherever he may sport himself and play."

To Sorrow
I bade good morrow,
And thought to leave her far away behind;
But cheerly, cheerly,
She loves me dearly;
She is so constant to me, and so kind:
I would deceive her,
And so leave her,
But ah! she is so constant and so kind.

KEATS

CCCX GRAMMACHREE

If I had thought thou couldst have died
I might not weep for thee;
But I forgot, when by thy side,
That thou couldst mortal be:

It never through my mind had past
  The time would e'er be o'er,
And I on thee should look my last,
  And thou shouldst smile no more!

And still upon that face I look,
  And think 'twill smile again;
And still the thought I will not brook,
  That I must look in vain!
But when I speak – thou dost not say
  What thou ne'er left'st unsaid;
And now I feel, as well I may,
  Sweet Mary! thou art dead!

If thou wouldst stay e'en as thou art,
  All cold and all serene—
I still might press thy silent heart,
  And where thy smiles have been!
While e'en thy chill bleak corse I have
  Thou seemest still mine own;
But there I lay thee in thy grave—
  And I am now alone!

I do not think, where'er thou art,
  Thou hast forgotten me;
And I, perhaps, may soothe this heart,
  In thinking too of thee:
Yet there was round thee such a dawn
  Of light ne'er seen before,
As fancy never could have drawn,
  And never can restore!

WOLFE

CCCXI THE GRAVES OF A HOUSEHOLD

They grew in beauty, side by side,
  They filled one home with glee;
Their graves are severed, far and wide,
  By mount, and stream, and sea.

The same fond mother bent at night
  O'er each fair sleeping brow;
She had each folded flower in sight—
  Where are those dreamers now?

One, 'midst the forests of the west,
By a dark stream is laid—
The Indian knows his place of rest,
Far in the cedar shade.

The sea, the blue lone sea, hath one,
He lies where pearls lie deep;
He was the loved of all, yet none
O'er his low bed may weep.

One sleeps where southern vines are dressed
Above the noble slain:
He wrapt his colours round his breast,
On a blood-red field of Spain.

And one—o'er her the myrtle showers
Its leaves, by soft winds fanned;
She faded 'midst Italian flowers—
The last of that bright band.

And parted thus they rest, who played
Beneath the same green tree;
Whose voices mingled as they prayed
Around one parent knee!

They that with smiles lit up the hall,
And cheered with song the hearth—
Alas! for love, if *thou* wert all,
And nought beyond, oh earth!

Mrs. Hemans

CCCXII BATTLE SONG

Day, like our souls, is fiercely dark;
What then? 'Tis day!
We sleep no more; the cock crows—hark
To arms! away!
They come! they come! the knell is rung
Of us or them;
Wide o'er their march the pomp is flung
Of gold and gem.
What collared hound of lawless sway
To famine dear—
What pensioned slave of Attila,
Leads in the rear?
Come they from Scythian wilds afar
Our blood to spill?

Wear they the livery of the Czar?
        They do his will.
Nor tasselled silk, nor epaulette,
        Nor plume, nor torse—
No splendour gilds, all sternly met
        Our foot and horse,
But dark and still, we inly glow,
        Condensed in ire!
Strike, tawdry slaves, and ye shall know
        Our gloom is fire.
In vain your pomp, ye evil powers,
        Insults the land;
Wrongs, vengeance, and *the cause* are ours,
        And God's right hand!
Madmen! they trample into snakes
        The wormy clod!
Like fire beneath their feet awakes
        The sword of God!
Behind, before, above, below,
        They rouse the brave;
Where'er they go, they make a foe,
        Or find a grave.

EBENEZER ELLIOT

CCCXIII IVRY

Now glory to the Lord of Hosts, from whom all glories are!
And glory to our sovereign liege, King Henry of Navarre!
Now let there be the merry sound of music and of dance,
Through thy cornfields green, and sunny vines, oh pleasant land of France!
And thou, Rochelle, our own Rochelle, proud city of the waters,
Again let rapture light the eyes of all thy mourning daughters.
As thou wert constant in our ills, be joyous in our joy,
For cold, and stiff, and still are they who wrought thy walls annoy.
Hurrah! hurrah! a single field hath turned the chance of war,
Hurrah! hurrah! for Ivry, and Henry of Navarre.
Oh! how our hearts were beating, when, at the dawn of day,
We saw the army of the League drawn out in long array;
With all its priest-led citizens, and all its rebel peers,
And Appenzel's stout infantry, and Egmont's Flemish spears.

There rode the brood of false Lorraine, the curses of our land;
And dark Mayenne was in the midst, a truncheon in his hand:
And, as we looked on them, we thought of Seine's empurpled flood,
And good Coligni's hoary hair all dabbled with his blood;
And we cried unto the living God, who rules the fate of war,
To fight for his own holy name, and Henry of Navarre.
The king is come to marshal us, in all his armour drest;
And he has bound a snow-white plume upon his gallant crest.
He looked upon his people, and a tear was in his eye;
He looked upon the traitors, and his glance was stern and high:
Right graciously he smiled on us, as rolled from wing to wing,
Down all our line, a deafening shout, "God save our lord the King."
"And if my standard-bearer fall, as fall full well he may—
For never saw I promise yet of such a bloody fray—
Press where ye see my white plume shine, amidst the ranks of war,
And be your oriflamme, to-day, the helmet of Navarre."
Hurrah! the foes are moving! Hark to the mingled din
Of fife, and steed, and trump, and drum, and roaring culverin.
The fiery Duke is pricking fast across Saint André's plain,
With all the hireling chivalry of Guelders and Almayne.
Now by the lips of those ye love, fair gentlemen of France,
Charge for the golden lilies—upon them with the lance!
A thousand spurs are striking deep, a thousand spears in rest,
A thousand knights are pressing close behind the snow-white crest;
And in they burst, and on they rushed, while, like a guiding star,
Amidst the thickest carnage blazed the helmet of Navarre.
Now, God be praised, the day is ours! Mayenne hath turned his rein.
D'Aumale hath cried for quarter. The Flemish Count is slain.
Their ranks are breaking like thin clouds before a Biscay gale;
The field is heaped with bleeding steeds, and flags, and cloven mail.
And then we thought on vengeance, and all along our van,
"Remember St Bartholomew," was passed from man to man;
But out spake gentle Henry: "No Frenchmen is my foe:
Down, down with every foreigner, but let your brethren go."

Oh! was there ever such a knight, in friendship or in war,
As our sovereign lord, King Henry, the soldier of Navarre!
Right well fought all the Frenchmen who fought for France to-day;
And many a lordly banner God gave them for a prey.
But we of the religion have borne us best in fight;
And the good lord of Rosny hath ta'en the cornet white.
Our own true Maximilian the cornet white hath ta'en,
The cornet white with crosses black, the flag of false Lorraine.
Up with it high; unfurl it wide; that all the host may know
How god hath humbled the proud house which wrought his church such woe.
Then on the ground, while trumpets sound their loudest points of war,
Fling the red shreds, a foot-cloth meet for Henry of Navarre.
Ho! maidens of Vienna! Ho! matrons of Lucerne!
Weep, weep, and rend your hair for those who never shall return.
Ho! Philip, send, for charity, thy Mexican pistoles,
That Antwerp monks may sing a mass for thy poor spearmen's souls!
Ho! gallant nobles of the League, look that your arms be bright;
Ho! burghers of Saint Genevieve, keep watch and ward to-night.
For our God hath crushed the tyrant, our God hath raised the slave,
And mocked the counsel of the wise, and the valour of the brave.
Then glory to his holy name, from whom all glories are;
And glory to our sovereign lord, King Henry of Navarre.

MACAULAY

CCCXIV THE CHAUNT OF THE BRAZEN HEAD

I think, whatever mortals crave,
With impotent endeavour,—
A wreath, a rank, a throne, a grave,—
The world goes round for ever;
I think that life is not too long;
And therefore I determine,
That many people read a song
Who will not read a sermon.

I think you've look'd through many hearts,
And mused on many actions,
And studied Man's component parts,
And Nature's compound fractions:
I think you've pick'd up truth by bits
From foreigner and neighbour;
I think the world has lost its wits,
And you have lost your labour.

I think the studies of the wise,
The hero's noisy quarrel,
The majesty of Woman's eyes,
The poet's cherish'd laurel,
And all that makes us lean or fat,
And all that charms or troubles,—
This bubble is more bright than that,
But still they are all bubbles.

I think the thing you call Renown,
The unsubstantial vapour
For which the soldier burns a town,
The sonnetteer a taper,
Is like the mist which, as he flies,
The horseman leaves behind him;
He cannot mark its wreaths arise,
Or if he does they blind him.

I think one nod of Mistress Chance
Makes creditors of debtors,
And shifts the funeral for the dance,
The sceptre for the fetters:
I think that Fortune's favour'd guest
May live to gnaw the platters,
And he that wears the purple vest
May wear the rags and tatters.

I think the Tories love to buy
"Your Lordship's" and "your Grace's,"
By loathing common honesty,
And lauding commonplaces:
I think that some are very wise,
And some are very funny,
And some grow rich by telling lies,
And some by telling money.

I think the Whigs are wicked knaves—
   (And very like the Tories)—
Who doubt that Britain rules the waves,
   And ask the price of glories;
I think that many fret and fume
   At what their friends are planning,
And Mr. Hume hates Mr. Brougham
   As much as Mr. Canning.

I think that friars and their hoods,
   Their doctrines and their maggots,
Have lighted up too many feuds,
   And far too many faggots:
I think, while zealots fast and frown,
   And fight for two or seven,
That there are fifty roads to Town,
   And rather more to Heaven.

I think that, thanks to Paget's lance,
   And thanks to Chester's learning,
The hearts that burn'd for fame in France
   At home are safe from burning:
I think the Pope is on his back;
   And, though 'tis fun to shake him,
I think the Devil not so black
   As many people make him.

I think that Love is like a play,
   Where tears and smiles are blended,
Or like a faithless April day,
   Whose shine with shower is ended:
Like Colnbrook pavement, rather rough,
   Like trade, exposed to losses,
And like a Highland plaid,—all stuff,
   And very full of crosses.

I think the world, though dark it be,
   Has aye one rapturous pleasure
Conceal'd in life's monotony,
   For those who seek the treasure;
One planet in a starless night,
   One blossom on a briar,
One friend not quite a hypocrite,
   One woman not a liar!

I think poor beggars court St. Giles;
  Rich beggars court St. Stephen;
And Death looks down with nods and smiles,
  And makes the odds all even:
I think some die upon the field,
  And some upon the billow,
And some are laid beneath a shield,
  And some beneath a willow.

I think that very few have sigh'd
  When Fate at last has found them,
Though bitter foes were by their side,
  And barren moss around them:
I think that some have died of drought,
  And some have died of drinking;
I think that nought is worth a thought,—
  And I'm a fool for thinking!

WINTHROP M. PRAED

CCCXV THE VICAR

Some years ago, ere time and taste
  Had turn'd our parish topsy-turvy,
When Darnel Park was Darnel Waste,
  And roads as little known as scurvy,
The man who lost his way, between
  St. Mary's Hill and Sandy Thicket,
Was always shown across the green,
  And guided to the Parson's wicket.

Back flew the bolt of lissom lath;
  Fair Margaret, in her tidy kirtle,
Led the lorn traveller up the path,
  Through clean-clipt rows of box and myrtle;
And Don and Sancho, Tramp and Tray,
  Upon the parlour steps collected,
Wagged all their tails, and seem'd to say—
  "Our master knows you—you're expected."

Uprose the Reverend Dr. Brown,
  Uprose the Doctor's winsome marrow;
The lady laid her knitting down,
  Her husband clasp'd his ponderous Barrow;

Whate'er the stranger's caste or creed,
  Pundit or Papist, saint or sinner,
He found a stable for his steed,
  And welcome for himself, and dinner.

If, when he reach'd his journey's end,
  And warm'd himself in Court or College,
He had not gain'd an honest friend
  And twenty curious scraps of knowledge,—
If he departed as he came,
  With no new light on love or liquor,—
Good sooth, the traveller was to blame,
  And not the Vicarage, or the Vicar.

His talk was like a stream, which runs
  With rapid change from rocks to roses:
It slipt from politics to puns,
  It pass'd from Mahomet to Moses;
Beginning with the laws which keep
  The planets in their radiant courses,
And ending with some precept deep
  For dressing eels, or shoeing horses.

He was a shrewd and sound Divine,
  Of loud Dissent the mortal terror;
And when, by dint of page and line,
  He 'stablish'd Truth, or startled Error,
The Baptist found him far too deep;
  The Deist sigh'd with saving sorrow;
And the lean Levite went to sleep,
  And dream'd of tasting pork to-morrow.

His sermon never said or show'd
  That Earth is foul, that Heaven is gracious,
Without refreshment on the road
  From Jerome, or from Athanasius:
And sure a righteous zeal inspired
  The hand and head that penn'd and plann'd them,
For all who understood admired,
  And some who did not understand them.

He wrote, too, in a quiet way,
  Small treatises, and smaller verses,
And sage remarks on chalk and clay,
  And hints to noble Lords—and nurses;

True histories of last year's ghost,
  Lines to a ringlet or a turban,
And trifles for the Morning Post,
  And nothings for Sylvanus Urban.

He did not think all mischief fair,
  Although he had a knack of joking;
He did not make himself a bear,
  Although he had a taste for smoking;
And when religious sects ran mad,
  He held, in spite of all his learning,
That if a man's belief is bad,
  It will not be improved by burning.

And he was kind, and loved to sit
  In the low hut or garnish'd cottage,
And praise the farmer's homely wit,
  And share the widow's homelier pottage:
At his approach complaint grew mild;
  And when his hand unbarr'd the shutter,
The clammy lips of fever smiled
  The welcome which they could not utter.

He always had a tale for me
  Of Julius Cæsar, or of Venus;
From him I learnt the rule of three,
  Cat's cradle, leap-frog, and *Quæ genus*.
I used to singe his powder'd wig,
  To steal the staff he put such trust in,
And make the puppy dance a jig,
  When he began to quote Augustine.

Alack the change! in vain I look
  For haunts in which my boyhood trifled,—
The level lawn, the trickling brook,
  The trees I climb'd, the beds I rifled:
The church is larger than before;
  You reach it by a carriage entry;
It holds three hundred people more,
  And pews are fitted up for gentry.

Sit in the Vicar's seat: you'll hear
  The doctrine of a gentle Johnian,
Whose hand is white, whose tone is clear,
  Whose praise is very Ciceronian.

Where is the old man laid?—look down,
And construe on the slab before you,
"*Hic jacet Gvlielmvs Brown,*
Vir nullâ non donandus lauru."

WINTHROP M. PRAED

CCCXVI

SONG OF THE SHIRT

With fingers weary and worn,
With eyelids heavy and red,
A woman sat in unwomanly rags,
Plying her needle and thread—
Stitch—stitch—stitch!
In poverty, hunger, and dirt,
And still with a voice of dolorous pitch
She sang the "Song of the Shirt."

"Work—work—work!
While the cock is crowing aloof;
And work—work—work
Till the stars shine through the roof!
It's oh to be a slave
Along with the barbarous Turk,
Where woman has never a soul to save,
If this is Christian work!

"Work—work—work!
Till the brain begins to swim;
Work—work—work!
Till the eyes are heavy and dim,
Seam, and gusset, and band,—
Band, and gusset, and seam,
Till over the buttons I fall asleep,
And sew them on in a dream!

"O men with Sisters dear!
O men with Mothers and Wives!
It is not linen you're wearing out,
But human creatures' lives!
Stitch—stitch—stitch,
In poverty, hunger, and dirt,
Sewing at once, with a double thread,
A Shroud as well as a Shirt!

"But why do I talk of Death?
  That phantom of grisly bone,—
I hardly fear his terrible shape,
  It seems so like my own—
    It seems so like my own,
  Because of the fasts I keep;
O God! that bread should be so dear,
  And flesh and blood so cheap!

  "Work—work—work!
My labour never flags;
  And what are its wages? A bed of straw,
A crust of bread—and rags.
  That shattered roof,—and this naked floor,—
A table,—a broken chair,—
  And a wall so blank, my shadow I thank
For sometimes falling there.

  "Work—work—work!
From weary chime to chime,
  Work—work—work!
As prisoners work for crime.
    Band, and gusset, and seam,
  Seam, and gusset, and band,
Till the heart is sick, and the brain benumbed,
  As well as the weary hand.

  "Work—work—work!
In the dull December light,
  And work—work—work!
When the weather is warm and bright,
    While underneath the eaves
  The brooding swallows cling,
As if to show me their sunny backs
  And twit me with the spring.

  "Oh! but to breathe the breath
  Of the cowslip and primrose sweet—
With the sky above my head,
  And the grass beneath my feet;
    For only one short hour
  To feel as I used to feel
Before I knew the woes of want
  And the walk that costs a meal!

"Oh! but for one short hour!
  A respite, however brief!—
No blessèd leisure for Love or Hope,
  But only time for Grief!
A little weeping would ease my heart,
  But in their briny bed
My tears must stop, for every drop
  Hinders needle and thread."

With fingers weary and worn,
  With eyelids heavy and red,
A woman sat in unwomanly rags,
  Plying her needle and thread—
    Stitch—stitch—stitch!
  In poverty, hunger, and dirt,
And still with a voice of dolorous pitch,—
Would that its tone could reach the rich!—
  She sang this "Song of the Shirt."

TOM HOOD

CCCXVII THE LEE SHORE

Sleet and hail and thunder!
  And ye winds that rave
Till the sands thereunder
  Tinge the sullen wave,—

Winds that like a demon
  Howl with horrid note
Round the toiling seaman
  In his tossing boat!

From his humble dwelling
  On the shingly shore,
Where the billows swelling
  Keep such hollow roar;—

From that weeping woman,
  Seeking with her cries
Succour superhuman
  From the frowning skies;—

From the urchin pining
  For his father's knee;—
From the lattice shining
  Drive him out to sea!—

Let broad leagues dissever
  Him from yonder foam.
O God ! to think man ever
  Comes too near his home.

TOM HOOD

CCCXVIII MAN AND BOY

Oh, when I was a tiny boy,
My nights and days were full of joy,
  My mates were blithe and kind !—
No wonder that I sometimes sigh,
And dash the tear-drop from my eye,
  To cast a look behind !

A hoop was an eternal round
Of pleasure. In those days I found
  A top a joyous thing ;—
But now those past delights I drop,
My head, alas ! is all my top,
  And careful thoughts the string !

My joys are wingless all and dead ;
My dumps are made of more than lead ;
  My flights soon find a fall ;
My fears prevail, my fancies droop,
Joy never cometh with a hoop,
  And seldom with a call !

My football's laid upon the shelf ;
I am a shuttlecock myself
  The world knocks to and fro ;—
My archery is all unlearn'd,
And grief against myself has turn'd
  My arrows and my bow !

No skies so blue or so serene
As then ;—no leaves look half so green
  As clothed the playground tree !
All things I loved are alter'd so,
Nor does it ease my heart to know
  That change resides in me !

TOM HOOD

CCCXIX RUTH

She stood breast-high amid the corn,
Clasped by the golden light of morn,
Like the sweetheart of the sun,
Who many a glowing kiss had won.

On her cheek an autumn flush
Deeply ripened;—such a blush
In the midst of brown was born,
Like red poppies grown with corn.

Round her eyes her tresses fell,
Which were blackest none could tell,
But long lashes veiled a light
That had else been all too bright.

And her hat, with shady brim,
Made her tressy forehead dim;
Thus she stood amid the stooks,
Praising God with sweetest looks.

Sure, I said, Heav'n did not mean,
Where I reap thou shouldst but glean:
Lay thy sheaf adown and come,
Share my harvest and my home.

TOM HOOD

CCCXX TIME OF ROSES

It was not in the Winter
  Our loving lot was cast:
It was the time of roses—
  We pluck'd them as we pass'd!

That churlish season never frown'd
  On early lovers yet!
O, no—the world was newly crown'd
  With flowers, when first we met!

'Twas twilight, and I bade you go
  But still you held me fast:
It was the time of roses—
  We plucked them as we pass'd.

TOM HOOD

CCCXXI NIGHT AND DEATH

Mysterious Night! when our first parent knew
  Thee from report divine, and heard thy name,
  Did he not tremble for this lovely frame,
This glorious canopy of light and blue?
Yet 'neath a curtain of translucent dew,
  Bathed in the rays of the great setting flame,
  Hesperus with the host of heaven came,
And lo! Creation widened in man's view.

  Who could have thought such darkness lay concealed
Within thy beams, O Sun! or who could find,
  Whilst flow'r and leaf and insect stood revealed,
That to such countless orbs thou mad'st us blind!
  Why do we then shun Death with anxious strife?
  If Light can thus deceive, wherefore not Life?

BLANCO WHITE

CCCXXII GRAVES OF INFANTS

Infants' gravemounds are steps of angels, where
  Earth's brightest gems of innocence repose.
God is their parent, so they need no tear;
  He takes them to his bosom from earth's woes—
  A bud their lifetime and a flower their close.
Their spirits are the Iris of the skies,
  Needing no prayer; a sunset's happy close.
Gone are the bright rays of their soft blue eyes;
Flow'rs weep in dew-drops o'er them, and the gale gently sighs.

Their lives were nothing but a sunny shower,
  Melting on flowers as tears melt from the eye.
Each death
  Was toll'd on flowers as summer gales went by:
  They bow'd and trembled, yet they heaved no sigh;
And the sun smiled to show the end was well.
  Infants have naught to weep for ere they die,
All prayers are needless, beads they need not tell;
White flowers their mourners are, Nature their passing bell.

JOHN CLARE

CCCXXIII THE THRUSH'S NEST

Within a thick and spreading hawthorn bush
  That overhung a molehill, large and round,
I heard from morn to morn a merry thrush
  Sing hymns of rapture, while I drank the sound
With joy—and oft an unintruding guest,
  I watched her secret toils from day to day;
How true she warped the moss to form her nest,
  And modelled it within with wood and clay.
And by and by, like heath-bells gilt with dew,
  There lay her shining eggs as bright as flowers,
Ink-spotted over, shells of green and blue:
  And there I witnessed, in the summer hours,
A brood of nature's minstrels chirp and fly,
Glad as the sunshine and the laughing sky.

JOHN CLARE

CCCXXIV SONG

It is not Beauty I demand,
  A crystal brow, the moon's despair,
Nor the snow's daughter, a white hand,
  Nor mermaid's yellow pride of hair.

Tell me not of your starry eyes,
  Your lips that seem on roses fed,
Your breasts where Cupid tumbling lies,
  Nor sleeps for kissing of his bed.

A bloomy pair of vermeil cheeks,
  Like Hebe's in her ruddiest hours,
A breath that softer music speaks
  Than summer winds a-wooing flowers:

These are but gauds: nay, what are lips?
  Coral beneath the ocean stream,
Whose brink when your adventurer sips
  Full oft he perisheth on them.

And what are cheeks but ensigns oft,
  That wave hot youth to fields of blood?
Did Helen's breast, though ne'er so soft,
  Do Greece or Ilium any good?

Eyes can with baneful ardour burn;
  Poison can breath that erst perfumed;
There's many a white hand holds an urn
  With lover's hearts to dust consumed.

For crystal brows—there's naught within;
  They are but empty cells for pride;
He who the Siren's hair would win
  Is mostly strangled in the tide.

Give me, instead of beauty's bust,
  A tender heart, a loyal mind,
Which with temptation I could trust,
  Yet never link'd with error find.

One in whose gentle bosom I
  Could pour my secret heart of woes,
Like the care-burthen'd honey-fly
  That hides his murmurs in the rose.

My earthly comforter! whose love
  So indefeasible might be,
That, when my spirit won above,
  Hers could not stay, for sympathy.

Darley

CCCXXV MAY, 1840

A lovely morn, so still, so very still,
  It hardly seems a growing day of Spring,
  Though all the odorous buds are blossoming,
And the small matin birds were glad and shrill
Some hours ago; but now the woodland rill
  Murmurs along, the only vocal thing,
  Save when the wee wren flits with stealthy wing,
And cons by fits and bits her evening trill.
Lovers might sit on such a morn as this
  An hour together, looking at the sky,
Nor dare to break the silence with a kiss,
  Long listening for the signal of a sigh;
And the sweet Nun, diffused in voiceless prayer,
Feel her own soul through all the brooding air.

Hartley Coleridge

CCCXXVI THE SOWER'S SONG

Now hands to seedsheet, boys!
We step and we cast; Old Time's on wing,
And would ye partake of Harvest's joys,
The corn must be sown in Spring.
Fall gently and still, good corn,
Lie warm in thy earthy bed;
And stand so yellow some morn,
For beast and man must be fed.

Old Earth is a pleasure to see
In sunshiny cloak of red and green;
The furrow lies fresh; this Year will be
As years that are past have been.
Fall gently and still, good corn,
Lie warm in thy earthy bed;
And stand so yellow some morn,
For beast and man must be fed.

Old Mother, receive this corn,
The son of Six Thousand golden sires:
All these on thy kindly breast were born;
One more thy poor child requires.
Fall gently and still, good corn,
Lie warm in thy earthy bed;
And stand so yellow some morn,
For beast and man must be fed.

Now steady and sure again,
And measure of stroke and step we keep;
Thus up and thus down we cast our grain:
Sow well, and you gladly reap.
Fall gently and still, good corn,
Lie warm in thy earthy bed;
And stand so yellow some morn,
For beast and man must be fed.

THOMAS CARLYLE

CCCXXVII THE PLOUGH

A LANDSCAPE IN BERKSHIRE

Above yon sombre swell of land
Thou see'st the dawn's grave orange hue,
With one pale streak like yellow sand,
And over that a vein of blue.

The air is cold above the woods;
  All silent is the earth and sky,
Except with his own lonely moods
  The blackbird holds a colloquy.

Over the broad hill creeps a beam,
  Like hope that gilds a good man's brow;
And now ascends the nostril-stream
  Of stalwart horses come to plough.

Ye rigid Ploughmen, bear in mind
  Your labour is for future hours:
Advance—spare not—nor look behind—
  Plough deep and straight with all your powers!

R. HENGIST HORNE

CCCXXVIII AN OLD GAME-RHYME

I

Water, water wall-flower,
Growing up so high,
We are all maidens,
We must all die.
All except Mary Anne,
She is the whitest flower;
She can skip and she can sing,
And ding us, ding us ower!

II

A dis, a dis o' green grass
A daisy dis, a dis!
Come all ye pretty maidens
And dance along with this.
And you shall have a duck so blue,
And you shall have a drake,
And you shall have a pretty young man
A-dancing for your sake.

CCCXXIX BLOW HIGH, BLOW LOW

Blow high, blow low, let tempests tear
  The main-mast by the board;
My heart, with thoughts of thee, my dear,
  And love well stored,
Shall brave all danger, scorn all fear,

The roaring winds, the raging sea,
In hopes on shore
To be once more
Safe moor'd with thee!

Aloft while mountains high we go,
The whistling winds that scud along,
And surges roaring from below,
Shall my signal be,
To think on thee;
And this shall be my song:
Blow high, blow low! . . .

And on that night when all the crew
The mem'ry of their former lives
O'er flowing cans of flip renew,
And drink their sweethearts and their wives,
I'll heave a sigh, and think on thee;
And as the ship rolls on the sea,
The burden of my song shall be—
Blow high, blow low! . . .

CHARLES DIBDIN

CCCXXX MARINERS' SONG

To sea, to sea! The calm is o'er;
The wanton water leaps in sport,
And rattles down the pebbly shore;
The dolphin wheels, the sea-cows snort,
And unseen Mermaids' pearly song
Comes bubbling up, the weeds among.
Fling broad the sail, dip deep the oar:
To sea, to sea! the calm is o'er.

To sea, to sea! our wide-wing'd bark
Shall billowy cleave its sunny way,
And with its shadow, fleet and dark,
Break the caved Triton's azure day,
Like mighty eagle soaring light
O'er antelopes on Alpine height.
The anchor heaves, the ship swings free,
The sails swell full. To sea, to sea!

T. LOVELL BEDDOES

CCCXXXI WOLFRAM'S SONG

Old Adam, the carrion crow,
  The old crow of Cairo;
He sat in the shower, and let it flow
  Under his tail and over his crest;
    And through every feather
    Leak'd the wet weather;
  And the bough swung under his nest;
  For his beak it was heavy with marrow.
    Is that the wind dying? O no;
    It's only two devils, that blow
    Through a murderer's bones, to and fro,
      In the ghosts' moonshine.

Ho! Eve, my grey carrion wife,
  When we have supped on kings' marrow,
Where shall we drink and make merry our life?
  Our nest it is queen Cleopatra's skull,
    'Tis cloven and crack'd,
    And batter'd and hack'd,
  But with tears of blue eyes it is full:
  Let us drink then, my raven of Cairo!
    Is that the wind dying? O no;
    It's only two devils, that blow
    Through a murderer's bones, to and fro,
      In the ghosts' moonshine. BEDDOES

CCCXXXII DIRGE

The swallow leaves her nest,
The soul my weary breast;
But therefore let the rain
  On my grave
Fall pure; for why complain?
Since both will come again
  O'er the wave.

The wind dead leaves and snow
Doth hurry to and fro;
And, once, a day shall break
  O'er the wave,
When a storm of ghosts shall shake
The dead, until they wake
  In the grave. BEDDOES

CCCXXXIII HOW MANY TIMES

How many times do I love thee, dear?
Tell me how many thoughts there be
In the atmosphere
Of a new-fall'n year,
Whose white and sable hours appear
The latest flake of eternity:—
So many times do I love thee, dear!

How many times do I love again?
Tell me how many beads there are
In a silver chain
Of evening rain,
Unravelled from the tumbling main,
And threading the eye of a yellow star:
So many times do I love again!

BEDDOES

CCCXXXIV EPITAPH ON A ROBIN

Tread lightly here, for here, 'tis said,
When piping winds are hush'd around,
A small note wakes from underground,
Where now his tiny bones are laid.

No more in lone and leafless groves,
With ruffled wind and faded breast,
His friendless, homeless spirit roves;
—Gone to the world where birds are blest!
Where never cat glides o'er the green,
Or schoolboy's giant form is seen;
But Love, and Joy, and smiling Spring
Inspire their little souls to sing!

SAMUEL ROGERS

CCCXXXV CARPE DIEM

Youth, that pursuest with such eager pace
Thy even way,
Thou pantest on to win a mournful race:
Then stay! oh, stay!

Pause, and luxuriate in thy sunny plain;
Loiter,—enjoy!
Once past, Thou never wilt come back again,
A second Boy,

The hills of Manhood wear a noble face,
When seen from far;
The mist of light from which they take their grace
Hides what they are.

The dark and weary path those cliffs between
Thou canst not know,
And how it leads to regions never-green,
Dead fields of snow.

Pause, while thou mayst, nor deem that fate thy gain
Which, all too fast,
Will drive thee forth from this delicious plain,
A Man at last.

LORD HOUGHTON

CCCXXXVI THE MIRROR

I

It saw, it knew thy loveliness,
Thy burning lip and glancing eye,
Each lightning look, each silken tress
Thy marble forehead braided by,
Like an embodied music, twined
About a brightly breathing mind.

II

Alas! its face is dark and dim;
No more its lightless depth below
That glancing eye shall seem to swim,
That brow to breathe or glow;
Its treacherous depth—its heartless hue—
Forgets the form that once it knew.

III

With many a changing shape and face
Its surface may be marked and crossed—
Portrayed with as distinct a grace
As thine, whose loveliness is lost;
But there's one mirror, good and true,
That doth not lose what once it knew.

IV

My thoughts are with that beauty blest,
A breathing, burning, living vision,
That, like a dove with wings at rest,
Still haunts the heart it makes Elysian;

And days and times pass like a sleep.
Softly sad, and still, and deep;
And, oh! what grief would wakening be,
From slumber bright with dreams of thee!

RUSKIN

CCCXXXVII
THE SPLENDOUR FALLS ON CASTLE WALLS

The splendour falls on castle walls
And snowy summits old in story:
The long light shakes across the lakes,
And the wild cataract leaps in glory.
Blow, bugle, blow, set the wild echoes flying,
Blow, bugle; answer, echoes, dying, dying, dying.

O hark, O hear! how thin and clear,
And thinner, clearer, farther going!
O sweet and far from cliff and scar
The horns of Elfland faintly blowing!
Blow, let us hear the purple glens replying:
Blow, bugle; answer, echoes, dying, dying, dying.

O love, they die in yon rich sky,
They faint on hill or field or river:
Our echoes roll from soul to soul,
And grow for ever and for ever.
Blow, bugle, blow, set the wild echoes flying,
And answer, echoes, answer, dying, dying, dying.

TENNYSON

CCCXXXVIII TEARS, IDLE TEARS

Tears, idle tears, I know not what they mean,
Tears from the depth of some divine despair
Rise in the heart, and gather to the eyes,
In looking on the happy Autumn-fields,
And thinking of the days that are no more.

Fresh as the first beam glittering on a sail,
That brings our friends up from the underworld,
Sad as the last which reddens over one
That sinks with all we love below the verge;
So sad, so fresh, the days that are no more.

Ah, sad and strange as in dark summer dawns
The earliest pipe of half-awaken'd birds
To dying ears, when unto dying eyes
The casement slowly grows a glimmering square;
So sad, so strange, the days that are no more.

Dear as remember'd kisses after death,
And sweet as those by hopeless fancy feign'd
On lips that are for others; deep as love,
Deep as first love, and wild with all regret;
O Death in Life, the days that are no more.

TENNYSON

CCCXXXIX O SWALLOW, SWALLOW

"O Swallow, Swallow, flying, flying South,
Fly to her, and fall upon her gilded eaves,
And tell her, tell her what I tell to thee.

"O tell her, Swallow, that thou knowest each,
That bright and fierce and fickle is the South,
And dark and true and tender is the North.

"O Swallow, Swallow, if I could follow, and light
Upon her lattice, I would pipe and trill,
And cheep and twitter twenty million loves.

"O were I thou that she might take me in,
And lay me on her bosom, and her heart
Would rock the snowy cradle till I died.

"Why lingereth she to clothe her heart with love,
Delaying as the tender ash delays
To clothe herself when all the woods are green?

"O tell her, Swallow, that thy brood is flown:
Say to her, I do but wanton in the South,
But in the North long since my nest is made.

"O tell her, brief is life but love is long,
And brief the sun of summer in the North,
And brief the moon of beauty in the South.

"O Swallow, flying from the golden woods,
Fly to her, and pipe and woo her, and make her mine,
And tell her, tell her, that I follow thee."

TENNYSON

CCCXL

HOME THEY BROUGHT HER WARRIOR DEAD

Home they brought her warrior dead:
  She nor swoon'd, nor utter'd cry:
All her maidens, watching, said,
  "She must weep or she will die."

Then they praised him, soft and low,
  Call'd him worthy to be loved,
Truest friend and noblest foe;
  Yet she neither spoke nor moved.

Stole a maiden from her place,
  Lightly to the warrior stept,
Took the face-cloth from the face;
  Yet she neither moved nor wept.

Rose a nurse of ninety years,
  Set his child upon her knee—
Like summer tempest came her tears—
  "Sweet my child, I live for thee."

TENNYSON

CCCXLI

THE LADY OF SHALOTT

PART I

On either side the river lie
Long fields of barley and of rye,
That clothe the wold and meet the sky;
And thro' the field the road runs by
    To many-tower'd Camelot;
And up and down the people go,
Gazing where the lilies blow
Round an island there below,
    The island of Shalott.

Willows whiten, aspens quiver,
Little breezes dusk and shiver
Thro' the wave that runs for ever
By the island in the river
    Flowing down to Camelot.
Four gray walls, and four gray towers,
Overlook a space of flowers,
And the silent isle imbowers
    The Lady of Shalott.

By the margin, willow-veil'd,
Slide the heavy barges trail'd
By slow horses; and unhail'd
The shallop flitteth silken-sail'd
    Skimming down to Camelot:
But who hath seen her wave her hand?
Or at the casement seen her stand?
Or is she known in all the land,
    The Lady of Shalott?

Only reapers, reaping early
In among the bearded barley,
Hear a song that echoes cheerly
From the river winding clearly,
    Down to tower'd Camelot:
And by the moon the reaper weary,
Piling sheaves in uplands airy,
Listening, whispers "'Tis the fairy
    Lady of Shalott."

PART II

There she weaves by night and day
A magic web with colours gay.
She has heard a whisper say,
A curse is on her if she stay
    To look down to Camelot.
She knows not what the curse may be,
And so she weaveth steadily,
And little other care hath she,
    The Lady of Shalott.

And moving thro' a mirror clear
That hangs before her all the year,
Shadows of the world appear.
There she sees the highway near
    Winding down to Camelot:
There the river eddy whirls,
And there the surly village-churls,
And the red cloaks of market-girls,
    Pass onward from Shalott.

Sometimes a troop of damsels glad,
An abbot on an ambling pad,
Sometimes a curly shepherd-lad,
Or long-haired page in crimson clad,
    Goes by to tower'd Camelot;

And sometimes thro' the mirror blue
The knights come riding two and two:
She hath no loyal knight and true,
The Lady of Shalott.

But in her web she still delights
To weave the mirror's magic sights,
For often thro' the silent nights
A funeral, with plumes and lights
And music, went to Camelot:
Or when the moon was overhead,
Came two young lovers lately wed;
"I am half sick of shadows," said
The Lady of Shalott.

PART III

A bow-shot from her bower-eaves,
He rode between the barley sheaves,
The sun came dazzling thro' the leaves,
And flamed upon the brazen greaves
Of bold Sir Lancelot.
A redcross knight for ever kneel'd
To a lady in his shield,
That sparkled on the yellow field,
Beside remote Shalott.

The gemmy bridle glitter'd free,
Like to some branch of stars we see
Hung in the golden Galaxy.
The bridle bells rang merrily
As he rode down to Camelot:
And from his blazon'd baldric slung
A mighty silver bugle hung,
And as he rode his armour rung,
Beside remote Shalott.

All in the blue unclouded weather
Thick-jewell'd shone the saddle-leather,
The helmet and the helmet-feather
Burn'd like one burning flame together,
As he rode down to Camelot.
As often thro' the purple night,
Below the starry clusters bright,
Some bearded meteor, trailing light,
Moves over still Shalott.

His broad clear brow in sunlight glow'd;
On burnish'd hooves his war-horse trode;
From underneath his helmet flowed
His coal-black curls as on he rode,
As he rode down to Camelot.
From the bank and from the river
He flash'd into the crystal mirror,
"Tirra lirra," by the river
Sang Sir Lancelot.

She left the web, she left the loom,
She made three paces thro' the room,
She saw the water-lily bloom,
She saw the helmet and the plume,
She look'd down to Camelot.
Out flew the web and floated wide;
The mirror crack'd from side to side;
"The curse is come upon me," cried
The Lady of Shalott.

PART IV

In the stormy east-wind straining,
The pale yellow woods were waning,
The broad stream in his banks complaining,
Heavily the low sky raining
Over tower'd Camelot;
Down she came and found a boat
Beneath a willow left afloat,
And round about the prow she wrote
The Lady of Shalott.

And down the river's dim expanse—
Like some bold seër in a trance,
Seeing all his own mischance—
With a glassy countenance
Did she look to Camelot.
And at the closing of the day
She loosed the chain, and down she lay;
The broad stream bore her far away,
The Lady of Shalott.

Lying, robed in snowy white
That loosely flew to left and right—
The leaves upon her falling light—
Thro' the noises of the night
She floated down to Camelot:

And as the boat-head wound along
The willowy hills and fields among,
They heard her singing her last song,
        The Lady of Shalott.

Heard a carol, mournful, holy,
Chanted loudly, chanted lowly,
Till her blood was frozen slowly,
And her eyes were darken'd wholly,
        Turn'd to tower'd Camelot;
For ere she reach'd upon the tide
The first house by the water-side,
Singing in her song she died,
        The Lady of Shalott.

Under tower and balcony,
By garden-wall and gallery,
A gleaming shape she floated by,
A corse between the houses high,
        Silent into Camelot.
Out upon the wharfs they came,
Knight and burgher, lord and dame,
And round the prow they read her name,
        The Lady of Shalott.

Who is this? and what is here?
And in the lighted palace near
Died the sound of royal cheer;
And they cross'd themselves for fear,
        All the knights at Camelot;
But Lancelot mused a little space;
He said, "She has a lovely face;
God in his mercy lend her grace,
        The Lady of Shalott."

TENNYSON

CCCXLII

SONG

I

A spirit haunts the year's last hours
Dwelling amid these yellowing bowers:
        To himself he talks;
For at eventide, listening earnestly,
At his work you may hear him sob and sigh
        In the walks;
        Earthward he boweth the heavy stalks

Of the mouldering flowers:
Heavily hangs the broad sunflower
Over its grave i' the earth so chilly;
Heavily hangs the hollyhock,
Heavily hangs the tigerlily.

II

The air is damp, and hushed, and close,
As a sick man's room when he taketh repose
An hour before death;
My very heart faints and my whole soul grieves
At the moist rich smell of the rotting leaves,
And the breath
Of the fading edges of box beneath,
And the year's last rose.
Heavily hangs the broad sunflower
Over its grave i' the earth so chilly;
Heavily hangs the hollyhock,
Heavily hangs the tigerlily.

TENNYSON

CCCXLIII A FAREWELL

Flow down, cold rivulet, to the sea
Thy tribute wave deliver:
No more by thee my steps shall be,
For ever and for ever.

Flow, softly flow, by lawn and lea,
A rivulet then a river:
No where by thee my steps shall be,
For ever and for ever.

But here will sigh thine alder tree,
And here thine aspen shiver;
And here by thee will hum the bee,
For ever and for ever.

A thousand suns will stream on thee,
A thousand moons will quiver;
But not by thee my steps shall be,
For ever and for ever.

TENNYSON

CCCXLIV THE LOTOS-EATERS

I

"Courage!" he said, and pointed toward the land,
"This mounting wave will roll us shoreward soon."
In the afternoon they came unto a land,
In which it seemed always afternoon.
All round the coast the languid air did swoon,
Breathing like one that hath a weary dream.
Full-faced above the valley stood the moon;
And like a downward smoke, the slender stream
Along the cliff to fall and pause and fall did seem.

II

A land of streams! some, like a downward smoke,
Slow-dropping veils of thinnest lawn, did go;
And some thro' wavering lights and shadows broke,
Rolling a slumbrous sheet of foam below.
They saw the gleaming river seaward flow
From the inner land: far off, three mountain-tops,
Three silent pinnacles of aged snow,
Stood sunset-flushed: and, dew'd with showery drops,
Up-clomb the shadowy pine above the woven copse.

III

The charmed sunset lingered low adown
In the red West: thro' mountain clefts the dale
Was seen far inland, and the yellow down
Bordered with palm, and many a winding vale
And meadow, set with slender galingale;
A land where all things always seemed the same!
And round about the keel with faces pale,
Dark faces pale against that rosy flame,
The mild-eyed melancholy Lotos-eaters came.

IV

Branches they bore of that enchanted stem,
Laden with flower and fruit, whereof they gave
To each, but whoso did receive of them,
And taste, to him the gushing of the wave
Far, far away did seem to mourn and rave
On alien shores; and if his fellow spake,
His voice was thin, as voices from the grave;
And deep-asleep he seem'd, yet all awake,
And music in his ears his beating heart did make.

V

They sat them down upon the yellow sand,
Between the sun and moon upon the shore;
And sweet it was to dream of Father-land,
Of child, and wife, and slave; but evermore
Most weary seem'd the sea, weary the oar,
Weary the wandering fields of barren foam.
Then some one said, "We will return no more";
And all at once they sang, "Our island home
Is far beyond the wave; we will no longer roam."

TENNYSON

CCCXLV

NOW SLEEPS THE CRIMSON PETAL

I.

"Now sleeps the crimson petal, now the white;
Nor waves the cypress in the palace walk;
Nor winks the gold fin in the porphyry font:
The firefly wakens: waken thou with me.

"Now droops the milkwhite peacock like a ghost,
And like a ghost she glimmers on to me.

"Now lies the Earth all Danaë to the stars,
And all thy heart lies open unto me.

"Now slides the silent meteor on, and leaves
A shining furrow, as thy thoughts in me.

"Now folds the lily all her sweetness up,
And slips into the bosom of the lake:
So fold thyself, my dearest, thou, and slip
Into my bosom and be lost in me."

II

"Come down, O maid, from yonder mountain height:
What pleasure lives in height (the shepherd sang),
In height and cold, the splendour of the hills?
But cease to move so near the Heavens, and cease
To glide a sunbeam by the blasted Pine,
To sit a star upon the sparkling spire;
And come, for Love is of the valley, come,
For Love is of the valley, come thou down

And find him; by the happy threshold, he,
Or hand in hand with Plenty in the maize,
Or red with spirted purple of the vats,
Or foxlike in the vine; nor cares to walk
With Death and Morning on the silver horns,
Nor wilt thou snare him in the white ravine,
Nor find him dropt upon the firths of ice,
That huddling slant in furrow-cloven falls
To roll the torrent out of dusky doors:
But follow; let the torrent dance thee down
To find him in the valley; let the wild
Lean-headed Eagles yelp alone, and leave
The monstrous ledges there to slope, and spill
Their thousand wreaths of dangling water-smoke,
That like a broken purpose waste in air:
So waste not thou; but come; for all the vales
Await thee; azure pillars of the hearth
Arise to thee; the children call, and I
Thy shepherd pipe, and sweet is every sound,
Sweeter thy voice, but every sound is sweet;
Myriads of rivulets hurrying thro' the lawn,
The moan of doves in immemorial elms,
And murmuring of innumerable bees."

TENNYSON

CCCXLVI O LET THE SOLID GROUND

I

O let the solid ground
Not fail beneath my feet
Before my life has found
What some have found so sweet;
Then let come what come may,
What matter if I go mad
I shall have had my day.

2

Let the sweet heavens endure,
Not close and darken above me
Before I am quite quite sure
That there is one to love me;
Then let come what come may
To a life that has been so sad,
I shall have had my day.

TENNYSON

CCCXLVII GO NOT, HAPPY DAY

Go not, happy day,
  From the shining fields,
Go not, happy day,
  Till the maiden yields.
Rosy is the West,
  Rosy is the South,
Roses are her cheeks,
  And a rose her mouth.
When the happy Yes
  Falters from her lips,
Pass and blush the news
  O'er the blowing ships;
Over blowing seas,
  Over seas at rest,
Pass the happy news,
  Blush it thro' the West;
Till the red man dance
  By his red cedar-tree,
And the red man's babe
  Leap, beyond the sea.
Blush from West to East,
  Blush from East to West
Till the West is East,
  Blush it thro' the West.
Rosy is the West,
  Rosy is the South,
Roses are her cheeks,
  And a rose her mouth.

TENNYSON

CCCXLVIII CAVALIER TUNES

I. MARCHING ALONG

I

Kentish Sir Byng stood for his King,
Bidding the crop-headed Parliament swing:
And, pressing a troop unable to stoop
And see the rogues flourish and honest folk droop,
    March them along, fifty-score strong,
    Great-hearted gentlemen, singing this song.

II

God for King Charles! Pym and such carles
To the Devil that prompts 'em their treasonous parles!
Cavaliers up! Lips from the cup,
Hands from the pasty, nor bite take nor sup
Till you're—

Chorus.

Marching along, fifty-score strong,
Great-hearted gentlemen, singing this song.

III

Hampden to hell, and his obsequies' knell
Serve Hazelrig, Fiennes, and young Harry as well!
England, good cheer! Rupert is near!
Kentish and loyalists, keep we not here?

Chorus.

Marching along, fifty-score strong,
Great-hearted gentlemen, singing this song!

IV

Then, God for King Charles! Pym and his snarls
To the Devil that pricks on such pestilent carles!
Hold by the right, you double your might;
So, onward to Nottingham, fresh for the fight.

Chorus.

March we along, fifty-score strong,
Great-hearted gentlemen, singing this song!

ROBERT BROWNING

CCCXLIX IL BOOT AND SADDLE

I

Boot, saddle, to horse, and away!
Rescue my castle before the hot day
Brightens to blue from its silvery grey,

Chorus.

"Boot, saddle, to horse, and away!"

II

Ride past the suburbs, asleep as you'd say;
Many's the friend there, will listen and pray
"God's luck to gallants that strike up the lay—

Chorus.

"Boot, saddle, to horse, and away!"

III

Forty miles off, like a roebuck at bay,
Flouts Castle Brancepath the Roundheads array:
Who laughs, "Good fellows ere this, by my fay,
Chorus.
"Boot, saddle, to horse, and away!"

IV

Who? My wife Gertrude; that, honest and gay,
Laughs when you talk of surrendering, "Nay!
I've better counsellors; what counsel they?"
Chorus.
"Boot, saddle, to horse, and away!"

ROBERT BROWNING

CCCL "HOW THEY BROUGHT THE GOOD NEWS FROM GHENT TO AIX"

I

I sprang to the stirrup, and Joris, and he;
I galloped, Dirck galloped, we galloped all three;
"Good speed!" cried the watch, as the gate-bolts undrew;
"Speed!" echoed the wall to us galloping through;
Behind shut the postern, the lights sank to rest,
And into the midnight we galloped abreast.

II

Not a word to each other; we kept the great pace
Neck by neck, stride by stride, never changing our place
I turned in my saddle and made its girths tight,
Then shortened each stirrup, and set the pique right,
Rebuckled the cheek-strap, chained slacker the bit,
Nor galloped less steadily Roland a whit.

III

'Twas moonset at starting; but while we drew near
Lokeren, the cocks crew and twilight dawned clear;
At Boom, a great yellow star came out to see;
At Düffeld, 'twas morning as plain as could be;
And from Mecheln church-steeple we heard the half-chime,
So, Joris broke silence with, "Yet there is time!"

IV

At Aershot, up leaped of a sudden the sun,
And against him the cattle stood black every one,

To stare thro' the mist at us galloping past,
And I saw my stout galloper Roland at last
With resolute shoulders, each butting away
The haze, as some bluff river headland its spray:

V

And his low head and crest, just one sharp ear bent back
For my voice, and the other pricked out on his track;
And one eye's black intelligence,—ever that glance
O'er its white edge at me, his own master, askance!
And the thick heavy spume-flakes which aye and anon
His fierce lips shook upwards in galloping on.

VI

By Hasselt, Dirck groaned; and cried Joris, "Stay spur!
Your Roos galloped bravely, the fault's not in her,
We'll remember at Aix"—for one heard the quick wheeze
Of her chest, saw the stretched neck and staggering knees,
And sunk tail, and horrible heave of the flank,
As down on her haunches she shuddered and sank.

VII

So, we were left galloping, Joris and I,
Past Looz and past Tongres, no cloud in the sky;
The broad sun above laughed a pitiless laugh,
'Neath our feet broke the brittle bright stubble like chaff;
Till over by Dalhem a dome-spire sprang white,
And "Gallop," gasped Joris, "for Aix is in sight!"

VIII

"How they'll greet us!"—and all in a moment his roan
Rolled neck and croup over, lay dead as a stone;
And there was my Roland to bear the whole weight
Of the news which alone could save Aix from her fate,
With his nostrils like pits full of blood to the brim,
And with circles of red for his eye-socket's rim.

IX

Then I cast loose my buffcoat, each holster let fall,
Shook off both my jack-boots, let go belt and all,
Stood up in the stirrup, leaned, patted his ear,
Called my Roland his pet-name, my horse without peer;
Clapped my hands, laughed and sang, any noise, bad or good,
Till at length into Aix Roland galloped and stood.

X

And all I remember is—friends flocking round
As I sat with his head 'twixt my knees on the ground;
And no voice but was praising this Roland of mine,
As I poured down his throat our last measure of wine,
Which (the burgesses voted by common consent)
Was no more than his due who brought good news from
Ghent.

ROBERT BROWNING

CCCLI EARTH'S IMMORTALITIES

I

FAME

See, as the prettiest graves will do in time,
Our poet's wants the freshness of its prime;
Spite of the sexton's browsing horse, the sods
Have struggled thro' its binding osier rods;
Headstone and half-sunk footstone lean awry,
Wanting the brick-work promised by and by;
How the minute grey lichens, plate o'er plate,
Have softened down the crisp-cut name and date!

II

CCCLII LOVE

So, the year's done with,
(*Love me for ever!*)
All March begun with,
April's endeavour;
May-wreaths that bound me
June needs must sever;
Now snows fall round me,
Quenching June's fever—
(*Love me for ever!*)

BROWNING

CCCLIII MERTOUN'S SONG

I

There's a woman like a dew-drop, she's so purer than the
purest;
And her noble heart's the noblest, yes, and her sure faith's the
surest:

And her eyes are dark and humid, like the depth on depth of lustre
Hid i' the harebell, while her tresses, sunnier than the wild-grape cluster,
Gush in golden-tinted plenty down her neck's rose-misted marble:
Then her voice's music . . . call it the well's bubbling, the bird's warble!

II

And this woman says, "My days were sunless and my nights were moonless,
Parched the pleasant April herbage, and the lark's heart's outbreak tuneless,
If you loved me not!" And I who—(ah, for words of flame!) adore her,
Who am mad to lay my spirit prostrate palpably before her—
I may enter at her portal soon, as now her lattice takes me,
And by noontide as by midnight make her mine, as hers she makes me!

BROWNING

CCCLIV HOME THOUGHTS, FROM ABROAD

I

Oh, to be in England
Now that April's there,
And whoever wakes in England
Sees, some morning, unaware,
That the lowest boughs and the brushwood sheaf
Round the elm-tree bole are in tiny leaf,
While the chaffinch sings on the orchard bough
In England—now!

II

And after April, when May follows,
And the whitethroat builds, and all the swallows!
Hark, where my blossomed pear-tree in the hedge
Leans to the field and scatters on the clover
  Blossoms and dewdrops—at the bent spray's edge—
That's the wise thrush; he sings each song twice over,
Lest you should think he never could recapture
The first fine careless rapture!

BROWNING

CCCLV EVELYN HOPE

I

Beautiful Evelyn Hope is dead!
  Sit and watch by her side an hour.
That is her book-shelf, this her bed;
  She plucked that piece of geranium-flower,
Beginning to die too, in the glass;
  Little has yet been changed, I think:
The shutters are shut, no light may pass
  Save two long rays through the hinge's chink.

II

Sixteen years old when she died!
  Perhaps she had scarcely heard my name;
It was not her time to love; beside,
  Her life had many a hope and aim,
Duties enough and little cares,
  And now was quiet, now astir,
Till God's hand beckoned unawares,—
  And the sweet white brow is all of her.

III

Is it too late then, Evelyn Hope?
  What, your soul was pure and true,
The good stars met in your horoscope,
  Made you of spirit, fire and dew—
And, just because I was thrice as old
  And our paths in the world diverged so wide,
Each was nought to each, must I be told?
  We were fellow mortals, nought beside?

IV

No, indeed! for God above
  Is great to grant, as mighty to make,
And creates the love to reward the love:
  I claim you still, for my own love's sake!
Delayed it may be for more lives yet,
  Through worlds I shall traverse, not a few:
Much is to learn, much to forget
  Ere the time be come for taking you.

V

But the time will come,—at last it will,
  When, Evelyn Hope, what meant, I shall say,

In the lower earth, in the years long still,
  That body and soul so pure and gay?
Why your hair was amber, I shall divine,
  And your mouth of your own geranium's red—
And what you would do with me, in fine,
  In the new life come in the old one's stead.

VI

I have lived, I shall say, so much since then,
  Given up myself so many times,
Gained me the gains of various men,
  Ransacked the ages, spoiled the climes;
Yet one thing, one, in my soul's full scope,
  Either I missed or itself missed me:
And I want and find you, Evelyn Hope!
  What is the issue? let us see!

VII

I loved you, Evelyn, all the while.
  My heart seemed full as it could hold?

smile,

  And the red young m
So hush,—I will give you this leaf to keep:
  See, I shut it inside the sweet cold hand!
There, that is our secret: go to sleep!
  You will wake, and remember, and understand.

BROWNING

CCCLVI A MUSICAL INSTRUMENT

What was he doing, the great god Pan,
  Down in the reeds by the river?
Spreading ruin and scattering ban,
Splashing and paddling with hoofs of a goat,
And breaking the golden lilies afloat
  With the dragon-fly on the river.

He tore out a reed, the great god Pan,
  From the deep cool bed of the river;
The limpid water turbidly ran,
And the broken lilies a-dying lay,
And the dragon-fly had fled away,
  Ere he brought it out of the river.

High on the shore sate the great god Pan,
  While turbidly flowed the river;

And hacked and hewed as a great god can,
With his hard bleak steel at the patient reed,
Till there was not a sign of a leaf indeed
  To prove it fresh from the river.

He cut it short, did the great god Pan,
  (How tall it stood in the river!)
Then drew the pith, like the heart of a man,
  Steadily from the outside ring,
And notched the poor dry empty thing
  In holes, as he sate by the river.

"This is the way," laughed the great god Pan,
  (Laughed while he sate by the river),
"The only way, since gods began
To make sweet music, they could succeed."
Then, dropping his mouth to a hole in the reed,
  He blew in power by the river.

Sweet, sweet, sweet, O Pan!
  Piercing sweet by the river!
Blinding sweet, O great god Pan!
The sun on the hill forgot to die,
And the lilies revived, and the dragon-fly
  Came back to dream on the river.

Yet half a beast is the great god Pan,
  To laugh as he sits by the river,
Making a poet out of a man:
The true gods sigh for the cost and pain,—
For the reed which grows nevermore again
  As a reed with the reeds in the river.

ELIZABETH BARRETT BROWNING

CCCLVII DEATH AND LOVE

Unlike are we, unlike, O princely Heart!
  Unlike our uses and our destinies.
  Our minist'ring two angels look surprise
On one another, as they strike athwart
Their wings in passing. Thou, bethink thee, art
  A guest for queens to social pageantries,
  With gages from a hundred brighter eyes
Than tears even can make mine, to play thy part
Of chief musician. What hast thou to do
  With looking from the lattice-lights at me—

A poor, tired, wandering singer, singing through
  The dark, and leaning up a cypress tree?
The chrism is on thine head—on mine the dew—
  And Death must dig the level where these agree.

ELIZABETH BARRETT BROWNING

CCCLVIII THE GIFT

What can I give thee back, O liberal
  And princely giver, who has brought the gold
  And purple of thine heart, unstained, untold,
And laid them on the outside of the wall
For such as I to take or leave withal,
  In unexpected largesse? Am I cold,
  Ungrateful, that for these most manifold
High gifts, I render nothing back at all?
Not so; not cold,—but very poor instead.
  Ask God who knows. For frequent tears have run
The colours from my life, and left so dead
  And pale a stuff, it were not fitly done
To give the same as pillow to thy head.
  Go farther! let it serve to trample on.

ELIZABETH BARRETT BROWNING

CCCLIX THE CRY OF THE CHILDREN

Do ye hear the children weeping, O my brothers,
    Ere the sorrow comes with years?
They are leaning their young heads against their mothers,—
    And *that* cannot stop their tears.
The young lambs are bleating in the meadows;
  The young birds are chirping in the nest;
The young fawns are playing with the shadows;
  The young flowers are blowing toward the west—
But the young, young children, O my brothers,
    They are weeping bitterly!—
They are weeping in the playtime of the others,
    In the country of the free.

Do you question the young children in the sorrow,
    Why their tears are falling so?—
The old man may weep for his to-morrow
    Which is lost in Long Ago—

The old tree is leafless in the forest—
  The old year is ending in the frost—
The old wound, if stricken, is the sorest—
  The old hope is hardest to be lost:
But the young, young children, O my brothers,
    Do you ask them why they stand
Weeping sore before the bosoms of their mothers,
    In our happy Fatherland?

They look up with their pale and sunken faces,
    And their looks are sad to see,
For the man's grief abhorrent, draws and presses
    Down the cheeks of infancy—
"Your old earth," they say, "is very dreary";
  "Our young feet," they say, "are very weak!
Few paces have we taken, yet are weary—
  Our grave-rest is very far to seek.
Ask the old why they weep, and not the children,
    For the outside earth is cold,—
And we young ones stand without, in our bewildering,
    And the graves are for the old."

"True," say the young children, "it may happen
    That we die before our time.
Little Alice died last year—the grave is shapen
    Like a snowball in the rime.
We look'd into the pit prepared to take her—
  Was no room for any work in the close clay;
From the sleep wherein she lieth none will wake her,
  Crying, 'Get up, little Alice! it is day.'
If you listen by that grave, in sun and shower,
  With your ear down, little Alice never cries!—
Could we see her face, be sure we should not know her,
  For the smile has time for growing in her eyes,—
And merry go her moments, lull'd and still'd in
    The shroud, by the kirk-chime!
It is good when it happens," say the children,
    "That we die before our time."

"For oh," say the children, "we are weary,
    And we cannot run or leap—
If we cared for any meadows, it were merely
    To drop down in them and sleep.
Our knees tremble sorely in the stooping—
  We fall upon our faces, trying to go;

And, underneath our heavy eyelids drooping,
  The reddest flower would look as pale as snow.
For, all day, we drag our burden tiring,
    Through the coal-dark, underground—
Or, all day, we drive the wheels of iron
    In the factories, round and round.

"For, all day, the wheels are droning, turning,—
    Their wind comes in our faces,—
Till our hearts turn,—our head, with pulses burning,
    And the walls turn in their places—
Turns the sky in the high window blank and reeling—
  Turns the long light that droppeth down the wall—
Turn the black flies that crawl along the ceiling—
  All are turning, all the day, and we with all.—
And all day the iron wheels are droning;
    And sometimes we could pray,
'O ye wheels,' (breaking out in a mad moaning)
    'Stop! be silent for to-day!'"

Now tell the poor young children, O my brothers,
    To look up to Him and pray—
So the blessèd One, who blesseth all the others,
    Will bless them another day.
They answer, "Who is God that He should hear us,
  While the rushing of the iron wheels is stirr'd?
When we sob aloud, the human creatures near us
  Pass by, hearing not, or answer not a word!
And *we* hear not (for the wheels in their resounding)
    Strangers speaking at the door:
Is it likely God, with angels singing round Him,
    Hears our weeping any more?

"But, no!" say the children, weeping faster,
    "He is speechless as a stone;
And they tell us, of His image is the master
    Who commands us to work on.
Go to!" say the children,—"Up in Heaven,
  Dark, wheel-like, turning clouds are all we find.
Do not mock us; grief has made us unbelieving—
  We look up for God, but tears have made us blind."
Do you hear the children weeping and disproving,
    O my brothers, what ye preach?
For God's possible is taught by His world's loving—
    And the children doubt of each.

They look up, with their pale and sunken faces,
And their look is dread to see,
For they mind you of their angels in their places,
With eyes meant for Deity;—
"How long," they say, "how long, O cruel nation,
Will you stand, to move the world, on a child's heart,—
Stifle down with a mail'd heel its palpitation,
And tread onward to your throne amid the mart?
Our blood splashes upward, O our tyrants,
And your purple shows your path;
But the child's sob curseth deeper in the silence
Than the strong man in his wrath!"

ELIZABETH BARRETT BROWNING

CCCLX A DEAD ROSE

O Rose! who dares to name thee?
No longer roseate now, nor soft, nor sweet;
But pale, and hard, and dry, as stubble-wheat,—
Kept seven years in a drawer—thy titles shame thee.

The breeze that used to blow thee
Between the hedge-row thorns, and take away
An odour up the lane to last all day,—
If breathing now,—unsweeten'd would forgo thee.

The sun that used to smite thee,
And mix his glory in thy gorgeous urn,
Till beam appear'd to bloom, and flower to burn,—
If shining now,—with not a hue would light thee.

The dew that used to wet thee,
And, white first, grow incarnadined, because
It lay upon thee where the crimson was,—
If dropping now,—would darken where it met thee.

The fly that lit upon thee,
To stretch the tendrils of its tiny feet,
Along thy leaf's pure edges, after heat,—
If lighting now,—would coldly overrun thee.

The bee that once did suck thee,
And build thy perfumed ambers up his hive,
And swoon in thee for joy, till scarce alive,—
If passing now,—would blindly overlook thee.

The heart doth recognize thee,
Alone, alone! The heart doth smell thee sweet,
Doth view thee fair, doth judge thee most complete—
Though seeing now those changes that disguise thee.

ELIZABETH BARRETT BROWNING

CCCLXI GRIEF

I tell you, hopeless grief is passionless;
That only men incredulous of despair,
Half-taught in anguish, through the midnight air
Beat upward to God's throne in loud access
Of shrieking and reproach. Full desertness
In souls as countries lieth silent-bare
Under the blanching, vertical eye-glare
Of the absolute Heavens. Deep-hearted man, express
Grief for thy Dead in silence like to death—
Most like a monumental statue set
In everlasting watch and moveless woe
Till itself crumble to the dust beneath.
Touch it; the marble eyelids are not wet:
If it could weep, it could arise and go.

ELIZABETH BARRETT BROWNING

CCCLXII THE PRISONER

Still let my tyrants know, I am not doom'd to wear
Year after year in gloom and desolate despair;
A messenger of Hope comes every night to me,
And offers for short life, eternal liberty.

He comes with Western winds, with evening's wandering airs,
With that clear dusk of heaven that brings the thickest stars:
Winds take a pensive tone, and stars a tender fire,
And visions rise, and change, that kill me with desire.

Desire for nothing known in my maturer years,
When Joy grew mad with awe, at counting future tears:
When, if my spirit's sky was full of flashes warm,
I knew not whence they came, from sun or thunder-storm.

But first, a hush of peace—a soundless calm descends;
The struggle of distress and fierce impatience ends.
Mute music soothes my breast—unutter'd harmony
That I could never dream, till Earth was lost to me.

Then dawns the Invisible; the Unseen its truth reveals;
My outward sense is gone, my inward essence feels;
Its wings are almost free—its home, its harbour found,
Measuring the gulf, it stoops, and dares the final bound.

O dreadful is the check—intense the agony—
When the ear begins to hear, and the eye begins to see;
When the pulse begins to throb—the brain to think again—
The soul to feel the flesh, and the flesh to feel the chain.

Yet I would lose no sting, would wish no torture less;
The more that anguish racks, the earlier it will bless;
And robed in fires of hell, or bright with heavenly shine,
If it but herald Death, the vision is divine.

EMILY BRONTË

CCCLXIII LAST LINES

No coward soul is mine,
No trembler in the world's storm-troubled sphere:
I see Heaven's glories shine,
And faith shines equal, arming me from fear.

O God within my breast,
Almighty, ever-present Deity!
Life—that in me has rest,
As I—undying Life—have power in Thee!

Vain are the thousand creeds
That move men's hearts: unutterably vain;
Worthless as wither'd weeds,
Or idlest froth amid the boundless main,

To waken doubt in one
Holding so fast by thine infinity;
So surely anchor'd on
The steadfast rock of immortality.

With wide-embracing love
Thy Spirit animates eternal years,
Pervades and broods above,
Changes, sustains, dissolves, creates, and rears.

Though earth and man were gone,
And suns and universes ceased to be,
And Thou were left alone,
Every existence would exist in Thee.

There is not room for Death,
Nor atom that his might could render void:
Thou—Thou art Being and Breath,
And what Thou art may never be destroy'd.

EMILY BRONTË

CCCLXIV DARK ROSALEEN

O my Dark Rosaleen,
Do not sigh, do not weep!
The priests are on the ocean green,
They march along the deep.
There's wine from the royal Pope,
Upon the ocean green;
And Spanish ale shall give you hope,
My dark Rosaleen!
My own Rosaleen!
Shall glad your heart, shall give you hope,
Shall give you health, and help, and hope,
My Dark Rosaleen!

Over hills, and thro' dales,
Have I roam'd for your sake;
All yesterday I sail'd with sails
On river and on lake.

I dash'd across unseen,
For there was lightning in my blood,
My Dark Rosaleen!
My own Rosaleen!
O, there was lightning in my blood,
Red lightning lighten'd thro' my blood,
My Dark Rosaleen!

All day long, in unrest,
To and fro do I move,
The very soul within my breast
Is wasted for you, love!
The heart in my bosom faints
To think of you, my Queen,
My life of life, my saint of saints,
My Dark Rosaleen!
My own Rosaleen!
To hear your sweet and sad complaints,
My life, my love, my saint of saints,
My Dark Rosaleen!

Woe and pain, pain and woe,
  Are my lot, night and noon,
To see your bright face clouded so,
  Like to the mournful moon.
But yet will I rear your throne
  Again in golden sheen;
'Tis you shall reign, shall reign alone,
  My Dark Rosaleen!
  My own Rosaleen!
'Tis you shall have the golden throne,
'Tis you shall reign, and reign alone,
  My Dark Rosaleen!

Over dews, over sands,
  Will I fly, for your weal:
Your holy delicate white hands
  Shall girdle me with steel.
At home, in your emerald bowers,
  From morning's dawn till e'en,
You'll pray for me, my flower of flowers,
  My Dark Rosaleen!
  My fond Rosaleen!
You'll think of me thro' daylight hours,
My virgin flower, my flower of flowers,
  My Dark Rosaleen!

I could scale the blue air,
  I could plough the high hills,
O, I could kneel all night in prayer,
  To heal your many ills!
And one beamy smile from you
  Would float like light between
My toils and me, my own, my true,
  My Dark Rosaleen!
  My fond Rosaleen!
Would give me life and soul anew,
A second life, a soul anew,
  My Dark Rosaleen!

O, the Erne shall run red,
  With redundance of blood,
The earth shall rock beneath our tread,
  And flames wrap hill and wood,
And gun-peal and slogan-cry
  Wake many a glen serene,

Ere you shall fade, ere you shall die,
  My Dark Rosaleen!
  My own Rosaleen!
The Judgement Hour must first be nigh,
Ere you can fade, ere you can die,
  My Dark Rosaleen!

JAMES CLARENCE MANGAN

CCCLXV GONE IN THE WIND

Solomon, where is thy throne? It is gone in the wind.
Babylon, where is thy might? It is gone in the wind.
Like the swift shadows of noon, like the dreams of the blind.
Vanish the glories and pomps of the earth in the wind.

Man, canst thou build upon aught in the pride of thy mind?
Wisdom will teach thee that nothing can tarry behind:
Tho' there be thousand bright actions embalm'd and enshrined;
Myriads and millions of brighter, are snow in the wind.

Solomon, where is thy throne? It is gone in the wind.
Babylon, where is thy might? It is gone in the wind.
All that the genius of man hath achieved or design'd
Waits but its hour to be dealt with as dust by the wind.

Say what is pleasure? A phantom, a mask undefined:
Science? An almond whereof we can pierce but the rind:
Honour and affluence? Firmans that Fortune hath sign'd,
Only to glitter and pass on the wings of the wind.

Solomon, where is thy throne? It is gone in the wind.
Babylon, where is thy might? It is gone in the wind.
Who is the fortunate? *He who in anguish hath pined.*
He shall rejoice when his relics are dust in the wind.

Mortal, be careful with what thy best hopes are entwined:
Woe to the miners for Truth, where the lampless have mined!
Woe to the seekers on earth for what none ever find!
They and their trust shall be scatter'd like leaves to the wind!

Solomon, where is thy throne? It is gone in the wind.
Babylon, where is thy might? It is gone in the wind.
Happy in death are they only whose hearts have consign'd
All earth's affections and longings and cares to the wind.

Pity thou, reader, the madness of poor humankind
Raving of knowledge—and Satan so busy to blind!

Raving of glory, like me; for the garlands I bind,
Garlands of song, are but gather'd—and strewn in the wind.

Solomon, where is thy throne? It is gone in the wind.
Babylon, where is thy might? It is gone in the wind.
I, Abul-Namez, must rest; for my fire is declined,
And I hear voices from Hades like bells on the wind.

JAMES CLARENCE MANGAN

CCCLXVI THE TRAVELLER'S GUIDE

Traverse not the globe for lore! The sternest
But the surest teacher is the heart;
Studying that and that alone, thou learnest
Best and soonest whence and what thou art.

Moor, Chinese, Egyptian, Russian, Roman.
Tread one common down-hill path of doom;
Everywhere the names are man and woman,
Everywhere the old sad sins find room.

Evil angels tempt us in all places.
What but sands or snows hath earth to give?
Dream not, friend, of deserts and oases;
But look inwards, and begin to live!

JAMES CLARENCE MANGAN

CCCLXVII THE FAIR HILLS OF IRELAND

A plenteous place is Ireland for hospitable cheer,
Uileacan dubh O!
Where the wholesome fruit is bursting from the yellow barley ear;
Uileacan dubh O!
There is honey in the trees where her misty vales expand,
And her forest paths in summer are by falling waters fann'd,
There is dew at high noontide there, and springs i' the yellow sand,
On the fair hills of holy Ireland.

Curl'd he is and ringleted, and plaited to the knee—
Uileacan dubh O!
Each captain who comes sailing across the Irish Sea;
Uileacan dubh O!
And I will make my journey, if life and health but stand,
Unto that pleasant country, that fresh and fragrant strand,

And leave your boasted braveries, your wealth and high command,
For the fair hills of holy Ireland.

Large and profitable are the stacks upon the ground,
Uileacan dubh O!
The butter and the cream do wondrously abound;
Uileacan dubh O!
The cresses on the water and the sorrels are at hand,
And the cuckoo's calling daily his note of music bland,
And the bold thrush sings so bravely his song i' the forests grand,
On the fair hills of holy Ireland.

SIR SAMUEL FERGUSON

CCCLXVIII CEAN DUBH DEELISH

Put your head, darling, darling, darling,
Your darling black head my heart above;
O mouth of honey, with thyme for fragrance,
Who, with heart in breast, could deny you love?

O many and many a young girl for me is pining,
Letting her locks of gold to the cold wind free;
For me, the foremost of our gay young fellows;
But I'd leave a hundred, pure love, for thee!

Then put your head, darling, darling, darling,
Your darling black head my heart above;
O mouth of honey, with thyme for fragrance,
Who, with heart in breast, could deny you love?

SIR SAMUEL FERGUSON

CCCLXIX THE UNREALISED IDEAL

I

My only Love is always near,—
In country or in town
I see her twinkling feet, I hear
The whisper of her gown.

II

She foots it ever fair and young,
Her locks are tied in haste,
And one is o'er her shoulder flung,
And hangs below her waist.

III

She ran before me in the meads;
And down this world-worn track
She leads me on; but while she leads
She never gazes back.

IV

And yet her voice is in my dreams,
To witch me more and more;
That wooing voice! Ah me, it seems
Less near me than of yore.

V

Lightly I sped when hope was high,
And youth beguiled the chase;
I follow—follow still; but I
Shall never see her Face.

FREDERICK LOCKER

CCCLXX THE SUN-GOD

I saw the master of the Sun. He stood
High in his luminous car, himself more bright;
An Archer of immeasurable might:
On his left shoulder hung his quivered load;
Spurned by his steeds the eastern mountains glowed;
Forward his eagle eye and brow of Light
He bent, and while both hands that arch embowed,
Shaft after shaft pursued the flying night.

No wings profaned that godlike form: around
His neck high-held an ever-moving crowd
Of locks hung glistening: while such perfect sound
Fell from his bowstring that th' ethereal dome
Thrill'd as a dew-drop; and each passing cloud
Expanded, whitening like the ocean foam.

AUBREY DE VERE

CCCLXXI THE ELEMENTS

Man is permitted much
To scan and learn
In Nature's frame;
Till he wellnigh can tame

Brute mischiefs, and can touch
Invisible things, and turn
All warring ills to purposes of good.
Thus, as a god below,
He can control
And harmonize what seems amiss to flow
As sever'd from the whole
And dimly understood.

But o'er the elements
One Hand alone,
One Hand hath sway.
What influence day by day
In straiter belt prevents
The impious Ocean thrown
Alternate o'er the ever-sounding shore?
Or who hath eye to trace
How the Plague came?
Fore-run the doublings of the Tempest's race?
Or the Air's weight and flame
On a set scale explore?

Thus God hath will'd
That Man, when fully skill'd,
Still gropes in twilight dim;
Encompass'd all his hours
By fearfull'st powers
Inflexible to him:
That so he may discern
His feebleness,
And e'en for Earth's success
To Him in wisdom turn,
Who holds for us the keys of either home,
—Earth, and the world to come.

Cardinal Newman

CCCLXXII THE FORSAKEN MERMAN

Come, dear children, let us away;
Down and away below.
Now my brothers call from the bay;
Now the great winds shorewards blow;
Now the salt tides seawards flow;

Now the wild white horses play,
Champ and chafe and toss in the spray.
Children dear, let us away.
This way, this way.

Call her once before you go.
Call once yet.
In a voice that she will know:
"Margaret! Margaret!"
Children's voices should be dear
(Call once more) to a mother's ear:
Children's voices, wild with pain
Surely she will come again.
Call her once and come away.
This way, this way.
"Mother dear, we cannot stay."
The wild white horses foam and fret:
Margaret! Margaret!

Come, dear children, come away down.
Call no more.
One last look at the white-wall'd town,
And the little grey church on the windy shore.
Then come down.
She will not come though you call all day.
Come away, come away.

Children dear, was it yesterday
We heard the sweet bells over the bay?
In the caverns where we lay,
Through the surf and through the swell
The far-off sound of a silver bell?
Sand-strewn caverns, cool and deep,
Where the winds are all asleep;
Where the spent lights quiver and gleam;
Where the salt weed sways in the stream;
Where the sea-beasts ranged all round
Feed in the ooze of their pasture-ground;
Where the sea-snakes coil and twine,
Dry their mail and bask in the brine;
Where great whales come sailing by,
Sail and sail, with unshut eye,
Round the world for ever and aye?
When did music come this way?
Children dear, was it yesterday?

Children dear, was it yesterday
(Call yet once) that she went away?
Once she sate with you and me,
On a red gold throne in the heart of the sea,
And the youngest sate on her knee.
She comb'd its bright hair, and she tended it well,
When down swung the sound of the far-off bell.
She sigh'd, she look'd up through the clear green sea.
She said: "I must go, for my kinsfolk pray
In the little grey church on the shore to-day.
'Twill be Easter-time in the world—ah me!
And I lose my poor soul, Merman, here with thee."
I said: "Go up, dear heart, through the waves.
Say thy prayer, and come back to the kind sea-caves."
She smiled, she went up through the surf in the bay.
Children dear, was it yesterday?

Children dear, were we long alone?
"The sea grows stormy, the little ones moan.
Long prayers," I said, "in the world they say.
Come," I said, and we rose through the surf in the bay.
We went up the beach, by the sandy down
Where the sea-stocks bloom, to the white-wall'd town.
Through the narrow paved streets, where all was still,
To the little grey church on the windy hill.
From the church came a murmur of folk at their prayers,
But we stood without in the cold blowing airs.
We climb'd on the graves, on the stones, worn with rains,
And we gazed up the aisle through the small leaded panes.
She sate by the pillar; we saw her clear:
"Margaret, hist! come quick, we are here.
Dear heart," I said, "we are long alone.
The sea grows stormy, the little ones moan."
But, ah, she gave me never a look,
For her eyes were seal'd to the holy book.
Loud prays the priest; shut stands the door.
Come away, children, call no more.
Come away, come down, call no more.

Down, down, down.
Down to the depths of the sea.
She sits at her wheel in the humming town,
Singing most joyfully.
Hark, what she sings: "O joy, O joy,

For the humming street, and the child with its toy.
For the priest, and the bell, and the holy well.
For the wheel where I spun,
And the blessed light of the sun."
And so she sings her fill,
Singing most joyfully,
Till the shuttle falls from her hand,
And the whizzing wheel stands still.
She steals to the window, and looks at the sand;
And over the sand at the sea;
And her eyes are set in a stare;
And anon there breaks a sigh,
And anon there drops a tear,
From a sorrow-clouded eye,
And a heart sorrow-laden,
A long, long sigh.
For the cold strange eyes of a little Mermaiden,
And the gleam of her golden hair.

Come away, away, children.
Come, children, come down.
The salt tide rolls seaward.
Lights shine in the town.
She will start from her slumber
When gusts shake the door;
She will hear the winds howling,
Will hear the waves roar.
We shall see, while above us
The waves roar and whirl,
A ceiling of amber,
A pavement of pearl.
Singing, "Here came a mortal,
But faithless was she.
And alone dwell for ever
The kings of the sea."

But, children, at midnight,
When soft the winds blow;
When clear falls the moonlight;
When spring-tides are low:
When sweet airs come seaward
From heaths starr'd with broom;
And high rocks throw mildly
On the blanch'd sands a gloom:

Up the still, glistening beaches,
Up the creeks we will hie;
Over banks of bright seaweed
The ebb-tide leaves dry.
We will gaze, from the sand-hills,
At the white, sleeping town;
At the church on the hill-side—
  And then come back down.
Singing, "There dwells a loved one,
But cruel is she.
She left lonely for ever
The kings of the sea."

CCCLXXIII PARTING

Ye storm-winds of Autumn!
Who rush by, who shake
The window, and ruffle
The gleam-lighted lake;
Who cross to the hill-side
Thin-sprinkled with farms,
Where the high woods strip sadly
Their yellowing arms—
Ye are bound for the mountains!
Ah! with you let me go
Where your cold, distant barrier,
The vast range of snow,
Through the loose clouds lifts dimly
Its white peaks in air—
How deep is their stillness!
Ah, would I were there!

But on the stairs what voice is this I hear,
Buoyant as morning, and as morning clear?
Say, has some wet bird-haunted English lawn
Lent it the music of its trees at dawn?
Or was it from some sun-fleck'd mountain-brook
That the sweet voice its upland clearness took?
  Ah! it comes nearer—
  Sweet notes, this way!

Hark! fast by the window
The rushing winds go,
To the ice-cumber'd gorges,
The vast seas of snow!

There the torrents drive upward
Their rock-strangled hum ;
There the avalanche thunders
The hoarse torrent dumb.
—I come, O ye mountains !
Ye torrents, I come !

But who is this, by the half-open'd door,
Whose figure casts a shadow on the floor ?
The sweet blue eyes—the soft, ash-colour'd hair—
The cheeks that still their gentle paleness wear—
The lovely lips, with their arch smile that tells
The unconquer'd joy in which her spirit dwells—
Ah ! they bend nearer—
Sweet lips, this way !

Hark ! The wind rushes past us !
Ah ! with that let me go
To the clear waning hill-side
Unspotted by snow,
There to watch, o'er the sunk vale,
The frore mountain-wall,
Where the niched snow-bed sprays down
Its powdery fall.
There its dusky blue clusters
The aconite spreads ;
There the pines slope, the cloud-strips
Hung soft in their heads.
No life but, at moments,
The mountain-bee's hum.
—I come, O ye mountains !
Ye pine-woods, I come !

ARNOLD

CCCLXXIV ISOLATION : TO MARGUERITE

Yes ! in the sea of life enisled,
With echoing straits between us thrown,
Dotting the shoreless watery wild,
We mortal millions live *alone*.
The islands feel the enclasping flow,
And then their endless bounds they know.

But when the moon their hollows lights,
And they are swept by balms of spring,

And in their glens, on starry nights,
The nightingales divinely sing;
And lovely notes, from shore to shore,
Across the sounds and channels pour—

Oh! then a longing like despair
Is to their farthest caverns sent;
For surely once, they feel, we were
Parts of a single continent!
Now round us spreads the watery plain—
Oh might our marges meet again!

Who order'd, that their longing's fire
Should be, as soon as kindled, cool'd?
Who renders vain their deep desire?—
A God, a God their severance ruled!
And bade betwixt their shores to be
The unplumb'd, salt, estranging sea.

ARNOLD

CCCLXXV REQUIESCAT

Strew on her roses, roses,
And never a spray of yew.
In quiet she reposes:
Ah! would that I did too.

Her mirth the world required:
She bathed it in smiles of glee.
But her heart was tired, tired,
And now they let her be.

Her life was turning, turning,
In mazes of heat and sound.
But for peace her soul was yearning,
And now peace laps her round.

Her cabin'd, ample Spirit,
It flutter'd and fail'd for breath.
To-night it doth inherit
The vasty Hall of Death.

ARNOLD

CCCLXXVI QUA CURSUM VENTUS

As ships, becalm'd at eve, that lay
With canvas drooping, side by side,
Two towers of sail at dawn of day
Are scarce, long leagues apart, descried;

When fell the night, upsprung the breeze,
  And all the darkling hours they plied,
Nor dreamt but each the self-same seas
  By each was cleaving, side by side:

E'en so—but why the tale reveal
  Of those, whom year by year unchanged,
Brief absence join'd anew to feel,
  Astounded, soul from soul estranged?

At dead of night their sails were fill'd,
  And onward each rejoicing steer'd—
Ah, neither blame, for neither will'd,
  Or wist, what first with dawn appear'd!

To veer, how vain! On, onward strain,
  Brave barks! In light, in darkness too,
Thro' winds and tides one compass guides,—
  To that, and your own selves, be true.

But O blithe breeze! and O great seas,
  Though ne'er, that earliest parting past,
On your wide plain they join again,
  Together lead them home at last.

One port, methought, alike they sought,
  One purpose hold where'er they fare,—
O bounding breeze, O rushing seas,
  At last, at last, unite them there!

ARTHUR HUGH CLOUGH

CCCLXXVII SAY NOT THE STRUGGLE NAUGHT AVAILETH

Say not the struggle naught availeth,
  The labour and the wounds are vain,
The enemy faints not, nor faileth,
  And as things have been they remain.

If hopes were dupes, fears may be liars;
  It may be, in yon smoke conceal'd,
Your comrades chase e'en now the fliers,
  And, but for you, possess the field.

For while the tired waves, vainly breaking,
  Seem here no painful inch to gain,
Far back, through creeks and inlets making,
  Comes silent, flooding in, the main.

And not by eastern windows only,
  When daylight comes, comes in the light;
In front the sun climbs slow, how slowly!
  But westward, look the land is bright!

CLOUGH

CCCLXXVIII WHEN THE WORLD IS BURNING

When the world is burning,
Fired within, yet turning
  Round with face unscathed;
Ere fierce flames, uprushing.
O'er all lands leap, crushing,
  Till earth fall, fire-swathed;
Up amidst the meadows,
Gently through the shadows,
  Gentle flames will glide,
Small, and blue, and golden.
Though by bard beholden,
When in calm dreams folden,—
  Calm his dreams will bide.

Where the dance is sweeping,
Through the greensward peeping,
  Shall the soft lights start;
Laughing maids, unstaying,
Deeming it trick-playing,
High their robes upswaying,
  O'er the lights shall dart;
And the woodland haunter,
Shall not cease to saunter
  When, far down some glade,
Of the great world's burning,
One soft flame upturning
Seems, to his discerning,
  Crocus in the shade.

EBENEZER JONES

CCCLXXIX THE YEAR

The crocus, while the days are dark,
  Unfolds its saffron sheen;
At April's touch, the crudest bark
  Discovers gems of green.

Then sleep the seasons, full of might;
  While slowly swells the pod
And rounds the peach, and in the night
  The mushroom bursts the sod.

The winter falls; the frozen rut
  Is bound with silver bars;
The snow-drift heaps against the hut;
  And night is pierc'd with stars.

COVENTRY PATMORE

CCCLXXX TAMERTON CHURCH-TOWER

In love with home, I rove tired eyed
  The rainy North; but there
The distant hill-top in its pride,
  Adorn'd the brilliant air;

And as I passed from Tavistock,
  The scatter'd dwellings white,
The church, the golden weather-cock
  Were whelm'd in hazy light;

Dark rocks shone forth with yellow brooms;
  And, over orchard walls,
Gleam'd congregated apple-blooms,
  In white and ruddy balls;

The children did the good sun greet,
  With song and senseless shout;
The lambs did skip, their dams did bleat,
  In Tavy leapt the trout;

Across the fleeting eastern cloud,
  The splendid rainbow sprang,
And larks, invisible and loud,
  Within its zenith sang.

PATMORE

CCCLXXXI THE LOVER

How strange a thing a lover seems
  To animals that do not love!
Lo, where he walks and talks in dreams,
  And flouts us with his Lady's glove;

How foreign is the garb he wears;
  And how his great devotion mocks
Our poor propriety, and scares
  The undevout with paradox!
His soul, through scorn of worldly care,
  And great extremes of sweet and gall,
And musing much on all that's fair,
  Grows witty and fantastical;
He sobs his joy and sings his grief,
  And evermore finds such delight
In simply picturing his relief,
  That 'plaining seems to cure his plight;
He makes his sorrow, when there's none;
  His fancy blows both cold and hot;
Next to the wish that she'll be won,
  His first hope is that she may not;
He sues, yet deprecates consent;
  Would she be captured she must fly;
She looks too happy and content,
  For whose least pleasure he would die;
O, cruelty, she cannot care
  For one to whom she's always kind!
He says he's nought, but, oh, despair,
  If he's not Jove to her fond mind!
He's jealous if she pets a dove,
  She must be his with all her soul;
Yet 'tis a postulate in love
  That part is greater than the whole;
And all his apprehension's stress,
  When he's with her, regards her hair,
Her hand, a ribbon of her dress,
  As if his life was only there;
Because she's constant, he will change,
  And kindest glances coldly meet,
And, all the time he seems so strange,
  His soul is fawning at her feet;
Of smiles and simple heaven grown tired,
  He wickedly provokes her tears,
And when she weeps, as he desired,
  Falls slain with ecstasies of fears;
He blames her, though she has no fault,
  Except the folly to be his;
He worships her, the more to exalt

The profanation of a kiss;
Health's his disease; he's never well
But when his paleness shames her rose;
His faith's a rock-built citadel,
Its sign a flag that each way blows;
His o'erfed fancy frets and fumes;
And Love, in him, is fierce, like Hate,
And ruffles his ambrosial plumes
Against the bars of time and fate.

PATMORE

CCCLXXXII AMANDA

She wearies with a want unknown;
In sleep she sobs, and seems to float,
A water-lily, all alone
Within a lonely castle-moat.

And, as the full-moon spectral, lies
Within the crescent's gleaming arms,
The Present shows her careless eyes
A future dim with vague alarms.

She sees, and yet she scarcely sees:
For, life-in-life not yet begun,
Too many are its mysteries
For thought to pause on any one.

PATMORE

CCCLXXXIII SPRING

'Twas when the spousal time of May
Hangs all the hedge with bridal wreaths,
And air's so sweet that bosom gay
Gives thanks for every breath it breathes,
When like to like is gladly moved,
And each thing joins in Spring's refrain,
"Let those love now who never loved;
Let those who have loved love again;"
That I, in whom the sweet time wrought,
Lay stretch'd within a lonely glade,
Abandon'd to delicious thought
Beneath the softly twinkling shade.
The leaves, all stirring, mimick'd well
A neighbouring rush of rivers cold,

And, as the sun or shadow fell,
  So these were green and those were gold;
In dim recesses hyacinths droop'd,
  And breadths of primrose lit the air,
Which, wandering through the woodland, stoop'd
  And gather'd perfumes here and there;
Upon the spray the squirrel swung,
  And careless songsters, six or seven,
Sang lofty songs the leaves among
  Fit for their only listener, Heaven.

PATMORE

CCCLXXXIV A YOUNG FIR-WOOD

These little firs to-day are things
  To clasp into a giant's cap,
  Or fans to suit his lady's lap.
From many winters many springs
  Shall cherish them in strength and sap,
  Till they be marked upon the map,
A wood for the wind's wanderings.

All seed is in the sower's hands:
  And what at first was trained to spread
  Its shelter for some single head,—
Yea, even such fellowship of wands,—
  May hide the sunset, and the shade
  Of its great multitude be laid
Upon the earth and elder sands.

DANTE GABRIEL ROSSETTI

CCCLXXXV MY SISTER'S SLEEP

She fell asleep on Christmas Eve:
  At length the long-ungranted shade
  Of weary eyelids overweigh'd
The pain nought else might yet relieve.

Our mother, who had leaned all day
  Over the bed from chime to chime,
  Then raised herself for the first time,
And as she sat her down, did pray.

Her little work-table was spread
  With work to finish. For the glare
  Made by her candle, she had care
To work some distance from the bed.

Without, there was a cold moon up,
  Of winter radiance sheer and thin;
  The hollow halo it was in
Was like an icy crystal cup.

Through the small room, with subtle sound
  Of flame, by vents the fireshine drove
  And reddened. In its dim alcove
The mirror shed a clearness round.

I had been sitting up some nights,
  And my tired mind felt weak and blank;
  Like a sharp strengthening wine it drank
The stillness and the broken lights.

Twelve struck. That sound, by dwindling years
  Heard in each hour, crept off; and then
  The ruffled silence spread again,
Like water that a pebble stirs.

Our mother rose from where she sat:
  Her needles, as she laid them down,
  Met lightly, and her silken gown
Settled: no other noise than that.

"Glory unto the Newly-Born!"
  So, as said angels, she did say;
  Because we were in Christmas Day,
Though it would still be long till morn.

Just then in the room over us
  There was a pushing back of chairs,
  As some who had sat unawares
So late, now heard the hour, and rose.

With anxious softly-stepping haste
  Our mother went where Margaret lay,
  Fearing the sounds o'erheard—should they
Have broken her long watched-for rest!

She stooped an instant, calm, and turned;
  But suddenly turned back again;
  And all her features seemed in pain
With woe, and her eyes gazed and yearned.

For my part, I but hid my face,
  And held my breath, and spoke no word:
  There was none spoken; but I heard
The silence for a little space.

Our mother bowed herself and wept:
And both my arms fell, and I said,
"God knows I knew that she was dead."
And there, all white, my sister slept.

Then kneeling, upon Christmas morn
A little after twelve o'clock
We said, ere the first quarter struck,
"Christ's blessing on the newly born!"

D. G. ROSSETTI

CCCLXXXVI THE BLESSED DAMOZEL

The blessed damozel leaned out
From the gold bar of heaven;
Her eyes were deeper than the depth
Of waters stilled at even;
She had three lilies in her hand,
And the stars in her hair were seven.

Her robe, ungirt from clasp to hem,
No wrought flowers did adorn,
But a white rose of Mary's gift,
For service meetly worn;
Her hair that lay along her back
Was yellow like ripe corn.

Herseemed she scarce had been a day
One of God's choristers;
The wonder was not yet quite gone
From that still look of hers;
Albeit, to them she left, her day
Had counted as ten years.

(To one, it is ten years of years.
. . . Yet now, and in this place,
Surely she leaned o'er me—her hair
Fell all about my face. . . .
Nothing: the autumn fall of leaves.
The whole year sets apace.)

It was the rampart of God's house
That she was standing on;
By God built over the sheer depth
The which is space begun;
So high, that looking downward thence
She scarce could see the sun.

It lies in Heaven, across the flood
Of ether, as a bridge.
Beneath, the tides of day and night
With flame and darkness ridge
The void, as low as where this earth
Spins like a fretful midge.

Heard hardly, some of her new friends
Amid their loving games
Spoke evermore among themselves
Their virginal chaste names;
And the souls mounting up to God
Went by her like thin flames.

And still she bowed herself and stooped
Out of the circling charm;
Until her bosom must have made
The bar she leaned on warm;
And the lilies lay as if asleep
Along her bended arm.

From the fixed place of Heaven she saw
Time like a pulse shake fierce
Through all the worlds. Her gaze still strove
Within the gulf to pierce
Its path; and now she spoke as when
The stars sang in their spheres.

The sun was gone now; the curled moon
Was like a little feather
Fluttering far down the gulf; and now
She spoke through the still weather.
Her voice was like the voice the stars
Had when they sang together.

(Ah sweet! Even now, in that bird's song,
Strove not her accents there,
Fain to be hearkened? When those bells
Possessed the mid-day air,
Strove not her steps to reach my side
Down all the echoing stair?)

"I wish that he were come to me,
For he will come," she said.
"Have I not prayed in Heaven?—on earth,
Lord, Lord, has he not pray'd?

Are not two prayers a perfect strength?
  And shall I feel afraid?

"When round his head the aureole clings,
  And he is clothed in white,
I'll take his hand and go with him
  To the deep wells of light;
We will step down as to a stream,
  And bathe there in God's sight.

"We two will stand beside that shrine,
  Occult, withheld, untrod,
Whose lamps are stirred continually
  With prayer sent up to God;
And see our old prayers, granted, melt
  Each like a little cloud.

"We two will lie i' the shadow of
  That living mystic tree
Within whose secret growth the Dove
  Is sometimes felt to be,
While every leaf that His plumes touch
  Saith His Name audibly.

"And I myself will teach to him,
  I myself, lying so,
The songs I sing here; which his voice
  Shall pause in, hushed and slow,
And find some knowledge at each pause,
  Or some new thing to know."

(Alas! We two, we two, thou say'st!
  Yea, one wast thou with me
That once of old. But shall God lift
  To endless unity
The soul whose likeness with thy soul
  Was but its love for thee?)

"We two," she said, "will seek the groves
  Where the lady Mary is,
With her five handmaidens, whose names
  Are five sweet symphonies,
Cecily, Gertrude, Magdalen,
  Margaret and Rosalys.

"Circlewise sit they, with bound locks
  And foreheads garlanded;

Into the fine cloth white like flame
  Weaving the golden thread,
To fashion the birth-robes for them
  Who are just born, being dead.

"He shall fear, haply, and be dumb:
  Then will I lay my cheek
To his, and tell about our love,
  Not once abashed or weak:
And the dear Mother will approve
  My pride, and let me speak.

"Herself shall bring us, hand in hand,
  To Him round whom all souls
Kneel, the clear-ranged unnumbered heads
  Bowed with their aureoles:
And angels meeting us shall sing
  To their citherns and citoles.

"There will I ask of Christ the Lord
  Thus much for him and me:—
Only to live as once on earth
  With Love,—only to be,
As then awhile, for ever now
  Together, I and he."

She gazed and listened and then said,
  Less sad of speech than mild,—
"All this is when he comes." She ceased.
  The light thrilled towards her, fill'd
With angels in strong level flight.
  Her eyes prayed, and she smil'd.

(I saw her smile.) But soon their path
  Was vague in distant spheres:
And then she cast her arms along
  The golden barriers,
And laid her face between her hands,
  And wept. (I heard her tears.)

D. G. Rossetti

CCCLXXXVII SUDDEN LIGHT

I have been here before,
  But when or how I cannot tell:

I know the grass beyond the door,
The sweet keen smell,
The sighing sound, the lights around the shore.

You have been mine before,—
How long ago I may not know:
But just when at that swallow's soar
Your neck turned so,
Some veil did fall,—I knew it all of yore.

Then, now,—perchance again! . . .
O round mine eyes your tresses shake!
Shall we not lie as we have lain
Thus for Love's sake,
And sleep, and wake, yet never break the chain?

D. G. Rossetti

CCCLXXXVIII THE SEA-LIMITS

Consider the sea's listless chime:
Time's self it is, made audible,—
The murmur of the earth's own shell.
Secret continuance sublime
Is the sea's end: our sight may pass
No furlong further. Since time was,
This sound hath told the lapse of time.

No quiet, which is death's,—it hath
The mournfulness of ancient life,
Enduring always at dull strife.
As the world's heart of rest and wrath,
Its painful pulse is in the sands.
Last utterly, the whole sky stands,
Grey and not known, along its path.

Listen alone beside the sea,
Listen alone among the woods;
Those voices of twin solitudes
Shall have one sound alike to thee:
Hark where the murmurs of thronged men
Surge and sink back and surge again,—
Still the one voice of wave and tree.

Gather a shell from the strown beach
And listen at its lips: they sigh
The same desire and mystery,
The echo of the whole sea's speech.

And all mankind is thus at heart
Not anything but what thou art:
And Earth, Sea, Man, are all in each.

D. G. Rossetti

CCCLXXXIX A NEW YEAR'S BURDEN

Along the grass sweet airs are blown
Our way this day in Spring.
Of all the songs that we have known
Now which one shall we sing?
Not that, my love, ah no!—
Not this, my love? why, so!—
Yet both were ours, but hours will come and go.

The grove is all a pale frail mist,
The new year sucks the sun.
Of all the kisses that we kissed
Now which shall be the one?
Not that, my love, ah no!—
Not this, my love?—heigh-ho
For all the sweets that all the winds can blow!

The branches cross above our eyes,
The skies are in a net:
And what's the thing beneath the skies
We two would most forget?
Not birth, my love, no, no,—
Not death, my love, no, no,—
The love once ours, but ours long hours ago.

D. G. Rossetti

CCCXC AN OLD SONG ENDED

"*How should I your true love know*
From another one?"
"*By his cockle-hat and staff*
And his sandal shoon."

"And what signs have told you now
That he hastens home?"
"Lo! the spring is nearly gone,
He is nearly come."

"For a token is there nought,
Say, that he should bring?"
"He will bear a ring I gave
And another ring."

"How may I, when he shall ask,
Tell him who lies there?"
"Nay, but leave my face unveiled
And unbound my hair."

"Can you say to me some word
I shall say to him?"
"Say I'm looking in his eyes
Though my eyes are dim."

D. G. Rossetti

CCCXCI RIDING TOGETHER

For many, many days together
The wind blew steady from the East;
For many days hot grew the weather,
About the time of our Lady's Feast.

For many days we rode together,
Yet met we neither friend nor foe;
Hotter and clearer grew the weather,
Steadily did the East wind blow.

We saw the trees in the hot, bright weather,
Clear-cut, with shadows very black,
As freely we rode on together
With helms unlaced and bridles slack.

And often, as we rode together,
We, looking down the green-bank'd stream,
Saw flowers in the sunny weather,
And saw the bubble-making bream.

And in the night lay down together,
And hung above our heads the rood,
Or watch'd night-long in the dewy weather,
The while the moon did watch the wood.

Our spears stood bright and thick together,
Straight out the banners stream'd behind,
As we gallop'd on in the sunny weather,
With faces turn'd towards the wind.

Down sank our threescore spears together,
  As thick we saw the pagans ride;
His eager face in the clear fresh weather,
  Shone out that last time by my side.

Up the sweep of the bridge we dash'd together,
  It rock'd to the crash of the meeting spears,
Down rain'd the buds of the dear spring weather,
  The elm-tree flowers fell like tears.

There, as we roll'd and writhed together,
  I threw my arms above my head,
For close by my side, in the lovely weather,
  I saw him reel and fall back dead.

I and the slayer met together,
  He waited the death-stroke there in his place,
With thoughts of death in the lovely weather,
  Gapingly mazed at my madden'd face.

Madly I fought as we fought together;
  In vain: the little Christian band
The pagans drown'd, as in stormy weather,
  The river drowns low-lying land.

They bound my blood-stain'd hands together,
  They bound his corpse to nod by my side:
Then on we rode, in the bright March weather,
  With clash of cymbals did we ride.

We ride no more, no more together;
  My prison-bars are thick and strong,
I take no heed of any weather,
  The sweet Saints grant I live not long.

William Morris

CCCXCII THE EVE OF CRECY

Gold on her head, and gold on her feet,
And gold where the hems of her kirtle meet,
And a golden girdle round my sweet;—
    Ah! qu'elle est belle La Marguerite.

Margaret's maids are fair to see,
Freshly dress'd and pleasantly;
Margaret's hair falls down to her knee;—
    Ah! qu'elle est belle La Marguerite.

If I were rich I would kiss her feet,
I would kiss the place where the gold hems meet,
And the golden girdle round my sweet—
Ah! qu'elle est belle La Marguerite.

Ah me! I have never touch'd her hand;
When the arriere-ban goes through the land,
Six basnets under my pennon stand;—
Ah! qu'elle est belle La Marguerite.

And many a one grins under his hood:
"Sir Lambert de Bois, with all his men good,
Has neither food nor firewood;"—
Ah! qu'elle est belle La Marguerite.

If I were rich I would kiss her feet,
And the golden girdle of my sweet,
And thereabouts where the gold hems meet;—
Ah! qu'elle est belle La Marguerite.

Yet even now it is good to think,
While my few poor varlets grumble and drink
In my desolate hall, where the fires sink,—
Ah! qu'elle est belle La Marguerite.

Of Margaret sitting glorious there,
In glory of gold and glory of hair,
And glory of glorious face most fair;—
Ah! qu'elle est belle La Marguerite.

Likewise to-night I make good cheer,
Because this battle draweth near:
For what have I to lose or fear?
Ah! qu'elle est belle La Marguerite.

For, look you, my horse is good to prance
A right fair measure in this war-dance,
Before the eyes of Philip of France;—
Ah! qu'elle est belle La Marguerite.

And sometime it may hap, perdie,
While my new towers stand up three and three,
And my hall gets painted fair to see—
Ah! qu'elle est belle La Marguerite.

That folks may say: "Times change, by the rood,
For Lambert, banneret of the wood,
Has heaps of food and firewood;—
Ah! qu'elle est belle La Marguerite.

"And wonderful eyes, too, under the hood
Of a damsel of right noble blood:"
St. Ives, for Lambert of the wood!—
Ah! qu'elle est belle La Marguerite.

WILLIAM MORRIS

CCCXCIII SUMMER DAWN

Pray but one prayer for me 'twixt thy closed lips,
Think but one thought of me up in the stars,
The summer night waneth, the morning light slips,
Faint and grey 'twixt the leaves of the aspen, betwixt the cloud-bars,
That are patiently waiting there for the dawn:
Patient and colourless, though Heaven's gold
Waits to float through them along with the sun.
Far out in the meadows, above the young corn,
The heavy elms wait, and restless and cold
The uneasy wind rises; the roses are dun;
Through the long twilight they pray for the dawn,
Round the lone house in the midst of the corn.
Speak but one word to me over the corn,
Over the tender, bow'd locks of the corn.

WILLIAM MORRIS

CCCXCIV NEXT OF KIN

The shadows gather round me, while you are in the sun:
My day is almost ended, but yours is just begun:
The winds are singing to us both and the streams are singing still,
And they fill your heart with music, but mine they cannot fill.

Your home is built in sunlight, mine in another day:
Your home is close at hand, sweet friend, but mine is far away:
Your bark is in the haven where you fain would be:
I must launch out into the deep, across the unknown sea.

You, white as dove or lily or spirit of the light:
I, stain'd and cold and glad to hide in the cold dark night:
You, joy to many a loving heart and light to many eyes:
I, lonely in the knowledge earth is full of vanities.

Yet when your day is over, as mine is nearly done,
And when your race is finish'd, as mine is almost run,
You, like me, shall cross your hands and bow your graceful head:
Yea, we twain shall sleep together in an equal bed.

CHRISTINA G. ROSSETTI

CCCXCV PASSING AWAY

Passing away, saith the World, passing away:
Chances, beauty and youth sapped day by day:
Thy life never continueth in one stay.
Is the eye waxen dim, is the dark hair changing to grey
That hath won neither laurel nor bay?
I shall clothe myself in Spring and bud in May:
Thou, root-stricken, shalt not rebuild thy decay
On my bosom for aye.
Then I answered, Yea.

Passing away, saith my Soul, passing away:
With its burden of fear and hope, of labour and play;
Harken what the past doth witness and say:
Rust in thy gold, a moth is in thine array,
A canker is in thy bud, thy leaf must decay,
At midnight, at cockcrow, at morning, one certain day
Lo, the Bridegroom shall come and shall not delay;
Watch thou and pray.
Then I answered, Yea.

Passing away, saith my God, passing away:
Winter passeth after a long delay:
New grapes on the vine, new figs on the tender spray,
Turtle calleth turtle in Heaven's May.
Though I tarry wait for Me, trust Me, watch and pray,
Arise, come away, night is past and lo it is day,
My love, My sister, My spouse, thou shalt hear Me say.
Then I answered, Yea.

CHRISTINA G. ROSSETTI

CCCXCVI A BIRTHDAY

My heart is like a singing bird
  Whose nest is in a watered shoot;
My heart is like an apple-tree
  Whose boughs are bent with thickest fruit;

My heart is like a rainbow shell
  That paddles in a halcyon sea;
My heart is gladder than all these
  Because my love is come to me.
Raise me a dais of silk and down,
  Hang it with vair and purple dyes;
Carve it in doves, and pomegranates,
  And peacocks with a hundred eyes;
Work it in gold and silver grapes,
  In leaves and silver fleurs-de-lys;
Because the birthday of my life
  Is come, my love is come to me.

CHRISTINA G. ROSSETTI

CCCXCVII UP-HILL

Does the road wind up-hill all the way?
  Yes, to the very end.
Will the day's journey take the whole long day?
  From morn till night, my friend.

But is there for the night a resting-place?
  A roof for when the slow dark hours begin.
May not the darkness hide it from my face?
  You cannot miss that inn.

Shall I meet other wayfarers at night?
  Those who have gone before.
Then must I knock, or call when just in sight?
  They will not keep you standing at that door.

Shall I find comfort, travel-sore and weak?
  Of labour you shall find the sum.
Will there be beds for me and all who seek?
  Yea, beds for all who come.

CHRISTINA G. ROSSETTI

CCCXCVIII A DIRGE

Naiad, hid beneath the bank
  By the willowy river-side,
Where Narcissus gently sank,
  Where unmarried Echo died,
Unto thy serene repose
Waft the stricken Anterôs.

Where the tranquil swan is borne,
  Imaged in a watery glass,
Where the sprays of fresh pink thorn
  Stoop to catch the boats that pass,
Where the earliest orchis grows,
Bury thou fair Anterôs.

Glide we by, with prow and oar:
  Ripple shadows off the wave,
And reflected on the shore
  Haply play about his grave.
Folds of summer-light enclose
All that once was Anterôs.

On a flickering wave we gaze,
  Not upon his answering eyes:
Flower and bird we scarce can praise,
  Having lost his sweet replies:
Cold and mute the river flows
With our tears for Anterôs.

W. Johnson-Cory

CCCXCIX AN INVOCATION

I never pray'd for Dryads, to haunt the woods again;
More welcome were the presence of hungering, thirsting men,
Whose doubts we could unravel, whose hopes we could fulfil,
Our wisdom tracing backward, the river to the rill;
Were such beloved forerunners one summer day restored,
Then, then we might discover the Muse's mystic hoard.

Oh, dear divine Comatas, I would that thou and I
Beneath this broken sunlight this leisure day might lie;
Where trees from distant forests, whose names were strange to thee,
Should bend their amorous branches within thy reach to be,
And flowers thine Hellas knew not, which art hath made more fair,
Should shed their shining petals upon thy fragrant hair.

Then thou shouldst calmly listen with ever-changing looks
To songs of younger minstrels and plots of modern books,
And wonder at the daring of poets later born,
Whose thoughts are unto thy thoughts as noon-tide is to morn;

And little shouldst thou grudge them their greater strength of soul,
Thy partners in the torch-race, though nearer to the goal.

As when ancestral portraits look gravely from the walls
Upon the youthful baron who treads their echoing halls;
And while he builds new turrets, the thrice ennobled heir
Would gladly wake his grandsire his home and feast to share;
So from Aegaean laurels that hide thine ancient urn
I fain would call thee hither, my sweeter law to learn.

Or in thy cedarn prison thou waitest for the bee:
Ah, leave that simple honey, and take thy food from me.
My sun is stooping westward. Entrancèd dreamer, haste:
There's fruitage in my garden, that I would have thee taste.
Now lift the lid a moment: now, Dorian shepherd, speak:
Two minds shall flow together, the English and the Greek.

W. JOHNSON-CORY

CD THE WOODLANDS

O spread ageän your leaves an' flow'rs
Lwonesome woodlands! zunny woodlands!
Here underneath the dewy show'rs
O warm-aïr'd spring-time zunny woodlands!
As when, in drong or open ground,
Wi' happy bwoyish heart I vound
The twitt'ren birds a buildèn round
Your high-bough'd hedges, zunny woodlands!

You gie'd me life, you gie'd me jaÿ,
Lwonesome woodlands! zunny woodlands!
You gie'd me health, as in my plaÿ
I rambled through ye, zunny woodlands!
You gie'd me freedom, vor to rove
In aïry meäd or sheädy grove
You gie'd me smilèn Fanny's love,
The best ov all o't, zunny woodlands!

My vu'st shrill skylark whiver'd high,
Lwonesome woodlands! zunny woodlands!
To zing below your deep-blue sky
An' white spring-clouds, O zunny woodlands!
An' boughs o' trees that woonce stood here,
Wer glossy green the happy-year

That gie'd me woone I lov'd so dear,
  An' now ha lost, O zunny woodlands!

O let me rove ageàn unspied,
  Lwonesome woodlands! zunny woodlands!
Along your green-bough'd hedges' zide,
  As then I rambled, zunny woodlands!
An' where the missèn trees woonce stood,
Or tongues woonce rung among the wood,
My memory shall meàke em good,
  Though you've a-lost em, zunny woodlands!

WM. BARNES

CDI THE SETTLE

Aa! naïghbour John, since I an' you
Wer youngsters, ev'ry thing is new.
My father's vires wer all o' logs
O' cleft-wood, down upon the dogs
Below our clavy, high, an' brode
Enough to teäke a cart an' lwoad,
Where big an' little all zot down
At bwoth zides, an' bevore, all roun'.
An' when I zot among em, I
Could zee all up ageän the sky
Drough chimney, where our vo'k did hitch
The zalt-box an' the beäcon-vlitch,
An' watch the smoke on out o' vier,
All up an' out o' tun, an' higher.
An' there were beäcon up on rack,
An' pleätes an' dishes on the tack;
An' roun' the walls were eärbs a-stowed
In peäpern bags, an' blathers blowed.
An' just above the clavy-bwoard
Wer father's spurs, an' gun, an' sword;
An' there wer then, our gre'test pride,
The settle by the vier zide.
  Ah! gi'e me, if I wer a squier,
  The settle an' the gre't wood vier.

But they've a-walled up now wi bricks
The vier pleäce vor dogs an' sticks,
An' only left a little hole
To teäke a little greäte o' coal,

So small that only twos or drees
Can jist push in an' warm their knees.
An' then the carpets they do use,
Bën't fit to tread wi' ouer shoes;
An' chairs an' couches be so neat,
You mussen teäke em vor a seat:
They be so fine, that vo'k must pleäce
All over em an outer ceäse,
An' then the cover, when 'tis on,
Is still too fine to loll upon.
  Ah! gi'e me, if I wer a squier,
  The settle an' the gre't wood vier.

Carpets, indeed! You coulden hurt
The stwone-vloor wi' a little dirt;
Vor what wer brought indoors by men,
The women soon mopp'd out ageän.
Zoo we did come vrom muck an' mire,
An' walk'd in straïght avore the vier;
But now, a man's a-kept at door
At work a pirty while, avore
He screäp'd an' rubb'd, an' cleän' an fit
To goo in where his wife do zit.
An' then if he should have a whiff
In there, 'twould only breed a miff:
He cän't smoke there, vor smoke won't goo
'Ithin the sooty little flue.
  Ah! gi'e me, if I wer a squier,
  The settle an' the girt wood vier.

WM. BARNES

CDII IN THE STILLNESS O' THE NIGHT

Ov all the housen o' the pleäce,
  There's woone where I do like to call
  By day or night the best ov all,
To zee my Fanny's smilèn feäce;
An' there the steätely trees do grow,
A-rockèn as the win' do blow,
While she do sweetly sleep below,
  In the stillness o' the night.

An' there, at evenèn, I do goo
  A-hoppèn over geätes an' bars,
  By twinklèn light o' winter stars,
When snow do clumper to my shoe;
An' zometimes we do slyly catch
A chat an hour upon the stratch
An' peärt wi' whispers at the hatch
  In the stillness o' the night.

An' zometimes she do goo to zome
  Young naïghbours' housen down the pleäce,
  An' I do get a clue to treäce
Her out, an' goo to zee her hwome;
And I do wish a vield a mile,
As she do sweetly chat an' smile
Along the drove, or at the stile,
  In the stillness o' the night.

Wm. Barnes

CDIII

MOTHER WEPT

Mother wept, and father sigh'd;
  With delight aglow
Cried the lad, "To-morrow," cried,
  "To the pit I go."

Up and down the place he sped,—
  Greeted old and young;
Far and wide the tidings spread;
  Clapt his hands and sung.

Came his cronies; some to gaze
  Wrapp'd in wonder; some
Free with counsel; some with praise;
  Some with envy dumb.

"May he," many a gossip cried,
  "Be from peril kept."
Father hid his face and sigh'd,
  Mother turn'd and wept.

Joseph Skipsey

CDIV

A DREAM

I heard the dogs howl in the moonlight night;
I went to the window to see the sight;

All the Dead that ever I knew
Going one by one and two by two.

On they pass'd, and on they pass'd;
Townsfellows all, from first to last;
Born in the moonlight of the lane,
Quench'd in the heavy shadow again.

Schoolmates, marching as when we play'd
At soldiers once—but now more staid;
Those were the strangest sight to me
Who were drown'd, I knew, in the awful sea.

Straight and handsome folk; bent and weak, too;
Some that I loved, and gasp'd to speak to;
Some but a day in their churchyard bed;
Some that I had not known were dead.

A long, long crowd—where each seem'd lonely,
Yet of them all there was one, one only,
Raised a head or look'd my way:
She linger'd a moment,—she might not stay.

How long since I saw that fair pale face!
Ah! Mother dear! might I only place
My head on thy breast, a moment to rest,
While thy hand on my tearful cheek were prest!

On, on, a moving bridge they made
Across the moon-stream from shade to shade,
Young and old, women and men!
Many long-forgot, but remember'd then.

And first there came a bitter laughter;
A sound of tears the moment after;
And then a music so lofty and gay,
That every morning, day by day,
I strive to recall it if I may.

WILLIAM ALLINGHAM

CDV THE FAIRIES

Up the airy mountain,
  Down the rushy glen,
We daren't go a-hunting
  For fear of little men;

Wee folk, good folk,
  Trooping all together;
Green jacket, red cap,
  And white owl's feather!

Down along the rocky shore
  Some make their home,
They live on crispy pancakes
  Of yellow tide foam;
Some in the reeds
  Of the black mountain lake,
With frogs for their watch-dogs,
  All night awake.

High on the hill-top
  The old king sits;
He is now so old and gray
  He's nigh lost his wits.
With a bridge of white mist
  Columbkill he crosses,
On his stately journeys
  From Slieveleague to Rosses:

Or going up with music
  On cold starry nights,
To sup with the Queen
  Of the gay Northern lights.
They stole little Bridget
  For seven years long;
When she came down again
  Her friends were all gone.

They took her lightly back,
  Between the night and morrow,
They thought that she was fast asleep,
  But she was dead with sorrow.
They have kept her ever since
  Deep within the lake,
On a bed of flag-leaves,
  Watching till she wake.

By the craggy hill-side,
  Through the mosses bare,
They have planted thorn-trees
  For pleasure here and there.

Is any man so daring
  As dig them up in spite,
He shall find their sharpest thorns
  In his bed at night.

Up the airy mountain.
  Down the rushy glen,
We daren't go a-hunting
  For fear of little men;
Wee folk, good folk
  Trooping all together;
Green jacket, red cap,
  And white owl's feather!

ALLINGHAM

CDVI SONGS FROM "PHANTASTES"

I

Alas, how easily things go wrong!
A sigh too much, or a kiss too long,
And there follows a mist and a weeping rain,
And life is never the same again.

Alas, how hardly things go right!
'Tis hard to watch in a summer night,
For the sigh will come, and the kiss will stay,
And the summer night is a winter day.

CDVII

II

Oh, well for him who breaks his dream
  With the blow that ends the strife;
And, waking, knows the peace that flows
  Around the pain of life!

We are dead, my brothers! Our bodies clasp,
  As an armour, our souls about;
This hand is the battle-axe I grasp,
  And this my hammer stout.

Fear not, my brothers, for we are dead;
  No noise can break our rest;
The calm of the grave is about the head,
  And the heart heaves not the breast.

And our life we throw to our people back,
  To live with, a further store;
We leave it them, that there be no lack
  In the land where we live no more.

Oh, well for him who breaks his dream
  With the blow that ends the strife;
And, waking, knows the peace that flows
  Around the noise of life!

GEORGE MACDONALD

CDVIII THE COMMON GRAVE

Last night beneath the foreign stars I stood,
And saw the thoughts of those at home go by
To the great grave upon the hill of blood,
Upon the darkness they went visibly,
Each in the vesture of its own distress.
Among them came One, frail as a sigh,
And like a creature of the wilderness
Dug with her bleeding hands. She neither cried
Nor wept; nor did she see the many stark
And dead that lay unburied at her side.
All night she toiled; and at that time of dawn,
When Day and Night do change their More and Less,
And day is more, I saw the melting Dark
Stir to the last, and knew she laboured on.

SYDNEY DOBELL

CDIX THE OLD HOUSE

Beneath those buttressed walls with lichen grey,
  Beneath the slopes of trees whose flickering shade
  Darkens the pools by dun green velveted,
The stream leaps like a living thing at play,—
In haste it seems: it cannot cannot stay!
  The great boughs changing there from year to year,
  And the high jackdaw-haunted eaves, still hear
The burden of the rivulet—Passing away!

And some time certainly that oak no more
  Will keep the winds in check; his breadth of beam
Will go to rib some ship for some far shore;
  Those coigns and eaves will crumble, while that stream

Will still run whispering, whispering night and day,
That oversong of Father Time—Passing away!

William Bell Scott

CDX AUTUMN EVENSONG

The long cloud edged with streaming gray
Soars from the west;
The red leaf mounts with it away
Showing the nest
A blot among the branches bare:
There is a cry of outcasts in the air.

Swift little breezes, darting chill,
Pant down the lake;
A crow flies from the yellow hill
And in its wake
A baffled line of labouring rooks:
Steel-surfaced to the light the river looks.

Pale on the panes of the old hall
Gleams the lone space
Between the sunset and the squall;
And on its face
Mournfully glimmers to the last:
Great oaks grow mighty minstrels in the blast.

Pale the rain-rutted roadways shine
In the green light
Behind the cedar and the pine:
Come thundering night!
Blacken broad earth with hoards of storm,
For me yon valley cottage beckons warm.

George Meredith

CDXI SHAKESPEARE

Thy greatest knew thee, Mother Earth: unsoured
He knew thy sons. He probed from hell to hell
Of human passions, but of love deflowered
His wisdom was not, for he knew thee well.
Thence came that honeyed corner at his lips,
The conquering smile wherein his spirit sails
Calm as the God who the white sea-wave whips;
Yet full of speech and intershifting tales

Close mirrors of us: thence had he the laugh
We feel is thine, broad as ten thousand beeves
At pasture: thence thy songs, that winnow chaff
From grain, bid sick Philosophy's last leaves
Whirl if they have no response—they enforced
To fatten Earth when from her soul divorced.

George Meredith

CDXII THE FOUNTAIN OF TEARS

If you go over desert and mountain,
  Far into the country of sorrow,
  To-day and to-night and to-morrow,
And maybe for months and for years;
  You shall come, with a heart that is bursting
  For trouble and toiling and thirsting,
You shall certainly come to the fountain
At length,—to the Fountain of Tears.

Very peaceful the place is, and solely
  For piteous lamenting and sighing,
  And those who come living or dying
Alike from their hopes and their fears;
  Full of cypress-like shadows the place is,
  And statues that cover their faces:
But out of the gloom springs the holy
And beautiful Fountain of Tears.

And it flows and it flows with a motion
  So gentle and lovely and listless,
  And murmurs a tune so resistless
To him who hath suffered and hears—
  You shall surely—without a word spoken,
  Kneel down there and know your heart broken,
And yield to the long curb'd emotion
That day by the Fountain of Tears.

For it grows and it grows, as though leaping
  Up higher the more one is thinking;
  And even its tunes go on sinking
More poignantly into the ears:
  Yea, so blessèd and good seems that fountain,
  Reached after dry desert and mountain,
You shall fall down at length in your weeping
And bathe your sad face in the tears.

Then, alas! while you lie there a season,
  And sob between living and dying,
  And give up the land you were trying
To find 'mid your hopes and your fears;
  —O the world shall come up and pass o'er you
  Strong men shall not stay to care for you,
Nor wonder indeed for what reason
Your way should seem harder than theirs.

But perhaps, while you lie, never lifting
  Your cheek from the wet leaves it presses,
  Nor caring to raise your wet tresses
And look how the cold world appears,—
  O perhaps the mere silences round you
  All things in that place grief hath found you,
Yea, e'en to the clouds o'er you drifting
May soothe you somewhat through your tears.

You may feel, when a falling leaf brushes
  Your face, as though some one had kissed you;
  Or think at least some one who missed you
Hath sent you a thought,—if that cheers;
  Or a bird's little song faint and broken,
  May pass for a tender word spoken:
—Enough, while around you there rushes
That life-drowning torrent of tears.

And the tears shall flow faster and faster,
  Brim over, and baffle resistance,
  And roll down bleared roads to each distance
Of past desolation and years;
  Till they cover the place of each sorrow,
  And leave you no Past and no morrow:
For what man is able to master
And stem the great Fountain of Tears?

But the floods of the tears meet and gather;
  The sound of them all grows like thunder:
  —O into what bosom, I wonder
Is poured the whole sorrow of years?
  For Eternity only seems keeping
  Account of the great human weeping:
May God then, the Maker and Father—
May He find a place for the tears!

ARTHUR O'SHAUGHNESSY

CDXIII AT MIDNIGHT

They were two poor young girls, little older than children,
Who passed through the midnight streets of the city
Singing.

Poorly clad, morning-eyed, with a strange look of shyness,
Linked arms, and round cheeks, and smooth heads bent together,
Singing.

Singing, great Heaven! with their fresh childish voices,
Some low-murmured ditty, half hymn-tune, half love-song,
Singing,

Always by hushed square, and long street deserted,
As from school by the old village street on fair evenings,
Singing,

Singing, and knowing it not, the old burden
That is born out of secular wrongs and oppressions,
Singing,

Of selfish riches, of misery and hunger,
Of sin that is bred of the wants of the wretched,
Singing,

Of poor bribes that purchase souls, of the endless,
Perpetual harvest of pain and of evil,
Singing.

So they passed to the flaring sin-befouled places,
And amid the thick throng of the fallen I lost them,
Singing,

A hymn-tune, a love-song, a prayer chanted backward,
A witch spell unholy, a sweet suffrage saintly
Singing.

Sir Lewis Morris

CDXIV WHEN SPARROWS BUILD

When sparrows build, and the leaves break forth
My old sorrow wakes and cries,
For I know there is dawn in the far, far north,
And a scarlet sun doth rise!

Like a scarlet fleece the snow-field spreads,
And the icy founts run free,
And the bergs begin to bow their heads,
And plunge, and sail in the sea.

O my lost love, and my own, own love,
And my love that loved me so!
Is there never a chink in the world above
Where they listen for words from below?
Nay, I spoke once, and I grieved thee sore,
I remember all that I said,
And now thou wilt hear me no more—no more
Till the sea gives up her dead.

Thou didst set thy foot on the ship, and sail
To the ice-fields and the snow;
Thou wert sad, for thy love did naught avail,
And the end I could not know;
How could I tell I should love thee to-day,
Whom that day I held not dear?
How could I know I should love thee away
When I did not love thee anear?

We shall walk no more through the sodden plain
With the faded bents o'erspread,
We shall stand no more by the seething main
While the dark wrack drives o'erhead;
We shall part no more in the wind and the rain,
Where thy last farewell was said;
But perhaps I shall meet thee and know thee again
When the sea gives up her dead.

JEAN INGELOW

CDXV THE DEAD

The dead abide with us! Though stark and cold
Earth seems to grip them, they are with us still
They have forged our chains of being for good or ill;
And their invisible hands these hands yet hold.
Our perishable bodies are the mould
In which their strong imperishable will—
Mortality's deep yearning to fulfil—
Hath grown incorporate through dim time untold.

Vibrations infinite of life in death,
  As a star's travelling light survives its star!
  So may we hold our lives, that when we are
The fate of those who then will draw this breath.
  They shall not drag us to their judgment-bar,
And curse the heritage which we bequeath.

MATHILDE BLIND

CDXVI THE RUNES

I

Read these faint runes of Mystery,
O Celt at home and o'er the sea;
The bond is loosed; the poor are free,
The world's great future rests with thee.

II

Till the soil, bid cities rise,
Be strong, O Celt; be rich, be wise;
But still, with those divine grave eyes,
Reveal the realm of Mysteries.

ROBERT BUCHANAN

CDXVII QUIET WATERS

O Rainbow, Rainbow, on the livid height,
  Softening the ashen outline into dream;
Dewy yet brilliant, delicately bright
  As pink wild-roses' leaves, why dost thou gleam
So beckoningly? Whom dost thou invite
  Still higher upward on the bitter quest?
What dost thou promise to the weary sight
  In that strange region whence thou issuest?
  Speak'st thou of pensive runlets by whose side
  Our dear ones wander sweet and gentle-eyed,
    In the soft dawn of a diviner Day?
  Art thou a promise? Come those hues and dyes
  From heavenly meads, near which thou dost arise
    Iris'd from Quiet Waters, far away!

ROBERT BUCHANAN

CDXVIII A SONG OF THE ROAD

The gauger walked with willing foot,
And aye the gauger played the flute;
And what should Master Gauger play
But *Over the hills and far away.*

Whene'er I buckle on my pack,
And foot it gaily in the track;
O pleasant gauger, long since dead,
I hear you fluting on ahead.

You go with me the self-same way—
The self-same air for me you play;
For I do think and so do you,
It is the tune to travel to.

For who would gravely set his face
To go to this or t'other place?
There's nothing under Heav'n so blue
That's fairly worth the travelling to.

On every hand the roads begin,
And people walk with zeal therein;
But wheresoe'er the highways tend,
Be sure there's nothing at the end.

Then follow you, wherever hie
The trembling mountains of the sky:
Or let the streams in civil mode
Direct your choice upon a road;

For one and all, or high or low,
Will lead you where you wish to go;
And one and all go night and day
Over the hills and far away!

ROBERT LOUIS STEVENSON

CDXIX REQUIEM

Under the wide and starry sky,
Dig the grave and let me lie.
Glad did I live and gladly die,
    And I laid me down with a will.
This be the verse you grave for me:
Here he lies where he longed to be;
Home is the sailor, home from sea,
    And the hunter home from the hill.

R. L. STEVENSON

CDXX GIVE A MAN A HORSE HE CAN RIDE

Give a man a horse he can ride,
  Give a man a boat he can sail;
And his rank and wealth, his strength and health
  Or sea nor shore shall fail.

Give a man a pipe he can smoke,
  Give a man a book he can read;
And his home is bright with a calm delight,
  Though the rooms be poor indeed.

Give a man a girl he can love,
  As I, O my Love, love thee;
And his hand is great with the pulse of Fate,
  At home, on land, on sea.

James Thomson

CDXXI ITYLUS

Swallow, my sister, O sister swallow,
  How can thine heart be full of the spring?
    A thousand summers are over and dead.
What hast thou found in the spring to follow?
  What hast thou found in thy heart to sing?
    What wilt thou do when the summer is shed?

O swallow, sister, O fair swift swallow,
  Why wilt thou fly after spring to the south,
    The soft south, whither thine heart is set?
Shall not the grief of the old time follow?
  Shall not the song thereof cleave to thy mouth?
    Hast thou forgotten ere I forget?

Sister, my sister, O fleet sweet swallow,
  Thy way is long to the sun and the south;
    But I, fulfilled of my heart's desire,
Shedding my song upon height, upon hollow,
  From tawny body and sweet small mouth
    Feed the heart of the night with fire.

I, the nightingale, all spring through,
  O swallow sister, O changing swallow,
    All spring through, till the spring be done,
Clothed with the light of the night on the dew,
  Sing, while the hours and the wild birds follow,
    Take flight and follow and find the sun.

Sister, my sister, O soft light swallow,
Though all things feast in the spring's guest-chamber,
How hast thou heart to be glad thereof yet?
For where thou fliest I shall not follow,
Till life forget and death remember,
Till thou remember and I forget.

Swallow, my sister, O singing swallow,
I know not how thou hast heart to sing:
Hast thou the heart? is it all past over?
Thy lord the summer is good to follow,
And fair the feet of thy lover the spring;
But what wilt thou say to the spring thy lover?

O swallow, sister, O fleeting swallow,
My heart in me is a molten ember,
And over my head the waves have met;
But thou wouldst tarry or I would follow,
Could I forget or thou remember,
Couldst thou remember and I forget.

O sweet stray sister, O shifting swallow,
The heart's division divideth us.
Thy heart is light as a leaf of a tree,
But mine goes forth among sea-gulfs hollow,
To the place of the slaying of Itylus,
The feast of Daulis, the Thracian Sea.

O swallow, sister, O rapid swallow,
I pray thee sing not a little space.
Are not the roofs and the lintels wet?
The woven web that was plain to follow,
The small slain body, the flower-like face,
Can I remember if thou forget?

O sister, sister, thy first-begotten!
The hands that cling and the feet that follow,
The voice of the child's blood crying yet,
"Who hath remembered me? who hath forgotten?"
Thou hast forgotten, O summer swallow,
But the world shall end when I forget.

Algernon Charles Swinburne

CDXXII

A MATCH

If love were what the rose is,
  And I were like the leaf,
Our lives would grow together
In sad or singing weather,
Blown fields or flowerful closes,
  Green pleasure or gray grief;
If love were what the rose is,
  And I were like the leaf.

If I were what the words are,
  And love were like the tune,
With double sound and single
Delight our lips would mingle,
With kisses glad as birds are
  That get sweet rain at noon;
If I were what the words are,
  And love were like the tune.

If you were life, my darling,
  And I your love were death,
We'd shine and snow together
Ere March made sweet the weather
With daffodil and starling
  And hours of fruitful breath;
If you were life, my darling,
  And I your love were death.

If you were thrall to sorrow,
  And I were page to joy,
We'd play for lives and seasons
With loving looks and treasons
And tears of night and morrow
  And laughs of maid and boy;
If you were thrall to sorrow,
  And I were page to joy.

If you were April's lady
  And I were lord in May,
We'd throw with leaves for hours
And draw for day with flowers,
Till day like night were shady
  And night were bright like day;
If you were April's lady,
  And I were lord in May.

If you were queen of pleasure,
  And I were king of pain,
We'd hunt down love together,
Pluck out his flying-feather,
And teach his feet a measure,
  And find his mouth a rein;
If you were queen of pleasure,
And I were king of pain.

A. C. SWINBURNE

CDXXIII THE OBLATION

Ask nothing more of me, sweet;
  All I can give you I give.
    Heart of my heart, were it more,
More would be laid at your feet:
  Love that should help you to live,
    Song that should spur you to soar.

All things were nothing to give
  Once to have sense of you more,
    Touch you and taste of you, sweet,
Think you and breathe you and live,
  Swept of your wings as they soar
    Trodden by chance of your feet.

I that have love and no more
  Give you but love of you, sweet:
    He that hath more, let him give;
He that hath wings let him soar;
  Mine is the heart at your feet
    Here, that must love you to live.

A. C. SWINBURNE

CDXXIV HOMER

I

The sacred keep of Ilion is rent
  By shaft and pit; foiled waters wander slow
Through plains where Simois and Scamander went
  To war with Gods and heroes long ago.
  Not yet to tired Cassandra, lying low
In rich Mycenæ, do the Fates relent:
  The bones of Agamemnon are a show,
And ruined in his royal monument.

The dust and awful treasures of the Dead,
  Hath Learning scattered wide, but vainly thee,
Homer, she meteth with her tool of lead,
  And strives to rend thy songs; too blind to see
The crown that burns on thine immortal head
  Of indivisible supremacy!

II

As one that for a weary space has lain
  Lulled by the song of Circe and her wine
  In gardens near the pale of Proserpine,
Where that Ægean isle forgets the main,
And only the low lutes of love complain,
  And only shadows of wan lovers pine,
  As such an one were glad to know the brine
Salt on his lips, and the large air again,—
So gladly, from the songs of modern speech
  Men turn, and see the stars, and feel the free
    Shrill wind beyond the close of heavy flowers,
    And through the music of the languid hours,
They hear like ocean on the western beach
  The surge and thunder of the Odyssey.

Andrew Lang

CDXXV EXTREME UNCTION

Upon the lips, the eyes, the feet,
  On all the passages of sense,
The atoning oil is spread with sweet
  Renewal of lost innocence.

The feet that lately ran so fast
  To meet desire, are soothly sealed:
The eyes, that were so often cast
  On vanity, are touched and healed.

From troublous sights and sounds set free,
  In such a twilight hour of breath,
Shall one retrace his life, or see
  Through shadows the true face of Death?

Vials of mercy! sacring oils!
  I know not where, nor when I come,
Nor through what wanderings and toils
  To crave of you Viaticum.

Yet when the walls of flesh grow weak,
In such an hour, it may well be,
Through mist and darkness light shall break,
And each anointed sense shall see!

ERNEST DOWSON

CDXXVI GLORIES

Roses from Paestan rosaries!
More goodly red and white was she:
Her red and white were harmonies,
Not matched upon a Paestan tree.

Ivories blaunched in Alban air!
She lies more purely blaunched than you:
No Alban whiteness doth she wear,
But death's perfection of that hue.

Nay! now the rivalry is done,
Of red, and white, and whiter still:
She hath a glory from that sun,
Who falls not from Olympus hill.

LIONEL JOHNSON

CDXXVII THE BEAUTY OF THE WORLD

I saw the beauty of the world
Before me like a flag unfurled,
The splendour of the morning sky,
And all the stars in company;
I thought, how beautiful it is!—
My soul said, There is more than this.

I saw the pomps of death and birth,
The generations of the earth;
I looked on saints and heroes crowned,
And love as wide as heaven is round;
I thought, How wonderful it is!—
My soul said, There is more than this.

Sometimes I have an awful thought
That bids me do the thing I ought,
It comes like wind, it burns like flame,
How shall I give that thought a name?
It draws me like a loving kiss—
My soul says, There is more than this.

I dreamed an angel of the Lord,
With purple wings and golden sword,
And such a splendour in his face
As made a glory in the place;
I thought, How beautiful he is!—
My soul said, There is more than this.

That angel's Lord I cannot see
Or hear, but He is Lord to me;
And in the heavens, and earth, and skies,—
The good which lives till evil dies,—
The love which I cannot withstand,—
God writes His name with His own hand.

WILLIAM BRIGHTY RANDS

CDXXVIII SPRING WIND

O full-voiced herald of immaculate Spring,
  With clarion gladness striking every tree
  To answering raptures, as a resonant sea
Fills rock-bound shores with thunders echoing—
O thou, each beat of whose tempestuous wing
  Shakes the long winter-sleep from hill and lea,
  And rouses with loud reckless jubilant glee
The birds that have not dared as yet to sing:—

O Wind that comest with prophetic cries,
  Hast thou indeed beheld the face that is
  The joy of poets and the glory of birds—
Spring's face itself:—hast thou 'neath bluer skies
Met the warm lips that are the gates of bliss,
  And heard June's leaf-like whisper of sweet words?

WILLIAM SHARP

CDXXIX A SUMMER AIR

O waving trees,
And waving wind,
And waving seas,
And waving mind—
Where, far and wide,
Am I to roam
To find my bride,
To reach my home?

My soul is my bride;
Ah, whither fled?
She hath not died,
Nor am I dead;
But somehow, somewhere,
A song she heard,
And she flashed through the air
A sun-fire bird.

My bride, she is
Where the rainbows are;
Sweet, sweet her kiss
Awaits afar:
My goal is where
The sea-waves meet
The sands of youth
Stirred by her feet.

O waving leaves,
O waving grass,
My heart grieves
That it may not pass.
"Summer is fleet,
Summer is long,"—
I know not, sweet,
'Tis an empty song.

Where, far and wide,
Across what foam,
On what strange tide
Shall I be come?
Meet me, O Bride,
Where, lost, I roam;
Leap to my side
And lead me home!

"Fiona Macleod"

CDXXX BY THE STATUE OF KING CHARLES AT CHARING CROSS

Sombre and rich, the skies,
Great glooms and starry plains;
Gently the night wind sighs;
Else a vast silence reigns.

The splendid silence clings
Around me: and around
The saddest of all Kings,
Crown'd, and again discrown'd.

Comely and calm, he rides
Hard by his own Whitehall.
Only the night wind glides:
No crowds, nor rebels, brawl.

Gone, too, his Court: and yet,
The stars his courtiers are:
Stars in their stations set;
And every wandering star.

Alone he rides, alone,
The fair and fatal King:
Dark night is all his own,
That strange and solemn thing.

Which are more full of fate:
The stars; or those sad eyes?
Which are more still and great:
Those brows, or the dark skies?

Although his whole heart yearn
In passionate tragedy,
Never was face so stern
With sweet austerity.

Vanquish'd in life, his death
By beauty made amends:
The passing of his breath
Won his defeated ends.

Brief life, and hapless? Nay:
Through death, life grew sublime.
Speak after sentence? Yea:
And to the end of time.

Armour'd he rides, his head
Bare to the stars of doom;
He triumphs now, the dead,
Beholding London's gloom.

Our wearier spirit faints,
Vex'd in the world's employ:
His soul was of the saints;
And art to him was joy.

King, tried in fires of woe!
Men hunger for thy grace:
And through the night I go,
Loving thy mournful face.

Yet, when the city sleeps,
When all the cries are still,
The stars and heavenly deeps
Work out a perfect will.

Lionel Johnson

CDXXXI ANNIE SMITH

Where have you been, Annie Smith, to-day,
  That your face and your eyes are so calm?
Did you hear in the church the minister pray?
  Did you join in the holy psalm?
Did he tell of the solemn joys of the blest,
  That your face is so calm and serene,
That you seem to have ended each earthly quest?
  In the church, Annie Smith, have you been?

Or did you stand on the shore, Annie Smith,
  And gaze away to the West?
Did you stand where the river becomes a frith,
  With your hands folded over your breast,
And gaze at the golden skyey gate
  As the sun passed through sublime?
Did you get this shadowy light of fate
  On your face at the sunset time?
Or are you an angel, Annie Smith,
  For a time from your blessedness riven,
To guide me over the cold, wan frith
  Of death to your happy heaven?

John Davidson

CDXXXII NEW YEAR'S DAY

The storm-wind sank, the moon rode high,
  Set round with silver haze,
Where, late, sky-spaces wonderful
  Showed green as chrysoprase.

Within the old grey church anon
  The gathered folk would sit;
I met the old year on the hill,
  And bade farewell to it.

The woods around stood stark and dim,
  But at my feet white birds
Fluttered, the wraiths of kindly deed,
  And sweet, remembered words.

Above me, from Orion's belt,
  A great gem flashed and fell,
Was it a seraph prince sped by,
  Michael, or Gabriel?

Then, though my lonely heart must mourn
  For some that come no more,
White sails of Hope I seemed to see
  Set to a sapphire shore.

As he who dreamed a New World sailed
  On an uncharted sea,
From Palos with his caravels
  Lured by a mystery.

So, under flaming Asian suns,
  Or by the still, white Pole,
That Great Adventure, the New Year,
  Beacons the human soul.

L. M. Little

CDXXXIII DAISY

Where the thistle lifts a purple crown
  Six foot out of the turf,
And the harebell shakes on the windy hill—
  O the breath of the distant surf!—

The hills look over on the South,
  And southward dreams the sea;
And, with the sea-breeze hand in hand,
  Came innocence and she.

Where 'mid the gorse the raspberry
  Red for the gatherer springs,
Two children did we stray and talk
  Wise, idle, childish things.

She listen'd with big-lipped surprise,
  Breast-deep 'mid flower and spine:
Her skin was like a grape, whose veins
  Run snow instead of wine.

She knew not those sweet words she spake,
  Nor knew her own sweet way;
But there's never a bird, so sweet a song
  Throng'd in whose throat that day!

O, there were flowers in Storrington
  On the turf and on the spray;
But the sweetest flower on Sussex hills
  Was the Daisy-flower that day!

Her beauty smooth'd earth's furrow'd face!
  She gave me tokens three:—
A look, a word of her winsome mouth,
  And a wild raspberry.

A berry red, a guileless look,
  A still word,—strings of sand!
And yet they make my wild, wild heart
  Fly down to her little hand.

For, standing artless as the air,
  And candid as the skies,
She took the berries with her hand,
  And the love with her sweet eyes.

The fairest things have fleetest end:
  Their scent survives their close,
But the rose's scent is bitterness
  To him that loved the rose!

She looked a little wistfully,
  Then went her sunshine way:—
The sea's eye had a mist on it,
  And the leaves fell from the day.

She went her unremembering way,
  She went, and left in me
The pangs of all the partings gone,
  And partings yet to be.

She left me marvelling why my soul
  Was sad that she was glad;
At all the sadness in the sweet,
  The sweetness in the sad.

Still, still I seem'd to see her, still
  Look up with soft replies,
And take the berries with her hand,
  And the love with her lovely eyes.

Nothing begins, and nothing ends,
  That is not paid with moan;
For we are born in other's pain,
  And perish in our own.

FRANCIS THOMPSON

CDXXXIV TO A SNOWFLAKE

What heart could have thought you?—
Past our devisal
(O filigree petal!)
Fashioned so purely
Fragilely, surely,
From what Paradisal
Imagineless metal,
Too costly for cost?
Who hammered you, wrought you,
From argentine vapour?—
"God was my shaper,
Passing surmisal,
He hammered, He wrought me,
From curled silver vapour,
To lust of His mind:—
Thou could'st not have thought me!
So purely, so palely,
Tinily, surely,
Mightily, frailly
Insculped and embossed,
With His hammer of wind
And His graver of frost."

FRANCIS THOMPSON

CDXXXV ENVOI TO BOOK SIXTH

Go, songs, for ended is our brief, sweet play;
  Go, children of swift joy and tardy sorrow:
And some are sung, and that was yesterday,
  And some unsung, and that may be to-morrow.

Go forth; and if it be o'er stony way,
  Old joy can lend what newer grief must borrow;
And it was sweet, and that was yesterday,
  And sweet is sweet, though purchasèd with sorrow.

Go, songs, and come not back from your far way;
  And if men ask you why ye smile and sorrow,
Tell them ye grieve, for your hearts know to-day;
  Tell them ye smile, for your eyes know to-morrow.

FRANCIS THOMPSON

INDEX OF FIRST LINES

Index of First Lines

INDEX OF POETS

WITH DATES OF BIRTH AND DEATH

[*The Nos. give the pages in which the poems of each writer are to be found.*]

GLOSSARY

OF OLD ENGLISH AND DIALECT WORDS

aglets, tags, points
aithis, oaths
al, all
anadem, wreath, garland: *cf.* diadem
ane, one
ant, and
arks, baskets
Auster, the south wind

bailey, Fr. bailli, bailiff
bak burd, backbone
baundoun, lordship
beadsman, almsman
Beltane, May Day (sometimes June 21)
bendes for-borne; bends so low with bearing the cross
bield, shelter
bienly, prosperously
bin, been
bink, bank
birks, birch-groves
black cow, the; ill fate
bleo, blee, colour
bloncket, blanket, woollen
bondyn, bound
bote, but, unless
braw, brave
breme, bravely
brent, burnt
brere, briar
briddes, birds
broachie, small broach, or pin
bruik, broke, spend
Brute's, Brutus's
burde, lady, maiden
buskets, bouquets
by dene, betimes, at once
bytand, biting
bytterly, bitterly

cantie, lively, jolly
carcanet, a jewelled collar
cassander, cassandra
chevring chirls, trembling trills
clavy, chimney-piece; *clavy-bwoard*, mantel-shelf
clote, yellow water-lily
coliander, ? coriander
corond, crowned
corse, body
cowplyt, coupled
creepie, low stool
crosce, cross
curted, curt, short-spoken

dears, dears, darlings
deeming, dooming, condemnation
deir, destroy
delved, dug
derne, secret
deye, die
donketh, dampeth
drad, dreaded
drong, thronged, thickly grown
drumlie, turbid, gloomy-looking

elles, ellys, else
ennewed, renewed
esperance, hope
essay, attempt
eternise, make eternal

faes, foes
falewe, turn yellow, fade
farly, wondrous
fauld, fold
feair, fair
feedand, fading
ferly fele, wondrous much
fille, Fr. girl
firstling, first flower
flagat, flagon, bottle
fleme, outcast, driven to fly
fond, find

folly, foolish
forget, forgotten
fors, force
forte, for to
foster, forester
frere, friar

gawsy, self-satisfied, sleek
geck, gibe
giffis, gives
girt woak tree, great oak tree
girt wood vire, great wood fire
gladieth, gladden
glister, glistening
glore, glory
go bet, go quick, hasten
governance, good guidance
gowan, daisy
graith, stuff, clothes
gre, wrap (?)
gree, palm, first place
gud, good
guiden, guide, direct

hadden, holding or bit of land
haef, half
haffits, cheeks and jowls
hait, hot
hals, neck
halt, hold
hap, chance
he, *heo*, she
heath-fowl, grouse
heeze, hoist, rise
hele, health, salvation
helen, heal
hendy, fair
hent, gained
her, hair
hert, heart
heu, hue
heugh, *haugh*, low bank of a stream
hevene, heaven
hie, high
hire, her
hock-carts, harvest carts or wains
hode, hood
holene, holly
hye, high

Ichabbe, I have
Icham, I am
Ichot, I wot, I know
imps, grafts, shoots
Isiphil, Isabel
i-slaw, slain
I-wisse, I wit, know

jay, joy

kail-worms, cabbage caterpillars
ken, know
knawis, knows

lacit, laced
laigh, lord
larded, garnished, trimmed
lawtie, loyalty
leäden, leaving
leal, loyal, true
lear, learning
leir, teach
lemmon, leman, lover
lent, turned
lesum, lawful
let, hindrance
levedi, lady
levys, lives
libbe, live
linns, cascades with pools below
litill braid, little space
lodge, find the deer in covert
loh, laughed
Lolledry, Lollardry
loof, hand
lossum, lovesome
lucken, looking
lud, voice
lustis, lusts, desires
lutel, little
lyht, alights

Madge-howlet, the owl
may, maiden
mayse, makes, causes
mene, moan
menksful, honorable
merimake, merry-making
mickle, great
mid, may
miff, tiff
mings, stores
minnie, little mother
missen, missing
mo, more
mon, man
moni, many

nard, spikenard

ner, near
nere, were not
nes, was not
noht, nought
nou, now

oo, aye

pardie, Fr. *par Dieu*
pearl paragone, the finest pearl
perquer, perquisite, belonging
pickle, a grain
pickle-hair, a scanty head of hair
piggésnie, piggie's eye, a term of endearment
pike-prods, thorn-points
pirty while, pretty while
pletyng, pleading
pomander, an apple stuck with cloves
pow, pate, head
purfilled, purfled

queme, please

raree show, show of marvels and monsters
rayleth, arrayeth
reytes, rushes
roches, rocks
rode, colour, hue
roune, tune

saikless, sackless, heedless
sare, sore
sawis, sows
seill, soul
semlokest, seemliest
sendal, silken stuff
shule, shall
sicker, sure, surely
sickerness, security, sureness
sike, sigh
skaith, hurt, trouble
slaiks, slacks, allays
soote, sweet
soth, sooth, truth
stanged, dragged heavily
start, first beginning
stere, stay
stour, struggle
suete, sweet
suffragane, nature's chosen one, elect lady
suit, hunting term for following up the deer
sustene, sustain
swyre, neck
syke, sickness

tabard, short coat
tabrere, tabor-player
taid, tied
tha, thou
thole, *tholien*; endure, bear
thurled, pierced
tickle, uncertain, insecure
toom, empty
train-bands, bands of soldiers in training
trayturly, treacherously
trentals, masses said in thirties
tressour, treasure
trone, throne
tun, chimney-top
twane, twain, two

vair, fair
vo'k, folk
vor, for
vust, first

wame, belly
warroke, a shepherd's name = Warwick
waukin, waking
wede, gone, faded
weders, weathers
wele, well
wende, turn
whilk, which
wlytheth, looketh, looks back
wode, *wod*; mad
won, abode
worchliche, worshipful
wore, weir
wots, knows
woweth, goeth
wurnliche, *wonderliche*; wonderful
wyterman, wise man

yearned, counted, prized
yode, went
yre, ire, anger

Richard Clay & Sons, Limited,
BRUNSWICK STREET, STAMFORD STREET, S.E.,
AND BUNGAY, SUFFOLK.

Lightning Source UK Ltd.
Milton Keynes UK
UKHW011302261118
332984UK00015B/948/P

9 781331 642978